CRACKS
IN THE
CEILING

Coming of age in a world of love,
tragedy, laughter and hardship.

JOHN COWELL

JOHN BLAKE

Published by John Blake Publishing Ltd, 3 Bramber Court, 2 Bramber Road,
London W14 9PB, England

First published in paperback in 2002

ISBN 1 903402 88 3

British Library Cataloguing-in-Publication Data: A catalogue record for this
book is available from the British Library.

Design by ENVY

Typeset by Mac Style Ltd, Scarborough, N. Yorkshire

Printed and bound in Great Britain by CPD (Wales)

1 3 5 7 9 10 8 6 4 2

Papers used by John Blake Publishing Ltd are natural, recyclable products
made from wood grown in sustainable forests. The manufacturing processes
conform to the environmental regulations of the country of origin.

Contents

1

Early Recollections

> Born in Bank Hall, my first day of life,
> Given a twin sister ... just like a wife.
> In a way it was great, but much to my loss,
> Right from the start she was to be boss.

These words are from a poem about my life. They are certainly true, but to be fair, my twin Mary was only the boss because I allowed her to be.

* * *

As a baby, I was quite robust with a thick crop of black hair, whereas Mary was very delicate and her hair was thin, blonde and wispy. On many occasions whilst Mum was pushing us in the pram, people would stop her and make comments: "Oh the little girl is much bigger than the boy isn't she? My, the little girl has got a lot more hair than the boy hasn't she?" My mum, Winifred Cowell, would quietly point out their mistake, leaving them a little embarrassed.

In spite of her size, Mary was always the boss, letting me know it in no uncertain terms. She would regularly pull my hair and clonk me with her rattle or anything else she could lay her hands on, but I took it all in my stride and hardly ever retaliated.

I was born in Bank Hall Hospital, Burnley, on April 11th 1939 at seven o'clock in the morning; Mary came into the world five hours later, at noon. Mum wasn't feeling too well following the births, as I was born feet first and Mary was breech, presenting buttocks first. Mum already had two older children, Maureen, who was four years and one month old, and Jimmy, aged twenty months. In the next bed to Mum in hospital, a lady had given birth to a little baby boy nine days previously. The lady was called Mrs Cheetham and she named her son Robert. Little did we know then, that although 'Bobby' and I were to have many differences, we would become lifelong friends.

Mum hadn't been too happy when she'd discovered she was pregnant for the third time. Her unhappiness stemmed from the fact that my dad wasn't the most supportive husband in the world; he much preferred the company of his drinking friends to that of his family, spending most of his time and money in the pub. He had a horse and cart and was a rag-and-bone man but also dealt in scrap iron, having many good business connections. Despite being a shrewd businessman with a flare for making money, he had an even greater flare for spending it, especially on his boozing cronies. He'd freely buy drinks for everyone in the pub, and relished the popularity that surrounded him. His name was John, but to his family and friends he was better known as 'Jack'. He also had another nickname around the town pubs: 'Barney'. He was well liked by all his drinking companions because of his generosity, but it was a different tale when it came to finding some housekeeping money ... poor Mum had to fight for every penny she got from him.

In her frustration at discovering that she was pregnant again, Mum became angry and raised her head to Heaven crying out, "No ... no, I don't want this baby, God! I know when I was a young girl I always dreamed of having four children of my own; but I'd imagined then that I would have the help and support of a loving, caring husband. But Jack thinks more of his so-called friends in the pubs than he does of his own little ones. I can't bear the thought of bringing another baby into this world ... please God, understand!"

Well, she got her answer all right ... it was as if God answered, *"Oh, so you don't want this baby, Winifred ... well, we'll just have to see about that won't we?"*

A few days later, whilst Mum was attending the antenatal clinic, one of the midwives approached her with a smile on her face.

"Well, well Mrs Cowell, haven't we got good news for you ... you're having twins!" Mum was flabbergasted.

"Oh dear!" she thought, "That just serves me right, doesn't it God ... testing Your infinite wisdom?" After the initial shock she was left with little option but to settle down into some sort of routine. Despite Dad's wanton ways, he always seemed to rally round at times like this. He stayed off the beer whilst Mum was in hospital and cared for the two older children, catering to their every need. When Dad was good, he was very good.

At the time, Mum and Dad lived in a council house at number 36 Dalton Street in the Bleak House Estate; it was Mum's pride and joy ... she used to call it her sunshine house. She'd only been married five years and had already moved six times, and this was the only decent place she'd ever lived in. Two of the previous five houses were in condemned slum areas with atrocious living conditions. Dalton Street, however, had a garden and three bedrooms, but most important of all … a bathroom. An added bonus was that Mum got on very well with the next-door neighbour, Mrs Alice King. Alice often looked after Maureen and Jimmy whilst Mum took Mary and me to the clinic – Mary needed sunlight treatment in order to build her up. My sister was placed on to a hospital trolley under a sunray lamp for about twenty minutes, and the rays aided the synthesis of certain vitamins, especially vitamin D needed for the building of strong, healthy bones and the prevention of rickets.

My oldest sister, Maureen, had only just turned four years old at the time, but was already coming into her own, doing little chores around the house and acting like a little mother to her younger siblings. She was a godsend to Mum. Whilst Mum was still in hospital she helped Dad with the housework and looked after Jimmy. She wasn't very big herself and used to stand at the sink on a wooden box to do the washing up. Maureen recalls standing at the front door when the ambulance arrived bringing Mum home from hospital. Mum stepped out followed by Dad, who was carrying Mary in one arm and me in the other. When Dad was like this things were great, but it wasn't long before he went back to his errant ways. In the following months Mum struggled, doing everything in her power to raise her young family alone.

*   *   *

In the September following my birth, Germany invaded Poland and three days later the Second World War began.

The Government introduced rationing and ration books were issued from specially designated government buildings. Air-raid shelters sprang up all over the town, in backyards, schools and workplaces. The voice of Winston Churchill was constantly on the wireless and warnings were plastered on billboards, alerting people to the impending danger, preparing them for war.

The Prime Minister, Neville Chamberlain, made an announcement over the wireless: "Unlike the First World War, this is not just going to be a soldiers' war, it's going to be a people's war too ... every man woman and child will be involved. Most attacks will be at night-time, so be prepared to spend many hours in the air-raid shelters provided in case of air attack."

*   *   *

Despite the war, things didn't change much for Mum. Maureen and Jimmy had just got over a bout of whooping cough when Mary and I contracted it. I was quite robust and soon recovered, whereas Mary, being so delicate, became seriously ill as the cough developed into croup. My sister fought for every breath she took and certainly would have died but for the constant vigil kept over her by Mum. Mary retched at every mouthful of food and gradually went back down to her birth weight ... Mum had to stay up night after night, painstakingly spoon-feeding her. Eventually, after five months of agonising torment, Mary started to show signs of improvement.

This was only one of many struggles that Mum endured, but through it all she persevered. Her biggest worry was that her children would be taken into care and separated from each other. She'd heard many bizarre tales of how children were being deported to Australia never to return, and she was determined to keep all her little ones together, no matter what the cost to herself.

"I want all my children to grow up knowing and loving one another," she would say, "I don't want them scattered to different parts of the globe." She also dreaded the fact that her children, like many others, would be taken into care and then fostered out, becoming skivvies to the more privileged folk.

*   *   *

Number 36 Dalton Street was certainly Mum's dream house but alas, her dream was about to be shattered. Because of Dad's drinking, Mum was forever short of money and consequently got into arrears with the rent. The Council, very strict about such matters, eventually served an eviction order on her. She wrote asking for leeway but they were unforgiving ... and shortly afterwards, the bailiff's van arrived. Mary and I were in our pram outside with Maureen gently rocking it; Mum was sat on the front step with Jimmy on her knee. The bailiff's workers were hardened men, but this pathetic sight touched them so much that even they couldn't carry out their grim task. However, the Council would not relent and served another notice; Mum, along with her young family, had to go. Dad did the job himself, loading all the furniture onto his cart.

As it happened, there was a family living just across the street from us – the Halsteads. Walter Halstead, fourteen years of age at the time, witnessed the whole sorry spectacle and he was moved to tears.

"This can't be true," he thought to himself. 'Surely to goodness the Council can't be throwing Mrs Cowell and her children out onto the street?" During the time spent in Dalton Street, young Walter used to run errands for Mum and he'd become quite attached to her family. He ran across and tapped Mum on the shoulder.

"What's happening Mrs Cowell, what are they doing with your furniture?"

Mum could see the concerned look on the young lad's face and tried to reassure him: "It's all right, young Walter, don't worry about it … we'll be all right, you'll see."

Walter was a very perceptive young lad and, despite Mum's assurance, he sensed the truth. He felt both mad and sad at the same time about the injustice of things, as he'd always looked up to Mum and admired her. In fact, he'd always had a kind of teenage crush on her because of striking features such as her long, flowing, dark hair. He knew in his heart that something cruel and heartless was happening; the memory of that terrible day was to remain with him for the rest of his life. He watched as Dad guided off the horse and cart with Mum and the four children perched in-between the sparse furniture.

"Goodbye kind lady," he muttered to himself as the cart turned right at the bottom of Dalton Street onto Coal Clough Lane. "Good luck and God bless." Walter didn't know it at the time, but he wasn't to set eyes on that poor family again for another sixty years.

Within the next fifteen months we moved another three times, living in appalling conditions at each new place, until finally we arrived at 14 Albion Street, where we lived for the next twenty years. It was during this upheaval that Mum discovered she was pregnant again. …

*   *   *

Albion Street was situated in the very heart of 'The Weavers' Triangle', so called because of the cluster of factories and tall factory chimneys that punctuated the skyline. Burnley, being a very important industrial town, had more factory chimneys than any other town of comparable size in the world; thick dense smoke constantly hung over it like a shroud. The main industry was cotton, as the damp climate of Burnley was ideal for its production. Day after day the tall chimneys belched out thick smoke and soot, which coated all the buildings and terraced houses with grime. Like many other milltowns, Burnley's Victorian buildings had been built during the Industrial Revolution of the 1800s. As a child, I could never remember living anywhere else other than this over-polluted area of town.

The Leeds and Liverpool Canal ran through the length of Burnley and was overlooked on both sides by large cotton mills and weaving sheds. Running parallel on the topside was Trafalgar Street, a main thoroughfare for traffic. The local people always knew Trafalgar Street as simply 'Trafalgar'. Built in close proximity to these dreary mills on the other side of Trafalgar was a labyrinth of cobbled streets that ran up to a railway embankment. Albion Street was much longer and steeper than any other street; it continued over the railway via a stone railway bridge, carrying on for another half-mile to the gates of Scott's Park.

Number 14 was below the railway bridge in the middle of the terraced block. It had two bedrooms, two downstairs rooms and two cellars. All the rooms were bare, without a strip of wallpaper on the walls. The plaster was crumbling and there was evidence of damp everywhere. Still, it was better than some of the hovels we had lived in.

The downstairs living room was the only room with lighting, an old antiquated gas-lamp that hung from the ceiling. The focal point of the room was a large black cast-iron fireplace with a mantelpiece. Pans could be placed on top of and into a built-in oven with a heavy door. The fire-grate was about fifteen inches off the floor to allow ashes to fall through the grid. On the other side, a water boiler with a hinged lid rested below a shelf on which kitchen utensils were stored.

It was a cold, draughty house, and the wind would howl up a flight of stone steps from the cellar below. The bare stone flags of the living-room floor didn't help matters either. When Mum looked around the house for the first time she fixed her gaze on the small pot sink that sat on cast-iron legs under the window. The flimsy, flea-ridden lace curtains billowed in the draught from the rotting windowsill.

"Well, at least I've got running water and a gas geyser," she told herself as her eyes wandered around the room. "Thank you, God, for small mercies!" She opened the back door to find a flight of fourteen steep stone steps. Taking up most of the yard space was a large air-raid shelter that housed the lavatory. "Bloomin' 'eck," she murmured, "I don't fancy going down there on a cold night … or any other night for that matter." Mum didn't like the situation very much, but being a realist she knew she had little option.

The living room was only small, though Dad helped improve the atmosphere of the place when he procured a large ornamental sideboard. It took up most of the space against the back wall, but Mum was quite pleased with the acquisition, because the reflection from its enormous mirror added depth to the room and made it feel much cosier.

After we went to bed, Maureen would help Mum to wash up and tidy the house and then help with the ironing, sock-darning and other chores. Mum never took her help for granted and was eternally grateful, thanking God every single night that Maureen had been her firstborn.

"Well God, it's not much but it's better than not having a roof over our heads. Please shine Thy holy light down onto this humble home and bless all who live in it. Please grant that all my young ones remain healthy and strong. I ask Thee for guidance to bring my children up in a proper manner and keep them free from evil. Also, if it's not asking too much, please let my husband come to his senses so we may rear our young family together." Unfortunately the latter part of the prayer was not answered ... at least, it seemed that way at the time.

One month after moving into Albion Street, Barry was born. Three little boys and two little girls, one big happy family ... but Dad's lifestyle remained unchanged. He still preferred the company of the yobbos in the pub to that of his young ones ... game of cards and a few pints of bitter were more to his taste than helping to raise his family. Still, Mum more than made up for his lack of support, making sure that none of her children went short of love.

Time passed by and Mum struggled on, using everything at her disposal to make it a happy home. Bath time was quite an ordeal in our house. One evening, after our Maureen had just helped Mum to bath Mary and me, she stood us on the old settee. Mary became over excited, laughing and giggling as she jumped up and down on the old, battered sofa. However, the merriment turned to tears when she hurt one of her big toes on a protruding spring.

"O-oh come here and let me kiss it better," Maureen said to her, reassuringly. "Bloomin' 'eck, what big tears, our little Mary ... we're gonna have to get out the mop and bucket!"

Then Maureen pretended she'd hurt her finger on the same spring, turning Mary's tears into laughter.

"My Maureen, can I kiss your finger better?" Mary giggled, her pain now forgotten.

"E-eh that's better, you're such a pretty little girl when you laugh. Now lift up your arms while I put on your nightie," smiled Maureen as she dressed Mary in some warm clean clothes that had been draped on the wooden rack, hanging from the ceiling over the warm fire. Mary and I then stood on a moth-eaten pegged rug in front of an old metal fireguard, which protected us from the flames.

Like Mary, Barry was always a delicate child, and in need of constant care and attention. He was forever contracting chest ailments and would suffer from asthma in his future years.

By now Mary and I were walking and had become very mischievous. To make matters worse, Jimmy was hyperactive and forever demanding Mum's undivided attention.

My earliest distinct memory dates back to when I was barely three years old when I got terrible stomach pains and was violently sick. Mum tried putting me on the potty, without a result and then aggravated the situation by giving me a dose of working medicine. The next thing I recall was waking up in a hospital cot with steel clips in my tummy after an emergency operation for a burst appendix and by all accounts had nearly died. I couldn't understand what was happening as Dad, Mum and Maureen were by my cot-side making a real fuss. It turned out that Dad and Maureen had been there all night awaiting my recovery. Mum had just arrived, having had to look after the other children.

I held out my arms beckoning Mum and she picked me up with tears in her eyes. "Oh thank you, God … thank you so much!" she whimpered, as she gave me a big hug.

Next it was Maureen's turn. "E-eh my little brother … come here and let me love you!"

Even Dad picked me up and gave me a gentle hug, muttering, "Eh my lad, thank goodness you're all reight … I thought we were gonna lose thi." I couldn't fully understand what all the fuss was about but, all the same, I enjoyed the attention!

A few days later Dad came and collected me and this too turned into a memorable occasion … it was the one and only time that I saw my Uncle Ted. "Right cock, afore we go home I'm gonna take you to see my brother Ted, who's on Ward Three." Uncle Ted was very poorly and confined to bed but all the same he gave me a hearty greeting.

"Eh, all reight, little un … by gum, I believe you've been in the wars. Never mind, you don't seem to have come to any harm. Anyroad, come here and let me have a reight look at thi." I was usually apprehensive in these kinds of situations, and needed a little friendly persuasion from Dad.

"Go on, our John, you know who it is, don't you … it's your Uncle Ted, mi brother?" I'd heard Dad talk about his brother Ted but, never having seen him before, I was still guarded. Ted, sensing my wariness, soon put me at ease.

"By 'eck lad, you've fairly grown since the last time I saw thi. Then again … you were nowt but a babe in arms, and now look at thi. Well, d'you know who I am then?" he grinned.

"U-um," I replied through pursed lips, "you're my Uncle Ted."

"Aye that's reight, lad. Anyroad, you'll have seen one o' these afore?" he said, showing me a flat cap.

"Yeah," I responded with a smile on my face, "it's a 'watta' … mi daddy has one."

Ted started to laugh, "Good lad … I can see we're gonna have to watch thi. Anyroad, you might have seen one afore, but not like this un … this one's magic!" He then took some sweets from a toffee bag on the top of his locker and dropped them into the cap along with some pennies. My eyes lit up … I was beginning to like my Uncle Ted. My pleasure increased even more when Ted shouted for one of the more able patients to come to his bedside.

"Will you take this little lad around the ward with this here cap and introduce him to t'other patients … his name's John and he'd like to meet 'em all." Ted handed me the cap saying, 'Go on young John … tha'll be all reight."

I was still feeling edgy as I looked up at this big man wearing pyjamas. With cap in hand, I glanced first at Uncle Ted and then Dad, as if asking for approval.

"Go on, our John, like your Uncle Ted said … you'll be all reight," he assured me.

As we set off round the ward, Ted remarked on what I had said to him, "A 'watta' … that's a good un, our Jack … I've never heard mi cap called that afore."

"Aye our Ted, he's probably heard me callin' it a 'ratter'."

"I'll tell thi what … he's a grand little lad and he certainly seems to be out o' the woods now, doesn't he?"

"He does that, Ted … touch wood. It's hard to believe that only a few days ago he frightened the life outta me, I thought he were a goner for sure … his eyes were rolling about in his head and he were just like a rag doll when I carried him into t'hospital."

In the meanwhile I was happily going around the ward getting the flat cap filled with pennies and sweets. After leaving the last bed I happily made my way back to Dad's side.

"Look what I've got, Daddy," I said with a large smile on my face, rubbing my hands in glee.

"By 'eck, cock, you have done well ... you've even got some thre'penny bits in there."

"Aye and think on, our Jack," put in Ted, "no borrowing out of it forra drink in the pub."

I left the ward holding Daddy's hand and on reaching the exit I turned and gave Uncle Ted a friendly wave. Sadly, that was the last time I ever saw him, for he died shortly afterwards.

*   *   *

My next vivid memory, which was to remain with me and in some ways affect me for life, was the time I spent in the Workhouse with my sister Mary and younger brother Barry. Dad had been involved with some villains and was serving time in Wakefield Prison for handling stolen goods, whilst Mum was in hospital 'buying' another baby.

I remember being shepherded into a barrack-type room with some other children by some matronly women in uniforms, who then started shouting and laying down strict rules. The most horrendous part, as far as I was concerned, was when all the children were shown a dark, eerie cubbyhole leading down some stone steps into the darkness. The formidable women then instilled fear into us all by threatening to put us in that awful place should we misbehave. The terrible threats rendered us all passive and afraid.

"Right, you little scruff bags," bellowed one of them, "this is the Bogey-hole and if you're bad that's where you'll go!"

Within a few days the inevitable happened ... I was dragged to the Bogey-hole by the scruff of my neck with threats of, "Right you little brat ... in you go and the Bogey-man's gonna come and get you!" I screamed incessantly, kicking out at the big woman, but to no avail; she was too strong for me and I finished up in the pitch-darkness, terrified and shivering. My fear intensified as I conjured up gory and gruesome images in my mind.

"Let me out of here, it's dark and I'm frikened," I wailed, "I don't want the Bogey-man to get me! ... I'm gonna tell mi mummy over you!" I kicked the door and screamed for all my worth, but it was useless ... I had to remain in that eerie place for what seemed hours.

Other cruel things happened in the Workhouse, but this particular incident left a lasting mark on my impressionable mind, and haunts me to this day. Both Mary and I hated being in that awful workhouse, but we had to stay there for two months until Dad was released from prison. We were highly delighted when he came to collect us and greeted him with open arms. On reaching home, however, our joy turned to perplexity when we discovered that there was an addition to the family.

Mum was in bed in the living room, cradling a little baby girl in her arms ... Barbara had been born. The family was now complete: Dad, Mum, three little boys and three little girls. This should have been enough to make any man happy, but not Dad ... no, not Dad.

2

FAMILY STRUGGLES

The memory of the Workhouse wasn't very pleasant, but Mum more than made up for it. I loved nothing more than sitting on her knee around the fireside whilst she told the most enlightening stories about her own upbringing and schooldays in Bacup. She was a raconteur of the highest order – her tales were both fascinating and poignant. She told them so explicitly and with such feeling that tears would well up in my eyes, while at other times I'd roll about laughing.

Our home was sparse and dire ... the bare stone floors, the one gaslight and just cold water to hand, but after Mum had finished telling her tales I would throw my arms around her neck, saying with real concern, "He-ey Mum, weren't you poor?" Then, despite myself, I'd prompt her to tell more: "Will you tell us agen about your little brother Jimmy who got killed in the pit when he were only a lad?" This was a really sad tale about how my grandmother had struggled to raise ten children under terrible conditions.

They lived in a two-roomed back-to-earth house, full of rising damp. Unlike a back-to-back house, the back-to-earth house was built into a hillside with only one door at the front. On entering, a staircase led to a solitary bedroom. The downstairs room had stone flag floors, a pot sink and a black cast-iron iron fireplace similar to the one in our house.

"There was no lighting," Mum began wistfully, "except from candles or an old paraffin lamp. Water had to be carried in a large bucket from a standpipe near to some communal toilets. U-um, and many a time during the winter months the standpipe was frozen solid so you can imagine what it was like then ... br-rr-r, it makes me shiver to think about it ... it was awful!"

I would often interrupt her tales asking, "Bloomin' 'eck, Mum, did you have to share the toilets with other people?"

"We did that, lad, and first we had to walk to the end of the block via a landing and down fifteen stone steps. Another thing, we could only have a bath on Wednesdays because all the neighbours took turns at sharing an old tin bath that hung on the wall outside. Aye, can you imagine carrying buckets of water from the standpipes and then having to heat it over the fire in a large double-handled pan? And also, to keep the fire going we had to lug coal from a cubbyhole that was at the top of the stairs."

"Do you mean the coal place was upstairs, Mum?" I quizzed her.

"Yes it was, the coal chap used to empty the bags down from a chute on Todmorden Road."

"Blimey Mam it musta seemed funny having to go upstairs for the coal."

"Well no, it didn't, our John, but don't forget we didn't know anything else."

"Yeah all right Mam, but it would've seemed funny to me."

The rest of Mum's story went something like this:

Large factories overlooked the small house, casting long shadows, which left it in permanent semi-darkness. There was a constant foisty smell in the air. Because of the dire circumstances my older brother Martin and two baby sisters, Teresa and Nellie, died, causing untold sorrow. My younger brother Jimmy was a godsend to mi mam, helping to support her in every way possible and especially so during the sorrowful times. He was a likeable lad and a well-known character around Bacup, working on the market stalls and selling the *Evening Telegraph* in the Town Square. Tragically, he was killed in a coal-mining accident just a few days before his seventeenth birthday. On the day of the funeral, hundreds of people lined the streets and followed the horse-drawn hearse to Bacup Cemetery. My poor mother didn't have young Jimmy to console her on this occasion; it was terrible... her hair turned snow white overnight following his death.

I was eighteen years old at the time and badly affected by my brother's death, which brought back painful memories of the deaths of my other brother and two baby sisters, which were due to the atrocious living conditions. It was awful ... simply awful!"

On other occasions, Mum told me about her own parents' childhood days and those of her grandmother.

I loved the tale of my great-grandmother Joanna. Unlike 'Cinderella', hers was a riches-to-rags story. It started back as far as 1869, in County Mayo, Ireland, where Joanna was born:

Joanna Lyons, the daughter of wealthy landowners and staunch Protestants, was just a slip of a girl of seventeen when she fell deeply in love with John Callaghan, an employee on her father's estate and a devout Catholic. When Joanna's father heard about the relationship he adamantly forbade it. However, Joanna and John eloped to England and married, whereupon Joanna's father disinherited her, leaving her completely penniless. The young couple subsequently had four children, but on writing home to her parents in Ireland, on each occasion, her letter was returned unopened ... she never heard from her parents again! The poverty had disastrous effects on their marriage and John left home, taking with him his eldest daughter Mary, who was later adopted and brought up by his relatives.

I interrupted Mum at this point. "Mary ... was that mi granma?"

"Yes that's right, and like you know, she was brought up in Stacksteads by the Tiddy family and raised in the Catholic faith."

"And when she grew up she met mi grandad in Bacup and they got married in a little church in Rawtenstall ... is that right, Mam?"

"Yes, that's right, our John ... it was called 'St James the Less'. Anyway, that's enough for one night ... it's bedtime now."

"A-ah Mam, just tell us a bit more ... please!"

She'd go on a little while longer and then I'd have to go to bed.

On other occasions when Mum took us all over to Bacup to visit our grandparents, my grandad would tell tales about the First World War and the appalling conditions in the trenches on the front line.

Grandad was always grumpy, but after listening to his harrowing tales I could well understand why.

"Besides," I would think, "my grandad isn't very well … what with all the gas bombs and having to spend fours years in them cold, wet trenches an' all. U-um, I think I'd be grumpy too if I'd had to go through all that lot!"

One tale that always touched me was the one Mum told me about the night her dad came home from that terrible war. She was nearly six years old at the time.

"It is very memorable," she would say, "because, number one … it was the first time I recall ever seeing my dad. Number two … he brought each one of us a present – mine was a little rag doll, the first I'd ever had. It was only a rag doll, but to me it was the most beautiful dolly in the world … I named her 'Joy' and treasured her right into my adult life. We also had a welcome-home party for Dad and for the first time in my life that little house echoed to the sound of joy and laughter."

"Bloomin' 'eck, Mam, I hope there's not a war when I grow up," I put in, "I wouldn't like to live in them cold, wet trenches."

"No, neither would I our John, my dad said it was like hell on earth! U-um, it wasn't just the war either. When the soldiers returned from that terrible place, the Government had a couldn't-care-less attitude and the men had to face appalling conditions. Mi poor dad came home full of expectations, but he had to pick up the threads of his life unsupported. What made it worse is that he'd been shot through his shoulder and was never able to use it again efficiently. The Government had promised this would be a land fit for heroes, but like many others who'd survived the terrible conditions on the Western Front, Dad found the country in a state of economic depression. For those who could find work the pay was poor and they had to work in all conditions for a meagre two shillings a day. Many a time Dad came home drenched to the skin. Against their pride, many of those heroic men ended up in the Workhouse."

Mother's storytelling totally enthralled me as I sat on her knee, listening intently.

"Go on, Mum, tell me some more ... how did you go on as a little girl at school?"

At that, Mum would describe the desperate deprivation of her own childhood. "Mind you," she would stress, "many other families languished in the same abject poverty." She paused for a moment in deep thought. "He-ey, mi poor mam and dad had nothing ... they didn't stand a chance. By 'eck, our John, things were hard, when I think about it, I don't know how we survived at all. Our Katie and I were forever in bother for fighting. We had to stick up for ourselves against girls from better-to-do families who were constantly attacking us with nasty comments and sarcastic remarks. Even the teachers seemed to look down on us. Mind you, we weren't the only ones ... many other children suffered the same plight as we did, constantly struggling to survive!" At this point Mum stopped briefly, a sad expression on her face. "In fact," she stressed, "just like my own family, many children died because of the appalling conditions!" She reflected sadly on one terrible incident, pausing for thought. "My best friend, Mary MacDevit, was one of those children ... she was only fourteen when a terrible tuberculosis epidemic, known in those days as consumption, swept through the town, killing her and two of her brothers and sisters. They all died within two months of each other."

"E-eh Mam that were a shame, I bet you missed her."

"I did that, lad," she murmured softly, "more than you'll ever know … it still brings tears to my eyes when I think about her."

"Were you workin' in the mill when it happened, Mam?"

"That's right, our John. In fact, I worked at Ross Mill with your Aunt Katie for about five years. The mill owners were slave drivers and by the time I was nineteen I'd decided I'd had enough. So I took myself off to London where I became a waitress in a big hotel. A kindly gentleman called Mr Baron, who'd previously lived in Bacup, introduced me to the trade. I'll never forget when he informed me that he'd found me a position and a place to stay."

"Flippin' 'eck Mam, is that where you met Dad?"

"No son, I worked down London for about eighteen months and then, after a short break back home in Bacup, I took myself off to Morecambe." She pondered again a little before adding, "Yeah, and that's where my troubles really began … I met your dad!"

I giggled at that remark, prompting her to tell me more.

"Well, we had a stormy courtship in Morecambe but I really loved him. I became pregnant with Maureen and, after a lot of consideration, we got married in Lancaster. After that we returned to Burnley, your dad's home town. Due to Jack's reckless behaviour we lived in atrocious conditions, moving from place to place. We were living in a little room in the Bridge Inn when Maureen was born. We then moved into a condemned house in the Croft area, near to your Aunt Lily's, and that's where our Jimmy was born. From there we moved uptown into Dalton Street on the Bleak House Estate."

"Dalton Street, Mum," I interrupted, "isn't that where me and Mary were born?"

"That's right, lad, so now you know the rest."

"E-eh Mam," I said, throwing my arms around her neck, "weren't it hard for you … you were so poor!"

I used to lie in bed at night and go over the stories in my head until sleep finally claimed me. I loved all these absorbing poignant tales and their fascination remains with me to this day.

*   *   *

Just after our fifth birthday, Mary and I went into the infants' class at St Thomas's School in the care of some mature nuns. I thought it was really funny to see those ladies walking about in penguin-type robes. Sister Mary Gonzala, an elderly nun, took a shine to me, treating me very kindly. The feeling was mutual and, from the beginning, a genuine friendship was formed between us. She regularly displayed her mark of affection by her kindness.

I was a very happy child, but one thing did trouble me … every time Dad came home drunk from the pub there were constant rows. During the arguments I would stand at the bottom of the stairs, quivering. Even at my young age, many anxious thoughts ran through my head.

"Oh please God, don't let Daddy hurt Mummy! Please Jesus mek mi daddy so he's not angry! When I'm a daddy, I'll never get drunk and frighten mi kids." I knew Dad was so very wrong acting the way he did. I used to tell myself that I would never be like that when I grew up.

Dad's behaviour meant that poor Mum had to virtually raise her young family on her own, but she more than made up for his shortcomings. She ruled us with a rod of iron and her word was law, but she would have gladly died for us. She gave each one of us love and affection in abundance and instilled a strict morale code into us. We all accepted this quite naturally and took everything in our stride. The simple values that she impressed upon us formed the fundamental bedrock of our lives.

Living in abject poverty, Mum strove to keep food on the table, using every method at her disposal ... even a meal of fish and chips from the chippy was a luxury she could ill afford. On some occasions we had to make do with dripping butties or jam and bread.

"Mam, will you make us some magic soldiers?" one or other of us would ask. She'd then spread some margarine onto freshly baked bread and cut it into segments.

"Here you are children, these are little magic soldiers. Now if you shut your eyes and wish, they can be anything you want them to be."

"Oh goodie, mine's gonna be a cream bun," said Barbara, excitedly.

"And I'm gonna have a chocolate cake," laughed Barry "yummy yummy!" Mum was always touched by our reaction. She'd look around the table and marvel at our enthusiasm and our fertile imaginations.

"Thank you God," she prayed with tears welling up in her eyes, "my little ones have so little and yet they're so happy ... they're grateful for every little morsel I give them." She had to smile to herself at the way we really did enjoy the scraps of food. At times like these she felt that, despite her plight, everything was worth it.

By now Mum had got to know the Trafalgar area quite well. She knew where all the shops were and, despite being regarded as overprotective towards her children, she generally got on well with the neighbours. She had a few rows, but these were usually sorted out and by and large there were no hard feelings.

* * *

Because of the blackout it became quite dangerous and scary trying to negotiate the outside fourteen stone steps on the way to the lavatory especially on moonless nights with the backstreet in total darkness.

A local joke at the time printed in the *Burnley Express*:

One night Mrs Smith, who lives in one of the many terraced houses, heard a knock on the backdoor. On opening it, there was a rather official-looking warden stood there.

"Hello officer, what can I do for thi?"

"Well, I'm here, Mrs Smith, to reprimand you cos you're showing a chink o' light through your curtains."

"Oh I'm sorry officer, I'll shut 'em right away and I'll mek sure it don't happen agen."

"Aye all right but think on it doesn't ... or I'll have to report thi."

"Righto officer, thank you very much ... bye."

Five minutes later there was another knock on the door and on opening it, Mrs Smith was surprised to see the same warden standing there, looking rather embarrassed.

"I'm sorry, Mrs Smith, but could you do me a favour please?"

"Certainly officer, what is it?"

"Well," he stuttered, "could you just open your curtains for a second ... I've put mi torch down somewhere and I can't find mi way outta the backyard!"

Many jokes like these filled the local newspapers in an effort to keep the people's morale high and the community spirit close knit. People took everything in their stride, even the daunting times they had to spend in the dark, dank air-raid shelters during an air-raid warning.

Mum refused to use an air-raid shelter, having weighed up the situation from every angle. In the case of threatened attack she would gather all of us together … if we were in bed she would leave us there.

"But what if a bomb drops onto t'house, Mummy?" Jimmy asked her anxiously one day. "We'll all be killed!"

"Yes, I know that our Jimmy, but if a bomb landed on th'air-raid shelter we'd be killed anyway."

"What are the air-raid shelters for, then?"

"Well, if a bomb landed on the house it wouldn't kill the people in th'air-raid shelter but they could be buried for days on end. They could face a horrible death, much worse than being killed instantly. No, I don't want that for my kids … if they're going to die let it be in the comfort and warmth of their own beds."

"But I don't want to die, Mummy!" said Jimmy, rather concerned.

"I know that son, nobody does, but it's the lesser of two evils … I'm just doing what I think is best under the circumstances. Anyway, don't fret yourself so, it's not going to happen."

*　*　*

As a child, I found life on Albion Street fascinating. With the goings on around our way and the many different characters in the area, there was never a dull moment. Nobody had anything much, but no matter – the close-knit community spirit and the friendliness more than made up for it.

Friends and neighbours alike helped each other, and if someone was ill, folk would rally round, making meals and doing anything else necessary for the family concerned. Constant round-the-clock care would be provided until the family could once again cope for themselves.

Some neighbours would go to great lengths, putting themselves out on a limb in order to help their fellow man … even to the extent of risking their own lives.

On one occasion that remains firmly lodged in my memory, a fire engine roared up Albion Street, its bells clanging. It stopped lower down the street to attend a house fire at number 9.

At the time, Mrs Florence Shackleton, whose husband was serving abroad in Egypt, lived next door at number 7. Living at home with her were her two sons, Jimmy and Tom, and her three daughters, Amy, Maud and Sally.

Mrs Shackleton smelt smoke, which appeared to be seeping through the walls from next door, and went to investigate. To her horror, she found the hallway ablaze, making it impossible for anyone to enter or leave the house. Her fears were intensified by the fact that a young couple with a baby girl had recently moved into the house and the child's cradle was in the front room.

"Oh my goodness," she gasped, "the baby's trapped!"

Without any thought of injury to herself, she got a stand-chair and smashed the window. Using the same chair as a step, she climbed onto the windowsill and into the smoky room. After fumbling about in the hazy fumes, she found the baby lying on an old battered settee. She immediately wrapped the child in her coat and then tried to make her escape. Alas, the floor caved in and she fell through to the cellar below, still protectively clutching the baby to her chest.

Meanwhile, another neighbour had called the fire brigade. After dousing the flames the firemen found Florence huddled in a corner of the cellar still cradling the little baby girl in her arms. Both Florence and the child were immediately taken to hospital and treated for smoke inhalation. By the grace of God, neither she nor the baby suffered any ill effects. However, Mrs Shackleton did suffer a minor back injury, which was to trouble her in the coming years. She had to wear a plaster cast for quite a long time afterwards.

The incident was the talking point around the neighbourhood but, despite a write-up in the *Burnley Express*, Mrs Shackleton never did get the recognition or commendation that she richly deserved.

But overall, things turned out fine and, like anything else, it did have its funny side. A neighbour, Mr Daly, later removed the plaster cast using the only tool he had ... a tin opener! Florence's children kept the plaster cast a long time afterwards as a souvenir and a reminder of their mother's outstanding bravery.

Florence's story is but a reminder of the resilience, determination and bravery people displayed in those trying times, as they all rallied together in friendship and mutual support.

*   *   *

Nobody had a television where we lived, yet no one lacked entertainment. Elderly folk and parents alike sat on their doorsteps and derived great pleasure from watching children playing street games. It was also amusing to watch the antics of the many different local characters – especially so at weekends, after the pubs had closed. Many men and women would come tottering over the footbridge at the bottom of Albion Street and individuals could easily be identified by their high-pitched voice or the song they were singing.

Jack Bickle, who lived across the street at number 27, never failed to make the kids laugh. He was partially sighted and wore thick-rimmed spectacles. One afternoon, after a session in the Malakoff Pub, he was tottering from side to side as he staggered up Albion Street; our Maureen and Winnie Clarke watched his progress, and finding it highly amusing to behold. He looked really funny, stopping for a breather every few yards, crouching over grasping his knees huffing and puffing.

"Hiya Jack, are you all right?" Maureen asked.

"Aye all reight cock … and you?"

"Yeah … I'm not so bad."

"Good … that's good," he mumbled. Then after a short pause, "Anyroad, canya tell me, cock … if I keep goin' up here, will I come to Scott's Park?"

"Yeah, you will, Jack," Winnie clipped in.

To their amusement he replied in a drawled-out voice, "Oh good, thanks a lot … I must be on the right street, then!"

* * *

One night, just a week before my sixth birthday, something happened that was to remain with me for the rest of my life. Dad arrived home in a paralytic state and as the depressing effects of the alcohol reached its peak he caused a right ruction. He was in the most obstreperous of moods and during a fierce struggle he put Jimmy, Mary, Barry and baby Barbara into the cellar top. Mum fiercely confronted him, scratching, biting and kicking him, but to no avail. A look of abject terror spread over Mum's face and the look of horror in her eyes chilled me to the bone ... that haunted look has remained with me to this day. I was stood in the living room and witnessed Mum hitting Dad over the head with a steel poker, splitting his head open. I was in a right state as the brutal scene unfolded before my eyes. He finished up lying on the floor of the lobby with his head in a pool of blood; thinking he was dead, I ran up to him and, kneeling by his side with tears rolling down my cheeks, begged for Jesus to let Daddy live. The police became involved and Mum was arrested and taken into custody at Burnley Police Station accused of causing grievous bodily harm.

Dad did live, but there was a big court case over the incident, and an article was written about it in the *Burnley Express*. It provided yet more scandal and gossip about us to be bandied around the neighbourhood. Still, not to worry, it was soon in the past and forgotten. In fact, it wasn't long before Dad got up to his gallivanting ways again!

* * *

Mary and I were just turned six years old when the most wonderful thing happened ... *the end of the war!* The good news was declared over the wireless throughout the country. In the face of defeat, Hitler had killed himself and Germany had surrendered. It was a night that was to remain forever in people's minds ... even those of the children.

We didn't have a wireless, but that didn't matter. It soon became apparent by the sound of many excited voices out on the street that something very special had happened. Almost every neighbour was outside chatting to each other on the stone flags or dancing merrily on the cobbles.

"What's up, Mummy," asked Barry, "why is everybody holding hands and laughing?"

"E-eh son, they're laughing because they're happy. You see, they've all just had some wonderful news ... the war's over son, the war's over!"

"Does that mean we don't have to be frightened o' being bombed any more, Mam?" asked Jimmy.

"That's right lad, we don't have to live in fear anymore ... we'll all be able to sleep safely in our beds at night."

Just then, droves of people came strolling down the street from above the railway-bridge. Young people lined the street five, six and seven abreast linked up to each other, skipping and dancing as they pranced along. Everyone was elated, cheering and singing as they passed the doorways.

"Come on everybody, get your glad rags on and get yourself down to the Town Hall ... we're gonna have a right rave up!"

Along with my brothers and sisters, I became very excited, wanting to join in the festivities. My excitement increased more so when Mum and Dad agreed to follow the happy crowd with all the family. I walked briskly along holding Dad and Mary's hand whilst Dad carried Barry on his shoulders. Maureen and Jimmy followed close behind as Mum pushed little Barbara in her pram.

"This is great," I thought as we walked along Trafalgar, "I've never been out with all mi family at the same time before."

"Keep close to each other, we don't want anyone getting lost in this crowd," said Dad as hundreds more flocked from off Patten Street and Gresham Place. On reaching Manchester Road, the crowd swelled to thousands as more people emerged from other districts.

"Bloomin' 'eck," said Mum now becoming quite perturbed, 'I've never seen anything like this in my life before." She stopped and expressed her concern to Dad. "Oh I'm sorry Jack but I daren't go any further with the two little ones ... I'm frightened that they may get crushed in that crowd. You go ahead with the others, but take care of them mind, and keep a close eye on them!"

"I'll keep an eye on them as well Mam," said Maureen, "don't worry about it, we'll be all right."

"Right Jack," said Mum, "I'll get going now and I'll make a little treat for you when you all get back home."

"Right our Jimmy, you heard what your mam said," asserted Dad, "you and Maureen stick close by me and I'll hold onto the twins' hands."

During the hustle and bustle even Dad was perturbed and the nearer we got to the Town Hall the more concerned he became. Not daring to go any nearer he stopped by the side of the Canal Tavern on the corner of Finsley Gate.

"All right kids, this is far enough ... I don't want any of you geddin' hurt."

"O-oh please Dad, let us go a bit nearer so we can see better," Jimmy, Mary and I pleaded.

"No, you can stay here ... you wouldn't be able to see anything down there anyroad among all that crowd! Anyway, whaddaya moaning at ... if you look across the road you can see all them firemen looking out from the Fire Station windows." Every single window of the fire brigade building was open as the firemen waved banners and cheered loudly.

Hundreds of kids, including Bobby Cheetham and his brothers, who lived on Finsley Gate, scrambled over the steel railings of Brunswick Church and clambered up onto the wide window ledges. Brunswick Church was directly facing the Town Hall on the other side of Manchester

Road, giving the children an excellent view. Other kids scurried hither and thither, climbing onto the tops of bus shelters or gas lamps to attain a better position.

"Oh can we go over there Dad with them other kids? Go on Dad ... please!" I pleaded.

He was nearly persuaded but thought better of it. "No, they're a lot bigger than you and things could get a bit rough. Anyroad, it's a long drop inside there ... if you fell off one o' them ledges you could be killed stone dead!"

"Oh go on Dad ... please! Bobby Cheetham's in there and he's only the same age as me," I begged.

"There's nowt I can do about that, our John, he wouldn't be in there if his dad were about."

"All right then, can we climb up onto one o' them gas lamps afore any o' t'other kids get here?"

"Aye all reight, I suppose so ... but be careful."

"Yeah!" Jimmy, Mary and I yelled simultaneously, running immediately to the three remaining gas-lamps, and scrambling up onto the crossbars.

I now had a very good view of everything that was going on. I could see right to the bottom of Manchester Road and there wasn't a space available anywhere. I had an excellent view of the Town Hall clock and was intrigued to see it lit up for the first time in my life. It gave me a wonderful feeling to see crowds of people swaying in harmony as they merrily chanted away. Children perched on their dads' shoulders gazed in wonderment at the colourful spectacle. By now the crowd was as far back as Trafalgar and people were stood shoulder to shoulder on all the adjacent streets. The bulk of the crowd was around the Town Hall and the Mechanics' Institute, awaiting the Mayor's speech. Then, after the Mayor finished speaking, the Town Hall clock started to chime twelve o'clock and a strange, wonderful silence descended on the place. No sooner had the last chime struck than something spectacular happened. The large crowd erupted spontaneously, breaking into the most festive of moods, holding hands and singing 'Auld Lang Syne' and other sentimental songs. Emotion was running high and everyone started to hug and kiss each other. It was a sight to behold, especially through the impressionable eyes of a child.

"Bloomin' 'eck," I chuckled, "this is better than New Year's Eve … I've never seen owt like it afore!" I felt a nice warm glow surge through my body as I sensed the feeling of all those happy folk. I glanced over to where Dad was standing with Maureen. "Good, he's not looking," I mumbled to myself, "I'm gonna go and get a bit closer."

I climbed down the gas lamp and intermingled with the crowd, finally getting right across from the Town Hall. I knew I'd be in bother with Dad, but that was the last thing on my mind … I was determined to join in the festivities. My excitement grew as brass bands appeared out of thin air, playing the wartime songs of Vera Lynn. I laughed heartily when I saw women dancing unashamedly in their nighties while men played mouth organs and clashed dustbin lids together. The thing that intrigued me most was when people formed lines and started to dance the conga as a musical rhythm reverberated around the place.

"Come on young fellow, do you want to join in?" said a kindly lady, "I'll make sure you're all right." I didn't need asking twice and enjoyed every minute of it as people danced along Elizabeth Street, Parker Lane, St James Street, Manchester Road and all the adjacent streets. I was actually witnessing a public expression of joy that the town had rarely seen before. My mind flashed back to the stories Mum had told me about my grandfather returning from the First World War and how Bacup had celebrated in a similar way. I was completely mesmerised by the goings on … it was a magical event. I'd only just turned six years old but even at that young age, I sensed in my heart that something very special was happening. It seemed to me that heaven was rejoicing and God's angels were singing alongside us.

"This is a very special night," I thought, "a moment that will never ever happen again." I knew instinctively that it was nigh impossible to understand the feelings of every single person on that most wonderful of all nights, unless you were actually there to witness the event yourself. At that moment the Town Hall Clock struck one o'clock, bringing me back to reality.

"O-oh flippin' 'eck, is it that time already," I mumbled, "mi dad'll kill me!" The inducement to stay was great, but I knew I was in enough trouble already. It took me about five minutes to sidle through the crowds and get back to the Canal Tavern.

"Where the bloody hell have you been," bawled Dad, "we've bin looking all o'er the flamin' place for thi!"

"I'm sorry Dad, I …."

"Never mind you're bleedin' sorry," he rapped, clipping me round the head, "get back there with t'others and do as you're told in future!" But Dad's anger didn't last long – he was too intent on enjoying the moment himself.

"Righto kids, come on, we'd best get going, your mam'll go mad if we stay out any longer." I wanted to protest but didn't push my luck … I'd got off very lightly as it was.

On reaching Trafalgar we could still hear the crowd heartily singing 'Hang out your washing on the Siegfried Line'. The merrymaking was still in full swing.

As we passed along Trafalgar there were still many people on the streets listening to their wirelesses and chatting away to each other; it was the same in Albion Street. It was a warm night and it felt as though it was only about nine o'clock. To add to the occasion, Mum had done some baking.

"Righto everybody, I know it's late but you can all have a bun, some broken biscuits and a cup of tea before you go to bed. It's been a very special day today and certainly one to celebrate."

"Hey Mam, does this remind you of when mi grandad came home from the war when you were a little girl?" I asked her.

"It certainly does, our John ... I was just thinking that before you got home."

On going to bed, Jimmy and I were too excited to sleep.

"Bloomin' 'eck our Jim I reight enjoyed miself ... did you?"

"Yeah it were great, our John, it's the best night I've ever had. Did you see all them blokes in night shirts dancing with them women in their nighties?"

"Yeah," I giggled, 'it were really funny, weren't it?" We talked a little more before finally dropping off ... it was certainly a night to remember, giving us something to talk about for a long time to come.

In spite of going to bed late, I was up early the next morning, eager to find out if anything else was going on. Many of the neighbours had already decorated the outside of their houses, draping Union Jacks and bunting from their windows. Within days every street and public building throughout the town was festooned with colourful trimmings and balloons to celebrate the joyous occasion.

I have a special memory of the first day we returned back to school. I was still in the infants' class and each of us children was given a large parcel. On opening mine, I got the surprise of my life.

"O-ooh, look what I've got, our Mary," I blurted out, excitedly, "a toy car!"

"Yeah and look what they've given me," she replied happily, cuddling a very pretty doll.

We were both elated and couldn't wait to get home to show off our new toys.

"Look what I've got from school, Mam!" shouted Mary unable to contain her excitement, "a little dolly and it goes to sleep when I lay her down."

I was just as eager to show Mum my present. "And they've given me a toy car, Mam, that I can wind up with a little key. Is it like that little car that mi grandad brought back from the war for mi Uncle Jimmy?"

Mum smiled at me as she reminisced a little, going back to that night so long ago. "U-um, it does seem rather coincidental … a doll for me and our Katie and a car for mi little brother Jimmy. Oh, how I loved that doll, it was the most …."

Her thoughts were interrupted as I tugged at her dress, "Well Mam … is it like mi Uncle Jimmy's car?"

Looking at my inquisitive face, her eyes welled up as she replied, "It is, love, it's very much like it … I hope you get as much pleasure from it as my little brother did."

"And does my dolly look like yours did, Mam?" asked Mary.

"Well no, Mary. You see, mine was only a rag dolly whereas yours is more like a real baby."

"But you loved your dolly, didn't you Mummy?"

"Oh yes, very much indeed," she replied, wistfully.

There was a happy atmosphere in the house. All my other brothers and sisters got presents too, the best ones that they had ever had.

Most people were happy because the stringent restrictions – regarding lights, curfews, and the like – were lifted, but the thing that most delighted me and all the other kids was the street party that was being organised for us.

"When's our party gonna be, Mam ... will it be this Saturday afternoon?"

"No John, it's not till the Saturday after."

"A-ah, why not? Rowley Street's having theirs this Saturday after the matinee."

"Look, there's nothing I can do about that ... anyroad what difference does it make?"

"U-umph, it's not fair, them getting theirs first."

"You won't think that the week after when you're having yours, will you?"

"No, I suppose not, Mam. Anyroad, I'm gonna go round there after the picture's finished to see if I can join in."

"Yeah, and fat chance there'll be of doing that, our John," she laughed, "there'll probably be loads of other kids with the same idea."

Still, after the Saturday matinee, my mates and I made our way to the bottom of Rowley Street ... we were well aware of the festivities and wanted a slice of the action.

The grown-ups were running the party, with two ladies acting as stewards to make sure no stray kids gatecrashed.

"Now you young uns ... tha knows only too well that this party is just for the Rowley Street kids."

None of us said anything, we didn't have to ... the expressions on our faces said it all. With bowed heads and bottom lips clenched under our top teeth, we showed our obvious disappointment.

One of the ladies succumbed to our abject appeal. "E-eh Lizzie, just look at 'em, how can we leave 'em out ... what dusta think?"

"Aye I suppose you're reight, Nellie ... they do look a pitiful sight don't they?"

To our delight Lizzie invited us to join in. "All reight kids, go and join the party and enjoy yourselves ... no getting up to any mischief, mind!"

Before she'd time to finish, we all scurried amongst the other excited youngsters. We stopped for a moment, looking in awe at all the food laid out on the tables. Never in our lives had we seen so many goodies ... cakes, mince pies, jam rolls, the lot!

"By 'eck," I thought, "just look at all the goodies ... u-um, they're real too, no need to pretend this time."

The following week was the time for the Albion Street party – and what a party it was! Just like Rowley Street, all the grown-ups waited upon the tables. Never before had the kids seen anything like it on our street. It gave Mum and all the other parents a lot of joy to see all their children so happy. The street echoed to the sound of laughter as never before. I was in my element – and to add to my happiness, I was given a silver shilling, as were all the other children.

The summer of 1945 was very memorable in more ways than one. Everything went great, the weather, the parties, and for the grown-ups ... V-J Day! This was a great excuse for yet another rave-up ... not that Dad needed an excuse.

"What's happening, Mam," I asked, curious as to why all the adults seemed to be scurrying about, "why are all the grown-ups so happy?"

"Ah well, our John, there's been another wonderful event ... the Japanese have surrendered unconditionally."

I didn't understand the full impact of this, but sensed it was good news.

But one thing I did know ... Dad was in a very jovial mood, as were lots of other men. They celebrated all right: every single pub in Burnley ran dry ... there wasn't a drop of beer to be had anywhere.

3

JUNIOR SCHOOL

At the age of seven, Mary and I moved up from the infants' class to the junior school, under the guidance of my idol ... Miss Quinn. I adored this lady from the first time I set eyes on her, and immediately began conjuring up romantic images of her in my mind.

"U-um, the beautiful Miss Quinn, she's just like a film star the same as Maureen O'Hara and Susan Hayward." I'd always been fond of Sister Mary Gonzala, but this was different ... very different!

Miss Quinn was very young, with dark wavy hair that seemed to bounce about buoyantly with every movement of her head. She also had the most beautiful complexion, with skin like silk, and the most pronounced smile. Every time she came near me I went all dithery. I was mesmerised and just couldn't take my eyes off her ... I was in love for the first time.

"Oh those eyes, those beautiful eyes ... I hope she likes me as much as I like her," I would murmur, in a trance. I even used to dream about her.

Besides teaching, one of Miss Quinn's duties was preparing all her pupils for their first Confession and first Holy Communion.

There was another set of twins in our class: Nora and Teresa O'Sullivan, who were just six days younger than Mary and I. Like us, these two girls were very close but, unlike the Cowells, they were seldom seen apart and even sat next to each other in class. The four of us took our vows of devotion to God very seriously, keeping up with our prayers and going to church every Sunday and on days of obligation.

I enjoyed many aspects of school life and everything was going fine until one day Miss Quinn came out with something that made me quite unhappy. She actually announced to the class that she was shortly to be married and would be leaving the school. I couldn't believe it ... my dream was shattered!

"How can she do this to me?" I thought as she flashed her engagement ring to some of the excited girls, "I always thought she'd wait for me until I'd grown up."

Nevertheless, she did get married, and as she'd said, she left the school ... I never ever saw her again. At first I felt very sad and still daydreamed about her. But the images I'd conjured up of her gradually diminished.

*　　*　　*

In 1947, hardly anybody had a television set; in fact, only the privileged few had a wireless. Although I was only seven, I used to be fascinated with the sound of voices coming out of these little receivers, and also a little confused.

"Mam," I would ask, "are there some little people in the back of those boxes?"

"No," she would reply with a smile on her face, "it's something to do with electricity." I wasn't convinced and would peep into the back of one every time I got the chance. The number of small wires inside the wooden box intrigued me, and added further to my confusion.

"U-um, I wonder why they call 'em wirelesses," I'd ponder, "there's thousands of wires in there."

Gradually, nearly every household rented one of these contraptions – for one shilling and thre'pence a week from Radio Rental. *Dick Barton Special Agent* used to keep the whole family pinned to their seat and we were all enthralled as narrator Valentine Dile recited *The Man in Black*. Comedy programmes such as *Life with the Lyons*, starring Bebe Daniels and Ben Lyons, had us in stitches, as did *Raise a Laugh*, starring Ted Ray. Another favourite was *Over the Garden Wall*, with Norman Evans; Beryl Reid and Jimmy Clitheroe were also popular radio comics at the time. Budding new talent was given a chance to shine every week on the *Carrole Levis Show*. Wilfred Pickles had a hit game show at the time, which regularly featured his famous catchphrase, "Give 'em the money, Barney!" As Barney was Dad's nickname, this particular phrase always created a laugh in our house.

Dad, like many others, always looked forward to the sports results at five o'clock on Saturday evening, which was always preceded with a special signature tune. Bobby Cheetham was the joker in my pack of mates, and was always coming up with riddles passed onto him by his older brothers.

"Which town is connected to the *Sports Report*?" he asked me one day.

"I haven't a clue, Bobby ... which one?"

"Durham," replied Bobby, with a smirk on his face.

"I don't get it ... how do you mean?"

"Well just listen to the music that's played afore the programme starts: 'Dur-ham dur-ham dur-ham dur-ham ... dur-ham dur-ham dur-ham. Ha, Ha!"

The wireless became one of our main sources of amusement, second only to the pictures. However, picture houses did not open on Sundays and so many people tuned in to Billy Cotton and his band on the BBC, a show that opened every week with the shout of "Wakey-Wakey!" from Billy himself.

There were plenty of picture places around at the time – at least one in every area of Burnley. The one in the Trafalgar area was the Alhambra, although lots of the kids preferred to go to the Temperance, which was a little further away, in the Croft area.

I always met up with my mates Ronnie Hopkinson, David Whittaker and Kenny Clayton on a Saturday afternoon to go the matinee at the Alhambra. On the way there we'd always talk about the previous week's episodes.

"Oh, I wonder how Johnny MacBrown's gonna escape from that burning building what he were trapped in?" I said.

"I don't know," laughed Ronnie, "but he always seems to manage it somehow, doesn't he?"

"Yeah," put in David, "I thought he were a gonna for sure the week afore, when he fell into that den o' snakes."

"Hey, you never know," said Kenny naively, "he might get killed for real this time." All the rest of us burst out laughing.

"You must be joking, Kenny," laughed Ronnie "they wouldn't be able to put any more chapters on then, would they?"

"Anyroad, never mind Johnny MacBrown … what about Flash Gordon and the Clay Men?" asked David,

'What about 'em?" I replied.

"Well, d'you think Flash'll be able to rescue Dale Evans from Emperor Ming's clutches before that dragon eats her?"

"Oh aye easy, just watch … he'll break its neck with his bare hands," replied Ronnie.

At that we all started laughing and then made our way into the pictures. As foreseen, our heroes performed the miracle of getting out of their predicament, only to finish up in another precarious one, leaving us all guessing until the following week. There was no shortage of cinema heroes: the Lone Ranger and Tonto, Zorro and Hoppalong Cassidy were also favourites of ours.

The Saturday matinee provided the opportunity for many boisterous kids to let off steam, especially at half-time, and one particular incident caused a bit of a riot. Some lads sneaked upstairs and peered over the balcony, and using peashooters, they fired dried peas onto the unsuspecting kids below, hitting them on the head, neck or face.

"Ouch!" howled David as a pea stung his left cheek. "Who did that?"

Things settled down a bit and then Ronnie let out a shout, "Ouch, that hurt!" Before long the cinema was in uproar as more cries rang out.

"Right, that's it," growled Ronnie as he spotted one of the lads peering over the balcony, "it's the Whittle Fielders, come on … let's go get 'em!" David, Kenny, Ronnie and I ran for the doorway leading to the upstairs with a few other lads following. Within a few minutes all hell let loose as we started battling with our fists, flailing the air trying to kill each other. The usherettes gradually restored order, but not before quite a few blows had been exchanged.

When a matinee finished it was easy to guess what film had been showing. If it had been Zorro, we all put our coats around our shoulders to form a cape and fenced with each other. One time, as we were leaving after a showing of *The Lone Ranger*, Ronnie turned to me:

"You kimmy savvy what I say?" he joked.

"Si bien, señor," I replied.

"Bueno, let's go … vamoose!" Ronnie set off along Trafalgar, slapping his backside and shouting, "Giddy up, giddy up." We all tried to catch him, but there was no chance … our make-believe horses couldn't catch Ronnie's steady steed.

One matinee that we all enjoyed was the day of the flood … and it wasn't on the screen! A water pipe burst in the toilets at the back of the cinema and water flowed down the aisles, banking up against the stage. All the kids on the front row were highly delighted as the water got deeper and deeper. Along with some other kids, Ronnie, David and I took off our clogs and socks and started to paddle, splashing everybody in sight, annoying the girls. Others floated ice-cream cartons and lollipop sticks on the water, pretending they were boats. Many lads started stamping their feet and whistling loudly whilst others hurled missiles through the air, hitting girls on the backs of their necks. The usherettes couldn't keep all the excited boisterous youngsters under control, and the film had to be abandoned. Complimentary tickets were given out for the following week.

Besides going to the Saturday matinee at the Alhambra, I also liked to go to the Temperance on Monday evening because they put on a mini-series ... my favourite was Superman and I couldn't wait for the programme to start. Talk about Johnny MacBrown's escapades – they were nothing compared to Superman's! One week he unwittingly opened a lead-lined box, which his arch-rival Lex Luthor had sent him. When he opened the box he was immediately exposed to deadly rays from a piece of kryptonite and the serial ended with everyone wondering whether Superman would live or die. I went along the following week with my mate, Bobby Cheetham, to find out.

"Bloomin' 'eck," commented Bobby, "I wonder how Superman escapes this week ... he were dying when we left him!"

"I'll bet thi owt that Lois Lane comes just in the nick o' time to save him," I replied.

"A-ah well, it'll mek a change from him rescuing her, won't it?" quipped Bobby. We both laughed and after the film finished the riddles continued.

"How many picture places in Burnley canya think of beginning with the letter 'T'?" asked Bobby.

"Well there's the Temp for a start, then the Tivoli and ... u-um!" After quite a bit of thought I answered, "Them's th'only two I can think of."

"Oh there's plenty more," sniggered Bobby.

I pondered a while longer, before saying, "Go on then, I give up ... tell me!"

Bobby burst out laughing, "Well, there's th'Alhambra, th'Empire, th'Empress, th'Imperial, th'Odeon ...!"

"Go on, get out of it you silly sod ... I thought you were serious." Both of us burst out laughing together.

The wisecracks weren't just one-sided; there were times when I caught Bobby on the hop.

"I'll tell you what it is, Bobby," I said one day in the schoolyard, "she's a right old trouble-maker is that Annie who lives on Kepple Street, isn't she?"

"Annie … Annie who?" he asked, looking puzzled.

I cracked up laughing, "Got ya, it's that Annie Mossity … ha, ha, ha! Do you get it? *Animosity!*"

"Annie Mossity," he mumbled, fiddling about with his hair, "I don't get it." And then the penny dropped. "Oh aye, I see what you mean … animosity … ha, ha, ha!"

"You must be slipping, Bobby, you were a bit slow on the uptake there … that's not like you."

Not to be beaten, Bobby went on, "I'll tell you somet that's funny, there's a little old woman who lives on Patten Street and she's really confused but comical with it."

"Oh yeah, I know who you mean … it's Mrs Smith who has a little dog called Patch."

"Aye that's reight but have you heard the latest?"

"No, Bobby, but I'm sure you're gonna tell me." So Bobby carried on:

Mrs Smith was sat around the fireplace when there was a knock on the door. When she opened the door a policeman was standing there.

"Good morning, Madam, would you be Mrs Smith?" he asked politely.

"That's reight officer … what can I do for thi?"

"Well," he said pausing for a second, "do you have a little dog called Patch?"

"Ye-es," she replied, a little puzzled.

"Well, I'm sorry to tell you Mrs Smith, but some of the neighbours have been complaining that Patch has been chasing some young kiddies on a bike."

To the policeman's surprise and bewilderment she answered in all seriousness, "Oh no officer, it couldn't o' bin my Patch. You see ... Patch hasn't got a bike!"

"Ha ha ha!" I cracked up, "That's great Bobby ... I love it!"

*   *   *

Another time, David, Kenny and I had been playing football on Whittlefield 'Reckory' and we were making our way home along Trafalgar.

As we passed the Alhambra, Kenny said, "Oh look what's on the pictures ... *Old Mother Riley's Ghost.*"

"Oh I'd love to see that," I replied. "Ronnie saw it t'other night and he told me it were really funny."

"Yeah ... he told me the same," said David.

"It's no good bothering," moaned Kenny, "there's no chance o' that, we're all skint."

"So what," said David, "how about dodging in through the side door from that ginnel which runs down the side o' the factory?"

"Good idea, David, there's always somebody coming outta there at half time," I agreed. So all three of us crept down the ginnel and waited patiently. Sure enough, after about ten minutes, some people came out. Nimbly as anything David nipped in the open door with me close behind. We walked tentatively down the middle aisle and made our way to some seats.

"Where's Kenny?" whispered David.

"I don't know, I thought he was behind me until we got here."

"Never mind, it doesn't matter ... he's probably chickened out." Just then, the film started and we both settled back to enjoy it. Little did we know that our little scam was about to be discovered. The film was hilarious and we were both laughing heartily when the beam from a torch highlighted us.

"You two lads," rapped the usher, "come out here now!"

"Flippin' 'eck," whispered David, "how the bloomin' 'eck has he found out about us?"

"I dunno, I haven't got a clue," I muttered.

"Right," growled the usher looking at David, "what's your name?"

"David Whittaker."

"And you'll be John Cowell then ... right?" he asked, shining the torch in my eyes.

I was still trying to figure out how we'd been rumbled. "Yeah, that's right ... whaddaya want to know for?" I asked, arrogantly.

"Because you've both sneaked into the pictures without paying, that's why."

"Oh no we haven't," replied David, rather cockily.

"All right then ... where's your tickets?" Both of us lied, saying we'd lost them.

"Oh have you now? Well come with me, we'll soon sort this out!"

"We'll be all reight, Johnny," whispered David, as we were marched upstairs, "he can't prove nowt." He couldn't have been more wrong; to our horror, there was a shock awaiting us. Bella Whittaker, David's mother, was stood by the pay-desk in the foyer and she was fuming.

David's face turned three shades paler, "Oh bloomin' 'eck, now I'm forrit ... I wonder how she's found out?"

"It must have bin Kenny," I muttered under my breath, "how else could she know?"

"Less o' that whispering you two, this is no laughing matter," rapped Bella. "And as for you," she growled clouting David about the head, "what have I told you about dodging in the pictures? It's stealing!"

"But Mam, we didn't …!"

Bella cut him short in mid-sentence. "Don't lie on top o' everything else … you're forrit when you get home as it is. Aye and that goes for you too Johnny Cowell!"

"But I haven't said nowt."

"And I don't want any back chat either, you're in trouble as well when you get home. Your mam weren't too happy about having to cough up money she didn't have."

The manager weighed up the situation and could see we were both going to get chastised when we got home.

"Right Mrs Whittaker, I can see that they're both gonna get their comeuppance … if you pay for the tickets, I am willing to let the matter go this time. But I can assure you that if it happens again, I'll call the police."

After paying the cashier, Bella got hold of each of us by the scruff of our necks and frog-marched us back home, where we were dealt with accordingly.

It turned out that Kenny had spilled the beans after all, but not intentionally. As he was walking up Albion Street our Mary had called across to him.

"Kenny, do you know where our John is? Mi mam's bin looking all oe'r the place for him, we haven't seen him all day."

"Aye, he's in th'Alhambra pictures watchin' *Old Mother Riley's Ghost* wi' David Whittaker."

"What's that," came a loud voice from behind him, "did I just hear you say our David's in th'Alhambra?" On turning, Kenny went grey; he knew he'd put his foot in it when he saw David's mam.

"Well … I … I'm not sure, I only think he is," he stuttered trying to get out of it. But it was useless. Bella was too wily for that.

"You can stop your fibbing, young Kenny Clayton. You're just trying to cover up for 'em now!"

Bella then went to see my mam, who gave her permission to sort it out.

We both got 'a reight good hiding'. And it was the last time that we dodged in the pictures ... at least for a while, anyway.

* * *

Only the very privileged children had toys. But it didn't seem to bother most kids; they made their own, games getting up to all kinds of tomfoolery. This was especially true about our Jimmy – give him a bag of dried peas and it would keep him occupied for hours on end. He didn't use the peas to fire from a peashooter or a pea-gun. No, he used them for playing his favourite game: soldiers.

Jimmy enjoyed nothing more than going upstairs into the back bedroom, where he would spread the peas onto the bare wooden floor. He'd put a handful in one corner of the room and a handful in another, finishing with little piles everywhere. By using old newspapers and discarded shoeboxes he'd form little garrisons and impregnable strongholds. Each pile represented a regiment of soldiers or a tribe of Indians, and each single file symbolised men on the march.

Jimmy's incredible imagination did the rest. His games varied between Cowboys and Indians, the North and South American Civil War and the English fighting the Germans. It didn't matter to Jimmy though, whichever armies fought against each other – it was still deadly serious.

If anyone walked into the bedroom they had to knock first.

"Right you can come in but watch where you're standing," he'd bellow, "there's a battalion under siege over there and loads of Indians in that corner." Sometimes Barry used to join him and quite enjoyed it, but I could never get into the game.

"Our Jimmy's upstairs again, Mum, playing soldiers with a bag o' dried peas," one or other of us would remark.

"You leave him be, at least it keeps him quiet and out of mischief," she'd reply.

Whether it was raining or brilliant sunshine, Jimmy preferred to stay inside in the back bedroom with his army. Mum didn't mind at all, because at least she always knew where to find him.

Our Maureen hardly ever got into mischief, but even she had her moments. She had a friend called Winnie Clarke, who lived two doors higher up at number 18. Winnie was just two months older than Maureen and they got on really well. So well in fact that Winnie practically lived at number 14 … she was like one of the family.

One day they were upstairs in Winnie's house playing make-believe.

"I'm bored," said Winnie, "can we not think of any other game to play?"

"What about Snakes and Ladders or Ludo?" suggested Maureen.

"No, I don't mean that sort of a game, Maureen … I mean something exciting and scary."

"What, like putting sheets o'er our heads and pretending to be ghosts, coming out of that cubbyhole?"

"Just hang on a minute, Maureen, you've just given me an idea."

"Oh yeah, whattaya thinking then?"

"Well, you know how your Jimmy's always playing at soldiers in the back bedroom with them dried peas?"

"Yeah … go on."

"Well, why don't we climb up into the roof space through the manhole that's in the top o' that cubbyhole?"

"U-um, but what's that got to do with our Jimmy?" asked Maureen, naively.

"A-ah well I've bin up into the loft space afore and it's possible to crawl right along the street from house to house."

"Are you sure, Winnie? I didn't think you'd be able to do that."

"I'm positive, I've done it loads o' times."

"Aye, all right, I believe you, but what's that got to do with our Jimmy?"

"Oh come off it, Maureen, you're not that thick, are you?"

"Hey, watch it, Winnie!"

"All right, all right, I'm only kidding. Anyroad, we can crawl through the loft space till we get over your back bedroom and we can make howling noises down through the manhole."

"Right, I'm forrit," mused Maureen, "we'll frighten our Jimmy to death!" So off they went, first climbing onto a chair and then lifting themselves up through the manhole.

"Bloomin' 'eck, Winnie, it's dark up here," protested Maureen, feeling a bit timid.

"Yeah I know, but there's a bit o' light coming in through the slates and if you leave the manhole cover off we'll manage. Mind, you'll have to mek sure to keep your weight on these little wooden joists or else you'll go through the ceiling." They both negotiated the little trek safely and then they lifted up the cover of number 14.

"Are you ready, Maureen?"

"I am that, Winnie … start blowing." They both took a deep breath and then tried hooting like an owl to create a ghostly sound.

"Hey who's that, who's up there?" wailed Jimmy. They stopped blowing for a while but as soon as he went quiet they started again.

"Right," whispered Winnie, "I think he's gone back to his dried peas … hoo-oo-oo!"

"That's it," bawled Jimmy, "I know somebody's up there cos the manhole cover's bin moved!" Once again the two girls went deadly quiet. However, their little prank backfired, as they discovered when they heard Jimmy shouting downstairs.

"Mam, you'd better come up here quick, I think somebody's tryin' to break into t'house through the loft."

"Quick," panicked Maureen, "we'd better get out of here, mi mam's coming!" Young Winnie nimbly scarpered through the roof space but Maureen fled rather clumsily. She was only halfway back when she missed her footing and her leg went right through the ceiling of number 16. As it happened Alice King was just making the bed at the time and lots of plaster landed on the top of her head.

"What the devil's going on," she screeched when she saw a leg dangling from the ceiling. She nearly popped out of her skin when, a minute later, Winnie came waltzing out of the cubbyhole.

"I'm sorry, Mrs King, we were only playing, we didn't mean to break your ceiling."

"Young Winnie Clarke, I should o' known … you're always geddin up to mischief. Anyroad, who else is up there with you?"

"My friend Maureen, from next door to you."

"What, you mean young Maureen Cowell?"

"Yes, Mrs King, we were only …."

Alice was furious, and cut in: "Never mind you were only … I don't want to hear any of your flimsy excuses!" She then bellowed loudly, ordering Maureen to come down through the manhole at once. Alice was all fired up, ready to tear a strip off Maureen, but when she saw the young girl she actually felt sorry for her. Maureen's face was dirty, her dress was torn and she had a big gash in her leg. Instead of scalding her, Alice warmed to her.

"Oh, young Maureen, just look at the state o' you. Come on, we'd best go downstairs and I'll get thi cleaned up afore your mam sees you." She bathed Maureen's leg, put a bandage on it and told her to wash her hands and face.

"All I can do with your dress is brush it down … I don't know what you're gonna tell your mam, though."

"But what about your roof, Mrs King, aren't you gonna tell her about it?"

"No lass, I think you're in enough trouble as it is already without me adding to it."

"But who's gonna mend it for you?"

"Don't worry about that, I'll get onto the landlord and tell him the ceiling collapsed. Not to worry yourself, lass, it were in need of a new one anyroad."

Both girls were eternally grateful to Alice and promised they'd do some shopping for her if she were ever stuck.

*   *   *

Jimmy, Barry and I all slept in the front bedroom in a double bed. Barry was always the warmest because he slept in the middle, and as the bed springs sagged Jimmy and I always rolled close to him.

Before getting into bed all three of us would kneel down by the bedside and say our prayers out loud without any embarrassment. All three sets of prayers were different.

My favourite prayer was quite simple and to the point:

If I should die before I wake,
I pray the Lord my soul to take.

Please God, look after Mum and Dad and all mi brothers
and sisters cos I want them to go to heaven as well.
Anyroad I'll try and be good tomorrow. And thank You
for making Mam happy today. I know she was cos she
went to bed this afternoon with mi dad, and when they
got up I heard Dad say, "E-eh, that were better than
arguing weren't it, love?"

Barry's prayers were always more serious, quoting a decade
of the 'Rosary', an 'Our Father" and a 'Glory be to the
Father' followed by an 'Act of Contrition'.

Jimmy's prayer was short and sweet: "I'm sorry for being
bad today and I promise You I won't put any worms down
any o' mi sisters' necks tomorrow … thank You God,
Amen."

After the prayers we'd usually chant a little song in
unison to keep the Devil at bay:

If you don't let him in at the window,
He's sure to come in through the door,
Or through the skylight in the dead of the night,
Or he'll work his way under the floor.

Once the prayer session was finished we got down to
serious business … 'I spy with my little eye'.

"Righto Barry, you're on first."

"Right … I spy with my little eye something beginning
with 'W'."

"A wall," said Jimmy.

"No, that's not it."

"A window," I said.

"Yeah that's it our John … you're on now."

"Bloomin' 'eck!" moaned Jimmy. "That was too flipping easy."

"Oh yeah, if it were that easy … why didn't you geddit?" I asked. "Anyroad it's my turn now, so I spy with my little eye something beginning with 'L'."

Various guesses were made in vain, "a leg – a latch – a light".

"We haven't got a light," I said.

"Course we have … what about the one from the candle," smirked Jimmy.

"Yeah all reight, but that's not it anyroad."

Silly guesses followed, "A lump in the bed", "a little door", but without success.

"All reight we give in … what is it?"

"A lion," I said, feeling pleased that I'd outsmarted them.

"Whaddaya talkin' about? There's no lions in the flippin' bedroom … not even a toy one!" protested Jimmy.

"Yeah there is," I gloated, "up there on the ceiling."

"On the ceiling … whaddaya talkin' about?"

"Well, just look up … can you see all them cracks?"

"Yeah, so what?"

"Well, look at that reight big one above your head and then move your eyes a little to the window. Just at the side o' that piece o' wood that's stickin' down, you can see a lion's face."

"Oh aye I can, but that's cheating … it's not a real one"

"Who said owt about it being a real one … there's no rule about that."

"Hey I should have got that," Barry blurted excitedly, "cos I can see loads o' different things up there in the ceiling. If you look over there you can see a castle, and in this corner there's a woman's face."

True enough, there were so many cracks in the plaster that many different faces, animals or objects could be conjured up. From then on the game of 'I spy' took on a new, more complex meaning....

* * *

Christmas was always the time for exchanging gifts, no matter how paltry they were. "It's the thought that counts," Mum would say, as we opened our flimsy parcels.

Using all our little scams to raise money, all my brothers and sisters managed to come up with something.

Our enterprising schemes always amused Dad. He was highly delighted one Christmas when I handed him an Oxo tin, lined with coloured paper full to the brim with tobacco. He wouldn't have been so pleased if he'd known where it had come from.

I'd come up with the idea four months previously, in September, after seeing a lad picking up discarded cigarette ends from the gutter.

"What are you doing?" I asked him.

"I'm collecting dockers for mi dad," he replied, stuffing the butts into a paper bag.

"You don't mean to say he's gonna smoke 'em, do you ... not after they've been in everybody else's gob?"

"No ... not like they are now, you silly sod! He'll break 'em up first and put all the bits in his bacco tin so he can roll his own fags later on."

"U-ugh ... that's disgusting! You don't know whose mouths them dog-ends have been in!"

"So what ... it doesn't seem to bother mi dad. As long as he's got a smoke, that's all he cares about."

As I made my way home, I got to thinking. What a good idea, I'll do that for Dad this Christmas … it'll save me a load o' money. Yeah, why not … he'll never know the difference."

I convinced myself that it was a good idea, and from then on I picked up dock-ends from wherever I could – the gutter, the pavement and even wastebins, but I was fussy … I never collected any soggy ones. I acquired the Oxo tin and lined the inside with red paper and painted fancy patterns on the outside. By the time December came the tin was full to the brim.

"Great, I've cracked it!" I congratulated myself, feeling quite smug. "All I need to do now is buy two packets of cigarette papers to put in the box and find a safe place to hide it." I had a good hiding place underneath some loose floorboards in the front bedroom, where I kept my treasured possessions. I felt very smug and couldn't wait for Christmas Day to see Dad's face. As it turned out, I didn't have to wait that long.

One night, about a week before the event, Dad stayed in and he was fidgety. He hadn't turned over a new leaf, he just didn't have any money to go boozing with … and worse still, he didn't have any fags either. As the evening passed he became irritable and made it obvious by tutting and blowing.

"For crying out loud Jack!" quipped Mum, 'You're like a bear with a sore backside … why don't you send our John to Wilding's Shop for five Woodbines?"

"Cos I've no flamin' money, woman!" he rapped. "What have I been trying to tell thi all bloody night?"

"All right, all right, keep your hair on, I'm only trying to help. Surely you've got eightpence? That's all it'll cost you."

"Eightpence, woman! It might as well be eight pound for all I care, I haven't got a red cent. Anyroad Winnie," he said, changing his tone, 'you don't happen to have …?"

"No Jack, I haven't," she cut him short, "it's no good asking me … I haven't got any money either. And besides, if I had I wouldn't give it to you to squander on fags."

"U-umph," he moaned, 'that's typical, innit … bloody typical. Anyroad, I might o' known what the answer would be."

"Well there you go then, why did you ask in the first place? Anyway, if you're so stuck why don't you get them on the tick until weekend?"

"You're joking, that woman wouldn't let me strap up to thre'pence. You know what she's like."

"Oh well, you'll just have to miss out for once, won't you? Anyroad, it'll happen do you good – your chest has been gurgling like a rusty old engine lately."

"Thank you very much Winnie, that's all I need," Dad grunted, growing even rattier.

This is where I stepped in. Their conversation got me to thinking. 'U-um, I've been raring to surprise Dad for ages," I mused, "Why not now? Yeah, why not indeed … I can't see me getting a better chance than right now."

So I slipped up to my bedroom, retrieved the gift and excitedly made my way downstairs. As I approached Dad he was sat in the armchair near to the cellar top, looking rather down in the dumps. His gloomy expression changed to one of surprise when I handed him the box.

"What's this then, our John," he asked. "It's not my birthday is it?"

"No it's not Dad," I replied smiling, "it doesn't have to be your birthday if I want to surprise you, does it? Anyroad, it's actually your Christmas present. I wasn't gonna give it you till next week, but I think now's as good a time as any."

"Oh aye, how come? Tha's never given me a prezzie afore Christmas Day before."

"Aye I know, Dad, but I can't bare to see you looking so miserable, what with having no fags an' all."

"Blimey, does it show that much, lad?"

"Yeah it does, Dad. Anyroad, I've a feeling that this might buck you up a little."

"By 'eck, cock you've got me all fired up and curious," he blurted out as he eagerly started to rip off the wrapping paper. "I think I like these little surprises," he giggled, like a little boy. Within a minute he was stood there with the tin box in his hands.

"Bloomin' 'eck, our John, you've certainly packed it well, there must be twenty elastic bands holding it together."

"Aye I know, Dad ... I just wanted to make sure it'd be all right."

"You're not kidding, our John," he joked, "you can say that again ... it's like geddin into Fort Knox."

Finally he opened the box and, much to my delight, he was ecstatic ... all my scheming seemed worthwhile.

"Oh great!" he shouted excitedly when he saw the tobacco tightly packed into the tin along with the cigarette papers. "Just look at this, Winnie, see what our John's bought me."

He gloated as he unfolded a cigarette paper and took a pinch of tobacco. The rapid mood change and the happy expression on Dad's face amused Mum.

"Just look at him now," she smiled at me, "he's like a dog with a bone. It doesn't take much, does it ... he can't wait to have a fag."

"Too true I can't," laughed Dad, "I'm gasping for a drag and this bacco smells fantastic. "Anyroad our John," he said turning to me, "it's good of you to think of me ... it must have cost you a bomb."

Luckily, I was prepared for this question.

"No, Dad it didn't, I only had to buy the fag paper. I got the bacco for nowt."

"For nowt," he queried, "how d'you mean for nowt?"

"Well, what it is" I replied convincingly, "for the last few months I've bin collecting all the dog-ends that you've been leaving in the ashtray. I didn't think you'd mind."

"Mind? You must be joking! I think you've done great. What a good idea, and enterprising too. Good lad ... I like the way you've used your initiative."

"Thanks, Dad. I'm glad you like it."

"Like it? I love it! This has made my day." But as Dad took a long drag on the self-made cigarette and pondered for a moment, my heart sank a little.

"Oh 'eck ... is he gonna catch on?" I thought, as he coughed and spluttered a bit. However, my concern was unfounded.

"By gum, that's grand," he murmured, "but it tastes different somehow. I can't quite put mi finger on it ... u-um, a little stronger, perhaps."

"Oh," I spluttered trying to think of something fast, "maybe the bacco has dried out a little in the tin, Dad. Happen I should have wrapped it in silver foil?"

"Aye, you're probably right, our John. Anyroad I'm not complaining," he sighed in sheer bliss as he took another long drag, "this is great ... thanks a lot, cock."

"'Thanks a lot!'" I thought, cringing a little, "He'd bloody well strangle me if he knew the truth."

Despite a feeling of guilt, I often giggled when I thought about the incident afterwards. But I never discussed it with anyone, for fear of Dad finding out!

* * *

One meal I always enjoyed was Sunday dinner. Mum always dished it out about five o'clock as a dinner-cum-tea. This suited me fine, as I often played football on Clifton Reckory with my mates and never got home until after six o'clock. One Sunday our Jimmy played as well and when we got home the others had already eaten.

"Sit yourselves down and I'll get your dinner out of the oven," said Mum.

"U-um, it smells good Mam," said Jimmy, "I'm starving. I could eat a scabby donkey."

"That'll do!" rapped Mum. "I'll not have you talking like that. Anyway, I hope it's not burned – don't blame me if it is."

"Don't worry about it Mam," I put in, "I'll scoff the lot, mi stomach thinks mi throat's bin cut."

We were both heartily scoffing when she placed a small plate on the table containing two pieces of sponge cake … one piece was noticeably bigger than the other.

"There, I've done a bit of baking," she said, "but make sure you eat your dinner before you have any cake."

My mouth watered at the thought of sinking my teeth into Mum's baking and I was determined to finish my dinner first so that I could take the big piece. That was my intention, but I didn't stand a chance. Jimmy shovelled the food down his throat so fast he almost choked. He'd finished before I was halfway through mine, then smugly pushed his dinner plate to one side and reached for the cake, taking the largest piece … I was fuming!

"Ar-rgh, just like you, you greedy sod!" I moaned. "You always take the biggest piece."

"Stop whining!" he sneered. "You're allus going on about somet."

"Oh aye, that's easy for you to say," I grunted, "so long as you're getting your own way all the time."

"All right then, clever clogs … if you'd o' finished first, which piece would you have taken?"

"I'd have taken the smallest piece," I replied, with a wry smile on my face.

The smile quickly turned to a pout as he laughed derisively, "Well then … you've nowt to moan about have you? Stop your whinging … you've got the smallest piece!"

*   *   *

Because of the general poverty, many youngsters were often hungry. Children of families in need did not have to pay for school dinners and even breakfast was supplied for the more impoverished. This was all very well, but there was a stigma attached to free school meals and the children who received such benefits were always on the receiving end of abuse from their peers. Every Monday morning they stood out like sore thumbs when the teacher collected the dinner monies straight after calling the register. During the obligatory head count she would ask the children for their dinner money.

The poorer kids would answer in embarrassment, "Free meals, Miss."

The more fortunate ones, from better-to-do families, would walk proudly over to the desk, hand over their money and stroll back to their seats, smirking at those on free meals.

"U-um," they'd mutter under their breath, "we pay for ours. At least we're not beggars like some in this class!"

Like children everywhere, the kids of Trafalgar played street games and got up to lots of mischief. Whether it be summer or winter they found a host of inventive games to play. These included skipping, tig, hopscotch, rounders, piggy-in-the-middle, ring-a-ring-a-roses and many more.

In one game, a circle was drawn near to the wall of a house and each child would place a coin within the ring. They'd then stand at the kerb and take turns at trying to knock the coins out of the circle with a ball.

One favourite game amongst the boys was playing 'bobbers' – marbles. Marian Pilkington could play it as well as any boy, and often challenged me.

"D'you want a game o' bobbers, Johnny Cowell?" she asked one day.

"Aye, all reight Marian, but I'm not using any of mi ironees. I'm gonna play with mi glass alleys."

"Reighto, I'm not bothered," she replied, pulling a glass marble out of her bobber bag.

"Bloomin' 'eck, Marian, you've got plenty o' bobbers on you today."

She gave a cheeky grin. "Yeah, I've just bin skinning some o' the Derby Street lads – they can't play bobbers for toffee, ha, ha, ha!"

"Oh aye, well don't expect any mercy from me, I'm not gonna give thi a start."

Marian simply laughed in reply. "Just throw your bobber, Johnny Cowell … we'll soon see who needs giving a start!"

For a while, we played ordinary marbles in the gutter. Then Marian changed the game. "How about playing nug, Johnny? It's better than this game."

"Go on then, I like playing that as well," I agreed.

For this game we used one of the sunken cobbles as the nug, which was like a hole in the ground. The idea was to land a marble into the nug, giving that player the opportunity to aim at their opponent's bobber.

Marian was the first to do it. "Reight Johnny watch this!" she gloated, skilfully aiming and hitting my bobber full in the face.

"Wow, good shot Marian. I think we're gonna have to call thi 'Dead-Eyed Dick'!"

She laughed, answering, "Right, do you still fancy your chances?" We played happily for a couple of hours with neither of us gaining the upper hand, each having the same amount of marbles, before deciding to call it a day.

Marian and I met up many times after that, enjoying the intriguing game and were both well matched, sometimes winning, sometimes losing. But the outcome didn't matter. We had a great respect for each other, and became good friends.

*   *   *

Despite the poor living conditions, the resilience of most children was evident by their happy and carefree attitude. There were hardly any burglaries and muggings were unheard of. Our front door was never locked, but nobody would dream of entering without permission, as everybody respected other people's property.

Many children went hungry and resorted to various scams to fill their bellies. One of these involved a visit the Fire Station. The large exit doors for the fire engines were situated on the Manchester Road side of the building. However, the poor kids would stand by a tunnel entrance on Finsley Gate, beckoning the firemen.

"Can we have a look at the fire engines, mister?" They knew that once inside they could revert to ruses aimed at getting a bit of food in their stomachs – and often their pleas were rewarded.

One of the crew usually took them under his wing – "Aye all reight cock, come on in. You can only have five minutes, mind." The kids enjoyed looking at the fire engines, but their main concern was food.

"U-um yummy yummy, that's a nice smell," one would hint, passing the canteen. The comment nearly always made the crew succumb to the kids' sorry plight.

"He-ey, just look at th'expression on their little faces … you can't help but feel sorry for 'em, canya?"

"Aye, they look like they've had nowt to eat for a month."

To the kids' delight they were usually given a meat pie and piece of cake, or something like.

"Just look at 'em …the poor little mites!" one of the men would comment, as the kids stuffed every last morsel of food into their mouths. The firemen got used to seeing the same faces but pretended not to notice.

"Right kids, now we don't want to see any of you around here agen for a while … you've got to give t'others a chance." Despite the friendly warning, some kids visited the station regularly.

*   *   *

Mother wasn't the only one to tell us tales about childhood – Dad did as well. As a child, he'd always lived in the Croft area of town.

"E-eh, I'll tell thi what our John," he would say nostalgically, "everybody were poor, but they were good days."

When he was in this kind of mood, I would encourage him to tell a tale. "Oh go on, Dad, tell us about when you were a little lad … please!"

"We-ell, I lived on Pickup Street down the Croft near the town centre. Just round the corner from us were Miller Street and Norton Street. It was at the top of Miller Street in a courtyard that Cece's made their ice-cream. Every morning you'd see loads of horse-and-carts pulling away, loaded up with th'ice-cream. Me and mi mates would go round there, trying to scrounge a free cornet or owt going before they set off. They used to put th'ice-cream into a metal cylinder and then place that into an even bigger one … a tub within a tub, if you like. The larger outer tub was filled with ice cubes to stop th'ice-cream from melting."

"Did they ever give you a free ice-cream, Dad?" I interrupted.

"Not so many times afore they set off, lad, but if they'd owt left at th'end o' the day we stood a good chance. Anyroad, it didn't really matter if they gave us one or not, cos there was another reason for waiting of 'em coming back."

"How d'you mean, Dad?"

"Well, you'll not believe this, but here goes. Just afore returning to the depot the ice-cream fella always drove the horse and cart into Boot Street, which had a small slope. This allowed the back o' the cart to tilt slightly backwards. The chap then pulled a plug from the bottom of the outer cylinder, so all the melted ice cubes could drain from the drum into the gutter and down a grate. Now, you can believe this or believe it not, but loads o' kids, including girls, would get down on their bellies and sup the ice water."

'What! From the gutter?"

"As I stand here, our John, that's the gospel truth!"

"U-ugh, I wouldn't o' fancied that! Anyroad, what did it taste like?"

"It might seem far-fetched but it's true. And in answer to your question … it was delicious."

"What, you mean to say that you supped it as well, Dad?"

"Aye I did that, all the kids did, and so would you o' done. I can't say why, but that ice-water had a taste of its own … it was absolutely delicious!"

"U-um, I don't know so much," I mumbled, "maybe. Anyroad, like you said, Dad, it does seem a bit far-fetched," I mused, adding jokingly, "Like a bucket of pee from China, ha, ha, ha!"

"You can laugh all you want, our John, but when I were a lad people were destitute and lots o' them kids were hungry. Anyroad, let me tell you about 'The Relief'."

"The Relief, Dad ... what's The Relief?"

"If you just shut your gob and listen I'll tell you."

"All reight Dad, I'm listening ... I'm listening."

"Well in them days the most needy, especially those with large families, had to apply to 'The Relief'. In earlier days, the office was situated in a narrow sloping ginnel, which ran from off Nicholas Street. The ginnel levelled out and this is where the official in charge would stand on a wooden platform, shouting out names from a register. Coincidentally, the official in charge was called 'Mr Penny'. He was a small man, who always wore a black billycock complemented by a black coat and waistcoat from which hung a watch and chain. To complete the outfit he wore pinstripe pants and black leather shoes. At the time the Relief was referred to as 'The Parish'. People always had an appointed time and would go and stand in the ginnel with t'others and wait for Mr Penny to call out their names.

"'Joe Smith.'

"'Here.'

"'Have you been working this week?'

"'No.'

"Joe would then go through to th'office and pick up his bit o' money. Later on, the premises were transferred to Finsley Gate.

"The main diet for most people on Relief was fish and chips from the chippy. Many a barbed comment would be thrown out: 'Aye, tha can allus tell them that's on Relief ... they've bin dragged up fro' the chip chop.'

"Young growing lads had big appetites and when sent to the chippy they'd poke a hole in the paper and pinch a few chips and often drink some of the vinegar. I always did this and mi dad would grumble when I got home.

"'The miserable bugger ... the bleedin' chips are geddin less and less every time tha goes to that chippy!'"

"Ha, ha, did he ever catch on it were you, Dad?"

"No, did he 'eck as like ... I'd o' got a reight old crack around back o' t'head if he had o' done."

"Going back to The Relief, Dad ... did they hand out the money freely?"

"Did they 'eck as like, you'd to be on the bread line afore you got owt. Let me tell thi what happened to a mate o' mine who tried to get a new pair o' clogs for his lad Billy."

"Good," I thought as Dad carried on with another saga, "my little scheme to get more tales from him has worked."

"Just let me get this right," he said pondering a little. "Little Billy was growing quickly and needed some new clogs. His dad applied for some Relief and had to go, with cap in hand, in front of the 'Board of Guardians' to try and get a new pair.

"'But there's nothing wrong with this pair,' pointed out one of the indignant guardians presiding on the panel, 'there's still plenty of wear in 'em.'

"'Yeah, I know that, but the lad's going through a growi'ng spell and they're hurting his feet.'

"Another grim official stroked his chin, saying, 'We can't just give clogs out at random, everything's got to be considered ... we need to sort out the wheat from the chaff.'

"'Whaddaya talkin' about,' rapped young Billy's dad, losing his patience, 'sort out the wheat from the chaff?

We're talking about a young growing lad here, not flamin' wheat growing in a field. Surely a bit o' common sense has to come into it … the lad'll be crippled if he wears these clogs much longer.'

"Young Billy got his clogs, but many others weren't so lucky. Loads o' people were turned away and got nowt … it were just the luck o' draw. Many of the poor kids had to mek do and finished up wi' crippled feet."

He paused for a moment before adding, "Yeah, our John, that's the way things were … everybody was poor! Your mam tells you tales about what it were like in Bacup when she were a lass, but it were just the same here in Burnley. People were destitute and lived in small, cramped, dilapidated back-to-back houses. There were no dustbins and we'd empty our rubbish into huge waste disposal bins that were kept at th'end of the block. Everywhere you went you saw lots o' kids with dirty faces and tousled hair. Mind you, despite their crass existence, people were proud … you never saw any graffiti on the walls or litter in the streets like you do nowadays. Aye, and the women used to donkey stone their front steps till they gleamed. One old lady used to swill the flags outside her house and she even donkey stoned some o' them. She was a bit eccentric, mind, and was forever chasing us kids off if we went anywhere near her flags … we nicknamed her Nellie Silverflags. There's no doubt about it … despite the poverty and deprivation the streets were a credit to the people who lived there."

I loved it when Dad was in this sort of mood. And I certainly took advantage of the situation, gleaning as much information from him as I could and soaking up many nostalgic memories.

4

YOUNGSTERS'
ESCAPADES

The summer holiday came and went, and now it was time to go up into Miss Drennan's class. In both the infants' class and Miss Quinn's, I had made many friends, including Desmond Lee, Bobby Cheetham, Keith Tattersall, Kenny Scully and Tommy Neville. But, like most lads, I had a best friend, who always sat next to me in class – my mate Ronnie Hopkinson.

Like children everywhere, the kids at St Thomas's School could be heartless and cruel. Along the way I found myself in many scrapes and despite not being a fighting lad, I had to face up to things because the Cowells were constantly singled out in the schoolyard. This stemmed mainly from the fact that Dad was a ragman and also because he'd just recently been sent to prison for the second time for getting involved in shady deals. It became apparent on the first day back after the holidays that we were in for a lot of abusive comments. At playtime, in the schoolyard, I was the first in the firing line from two lads called Peter Birtwhistle and Paul Whitham.

"Hiya Cowheel … canya dad fly?"

"What aya talking about Birtwhistle," I responded.

"Well, he's a bird isn't he … a jailbird, ha, ha, ha!"

"Yeah, and I bet he's in with all the murderers!" mocked Paul Whitham.

"Get lost!" I retaliated, "he's a better dad than yours, anyroad!"

"Oh aye … you mean when he's not in jail?"

"Don't stand for that, our kid," said our Jimmy who'd heard the stinging comments from across the playground, "get him thumped!"

"Lay off, our Jimmy!" I said, trying to play down the situation, "I'll handle it my way."

"Handle it your way," jeered Peter Birtwhistle, "what you mean is you're frightened to death!"

"Don't start somet you can't finish, Birtwhistle!" warned Jimmy.

"Why what will you do, Cowheel … put me in a padded cell with your dad?"

"A padded cell," queried Jimmy, "what the flamin' 'eck are you talking about?"

To the amusement of all the other kids, Peter Birtwhistle, burst out laughing and fired off another insult, "Well your dad'll be in a padded cell won't he … padded out wi' loads o' rags off the rag-cart? Ha, ha, ha!"

"*Enough said!*" Jimmy's composure changed from controlled to seething anger. "You swine!" he screeched, his face red with rage. He was fuming, almost frothing at the mouth, and immediately set into the lad with both fists flying.

It wasn't long before lots of kids formed a circle and the loud chanting of "A fight, a fight!" resounded through the schoolyard.

I could feel the tension building up inside me as the air became more and more charged. Within minutes, I too was rolling about the floor, fighting Paul Whitham. One of the reasons I didn't like fighting was because I often finished up on the losing end, but in this case it was different. My adrenaline was flowing, as it always did when I had been goaded into a fight.

"Right Whitham," I thought, 'it's either you or me!" I laid into him for all I was worth and didn't stop until he wailed he'd had enough. That was good enough for me … I was quite happy with the outcome. Whitham never bothered me again after that.

Other kids also threw out many hurtful comments: "Hiya Cowheel, hasta bin visiting your dad in jail this weekend … how did you get there, on the rag-cart?" Still, I never reacted to these remarks unless pushed to the very limit.

Our Mary, like Jimmy was fiery and she too had many run-ins with the girls. They could be very catty with their sly comments, but it didn't wear with Mary. Having the same temperament as Jimmy and a natural ability to fight, using her fists like a boy, she soon put the name-callers in their place.

Despite all the jeering and insults, we still loved Dad dearly and couldn't wait for him to be released from prison. One wintry day in February our Maureen arranged a special homecoming for him and had us rehearsing a little welcome home song for hours on end. When the singing stopped we pranced around in front of the fire in our nightwear and each one of us gave him a special hug before marching up the stairs. On that special night the show went down a treat, with Dad ending up in tears. Snowdrifts piled up to the windowsills and the icy winds outside cut through to the bone, but the atmosphere inside number 14 was warm and glowing.

* * *

Jimmy was forever battling with Michael, Joseph or Kevin Cheetham. One thing though: when two lads were fighting, nobody else ever intervened. Also there were strict rules, to which everybody strictly adhered: no kicking, no biting, no pulling hair. The two lads would get stuck in, trying to knock three bells out of each other. Still, after the fight had ended, they'd shake hands and then play happily together as though nothing had happened.

One thing that the bigger lads did was to constantly tease the younger ones, inciting them to fight. They'd then form a circle around the two fighting youngsters whilst at the same time keeping an eye out for the teacher. The head teacher was the renowned Miss Gordon, a strict disciplinarian, who ruled with a rod of iron.

Bobby Cheetham and I were forever on the end of these incitations and invariably had many confrontations, much to the bigger lads' amusement.

Miss Drennan was very strict and nicknamed 'The Battleaxe'. On reflection, it should have been 'Battlecane', because she was always wielding it. If anyone misbehaved she would throw a tantrum, which was often followed literally by a piece of chalk or the board duster.

But one day, Miss Drennan had the class in raptures. She was a very stout lady and always wore loose-fitting dresses. Whilst throwing one of her tantrums, she started to stamp her feet hard on the wooden floor and, to the amusement of all the class, her large bloomers fell down to her ankles.

She quickly whipped them back up again and ran out of the class in embarrassment. She was the laughing stock of the school for months afterwards!

* * *

Like all children at the time, my real adventures and life-forming experiences took place in the world beyond the school gates.

I was out with my two mates David and Ronnie and we were making our way to Thompson's Park when some bicycles in a shop window intrigued me. Before I'd realised it, my two mates were well in front.

On catching them up Ronnie said to me, "Hey look at this, David's found a tanner while you were looking in that window – thre'pence a piece."

"No, tuppence each," I replied, "there's three of us."

"You're joking … you weren't with us when we found it."

"A-ah that's not fair!" I complained. "You knew I was coming."

"It meks no difference, we're not splitting it three ways … we can both buy a thre'penny cornet now when we reach Thompson's Park."

"Please yourself, then," I said, "I'm not bothered o'er tuppence. I still think it's unfair, though."

I didn't fall out with them about it, and we carried on to the park, where we stayed for a few hours before making our way home. It was on the return journey that something happened which made Ronnie and David regret their selfishness. We walked through the town centre and as we were passing the *Burnley Express* Office on Bull Street, I once again became distracted by the contents of a shop window. As before, Ronnie and David walked on and they had reached Hargreaves Street before I decided to follow. I'd just set off when three blokes came tottering out of the back alley of the Clockface Hotel. It was obvious that they were merry, as they swaggered about with their arms around each other's shoulders and it became clear by their chatter that they had won some money on the horses.

"All reight young un, how's it going? What's the glum face for?" joked one of them as they bumped into me.

"I haven't got a glum face. It's your fault, you nearly knocked me down," I replied, cockily.

"E-eh, don't be so serious cock, I were only kidding," he laughed. "Anyroad, here's a tanner for upsettin' thi." I was aware that I shouldn't take money from strangers, but seeing as there were three of them I felt safe. Besides, it was broad daylight and there were plenty of people about.

"Hey Burt," quipped one of his mates, "you mean bugger ... is that all you're giving the young lad after what you've just won?" To my surprise he turned to me and handed me a shilling. "Here you are, cock ... go and enjoy yourself."

The third man, rather more intoxicated than the other two, fumbled through his pockets and pulled out a handful of loose change.

"Well lad," he mumbled, "I ain't just come up on t'horses, I've been winning at cards as well ... what dusta think about that?"

"I think you're very lucky," I answered trying my hardest to please him.

"Ha ha ha!" he laughed merrily, "You're reight about that, cock! Anyroad, it's your lucky day too, cos I'm gonna treat thi. Here you are, lad ... what dusta think about that?" he chuckled, handing me a silver coin!

I couldn't believe my eyes. There in the palm of my hand was a half-crown piece!

"Wow!" I yelped, jumping for joy, "Half a dollar, I've never had this much money in all mi life afore … mi mam'll be o'er the moon when I tell her!" The three men started laughing, highly amused at my obvious delight.

"Good lad, Billy, you've just med the young lad's day," said his two mates, laughing as they walked off. I gazed at the money in my hand, unable to believe my luck.

"I'm rich, I'm rich!" I giggled. 'I've never had this much money before … ever!"

Coming back to reality I chased after Ronnie and David, catching them up on Hammerton Street; I couldn't wait to tell them of my good fortune.

"Give o'er, you lying sod!" retorted Ronnie. "You mean to say they gave you four bob just like that?"

"It's the gospel truth, it happened just like I said!" I whooped, not being able to contain my delight.

"All reight, I believes you. Are we splitting it three ways, cos we're all together?"

"No, am I 'eck as like," I replied, adamantly, "I would have done if you'd have split that tanner with me earlier on. It were you who said I wasn't with you then … that means that you weren't with me now when this happened."

Both of them had to reluctantly agree. I couldn't wait to get home to give most of the money to Mum.

*   *   *

The folly of youth blinded us to the many perils that surrounded us. Playing on the railway was dangerous and strictly forbidden; anyone caught was liable to prosecution. The line had a double track, being part of the main Leeds to London railway. Nonetheless, this didn't deter many children, and both boys and girls frequently used it as a playground for general tomfoolery. The girls would make sandwiches and play happy families, having picnics on the grassy embankment. Being more boisterous, the lads often spoiled their fun by acting silly and sometimes fighting.

One day our Jimmy, Kenny Clayton, David Whittaker, Ronnie Hopkinson and I were frolicking about when another gang of lads came climbing over Patten Street's wall. They were from the King Street area on the other side of the footbridge. The leader of the group was called Bernard Aspinall and he was the 'cock' of St Thomas's School. At the time Bernard and Jimmy didn't get on very well and it wasn't long before this became apparent.

"All reight, Cowheel, hasta been out ragging with your dad lately?" sneered Bernard.

"Get lost Aspin … get back to scruffy King Street where you belong!" retaliated Jimmy.

"Oh yeah, and who's gonna make me then … you and who's army?"

"Don't be so fly, just cos you're with your gang!"

"Ha ha ha ha!" roared Bernard, "Don't mek me laugh. I could take thi on with one arm behind me back, Cowheel!" That did it, the veins stuck out in Jimmy's neck as he seethed with anger. Two seconds later, both lads were at it tooth and nail, tearing lumps out of each other. They were of a similar age and well matched and rolled about the sloping embankment grappling furiously. Consequently, they rolled over and over until they finished up at the side of the railway line. The fighting carried on for a while, with neither lad gaining the advantage. First one was on top, then the other, as they tumbled onto the first set of lines, thumping and gouging each other and then stumbled in-between the two gritty railway tracks.

All the lads from both gangs, including me, were enjoying the fight and loud jeering filled the air as we all yelled in frenzy:

"Come on, Jimmy, you've got him … you've got him!" "Come on Aspy … you'll murder him!"

I was as enthusiastic as the others – until I saw the signal rise!

"Our Jimmy … Bernard … stop it quick, there's a train coming!" I shouted at the top of my voice.

All the lads now became agitated, shouting similar things: "Come on, stop it … you'll be killed!" "Be quick, I can hear the train coming!" "Oh flippin 'eck, I can see the smoke from the train … tell 'em to give o'er!" The shouting increased as we saw the train coming round the bend, but to no avail … Jimmy and Bernard continued to rain blows on one another, each refusing to yield. By now I was scared … I feared for my brother's life and Bernard's too.

"Oh 'eck," I thought, "they're so intent on fighting they can't hear any of us." Without further ado, I dashed down onto the track. By now Jimmy and Bernard were grappling on the opposite line but still in a precarious position. Bernard was on top and appeared to be getting the best of our Jimmy.

"Stop it, Bernard, there's a train coming," I screeched as I tugged at his sleeve, "you're both gonna get killed!" Bernard, who didn't seem to hear me and must have thought I was trying to help our Jimmy, landed out, catching me with a solid back hander. By now the train was perilously close, but still the fighting continued. "Blow this for a tale!" I muttered, and made my way to the other embankment, clutching my cheek. The other lads watched in horror as the train sped by; it was a goods train and they had to wait in nervous anticipation while twenty wagons passed by. To their surprise and sheer delight, the fight was still ongoing. Finally, when both Jimmy and Bernard were totally exhausted, the fight ended. Jimmy was the worse for wear, and on the whole, Bernard was the overall winner ... still, some good came out of it.

"By 'eck Cowheel, that were a good scrap weren't it?" said Bernard, grinning all over his face. "I've got to put mi hand up ... I didn't know you had it in you."

"Aye all reight, but less o' the Cowheel ... Aspy!"

"Ha, ha, ha!" roared Bernard. Both lads shook hands, laughing heartily ... they remained good friends thereafter.

* * *

Another dangerous thing that the lads enjoyed was daring each other to walk the length of Albion Street's railway bridge wall, which overlooked the railway lines. It was a kind of ritual that all the lads went through for fear of being ridiculed by the others if they chickened out. In comparison to the backyard walls it was quite wide, but it was very frightening to stand up on it ... especially at the highest point over the railway track. I well remember the first and only time I attempted it; I was with my mates Ronnie, David and Kenny Clayton. A few older lads were playing by the bridge and they started to tease us younger ones.

"Come on you lot ... have you passed your test yet? Before you can be a member of any gang you have to walk on top o' the railway bridge from one end to t'other."

"I'll go first," I said, wanting to show off in front of my mates, "it should be easy, cos it's pretty wide." I was a show-off, but my little act of bravado failed. It didn't seem too bad at first when I set off, as it wasn't too much of a drop to the embankment. However, as I progressed over to the railway lines, the sight was too much. I became petrified and sensibly decided to quit. I'd to put up with some sneering remarks, but it didn't matter: my legs were trembling and I knew there was no way I'd attempt it again.

Then came Kenny's turn! He started the walk in a similar way to me and it soon became apparent that he too was scared. He started to panic and lost his balance, plummeting into the ferns. Luckily, the drop wasn't too far, but all the same, he couldn't stop himself from rolling over and over down the steep embankment, finishing up on the railway track. He ended up with a few cuts and bruises, but wasn't badly hurt. Nevertheless, much to David and Ronnie's delight, the bigger lads decided that the stunt was too dangerous after all.

"It's all reight you other young uns, there's no need to do it … we all believe you're brave."

The railway was also used as a shortcut to many of the other adjacent streets. Kenny Clayton and I would run the backyard walls and climb over the railway on our way to the tennis courts, where we used to play football; ironically, this place was also out of bounds. No matter, all the lads in the neighbourhood would congregate there for their favourite game. We were all keen supporters of Burnley Football Club and as we kicked the ball about on the tennis courts we would each pretend to be one of our heroes from Turf Moor. Mine was Tommy Cummings.

We also enjoyed many a good game of cricket on the backstreet – much to the annoyance of the neighbours. A dustbin made an ideal wicket and an old jersey or coat determined the length of the pitch. The walls on the Albion Street side were only small, but those on the Patten Street side were about eight feet high. The idea was to knock the ball past the bowler. If one knocked it over the shallow walls it was counted as four runs; however, if this happened twice, the runs counted but the player was out. On the other hand, if it was knocked over one of the high walls, the player was out for a score of six.

We also played ther games on the backstreet; one of these was wall running. Kids would run on top of the backyard walls, leaping from one to another as they negotiated the backyard gates. I became really fleet footed at this game and challenged others to a race. We'd start from Maggie Astin's house at the bottom of the backstreet and the winner was the first to reach the railway embankment. The challenge was that I would run the gauntlet on the walls whilst they ran the cobbles on the backstreet.

"One – two – three go!" The fast runners would be slightly in front of me, but on reaching the top of the back-street they had to climb a high railway wall whereas I simply sprang nimbly from the backyard wall and was over the wall onto the grassy verge in a flash.

With its foul-smelling backyards and dustbin ashes strewn all over the place, the backstreet wasn't the healthiest environment in the world. My two brothers and I had the job of keeping the backyard and the cellar clean. I was cleaning the cellar one day when I heard a lad's voice shouting down the coal-chute.

"Hey, is there any chance o' giving us our ball back?"

"Righto then … whereabouts is it?" I asked.

"It's gone down the space in front of your cellar window … I can see it on the stone ledge."

"Aye, reighto, just hang on a minute … I'll have to climb up forrit." On climbing up the ball was there, but I also spotted a penny … then something occurred to me.

"That penny must o' fallen down here when kids were trying to knock coins outta the circle with a ball. U-um, if there's one coin down here, there may be more." After throwing the ball back, I cleared away a few cobwebs and then got down to cleaning the ledge. "Bloomin' 'eck, some o' this muck must have been here since t'house was built," I thought. But my efforts were rewarded. To my delight, I found two shillings and thre'pence in pennies, ha'pennies, thre'penny bits and a tanner.

"Great!" I thought chuffed with myself. And it got me to thinking. "I'll ask Mrs King next door if she wants her cellar cleaning … there may be some money on her ledge too. U-um, even if there isn't, I can charge a bob for doing the job." I got the job and sure enough there was some more green mouldy coins amidst the dirt. Mind you, there weren't as much … about one shilling and thre'pence.

"Still," I murmured to myself, "counting the shilling payment, that's two and thre'pence. That's not bad … not bad at all."

From then on I set up quite a nice little scheme for myself, asking the neighbours on either side of the street if they wanted their cellars cleaning.

I knew my little scam would be short-lived, but I was quite happy, telling myself, "You've gotta make hay whilst the sun shines."

I only found thre'pence in one of the cellars, but still smiled as I mused to myself, "Oh never mind … 'Every little helps,' the old lady said as she wee'd in the sea."

* * *

As a young lad, I realised there was a lot of ill-feeling between Dad's sisters and Mum. I wasn't too sure where the blame lay, but the truth became abundantly clear when, on visiting each of my aunts, I always received the same cold reception.

One time I went to my Aunt Beatie's house. "Oh what do you want? We haven't time for the likes o' you." She carried on in the same vein, making snide remarks as though I wasn't even there. "U-umph, I can't do with scruffy kids ... just look at the holes in his socks and look at his pants ... I don't think they've ever seen a wash tub."

"Yeah," someone else chipped in, "he looks like he could do with a good meal and I don't think his hair's ever seen a brush or comb."

Then came the crunch that I wouldn't tolerate. "I hope he doesn't bring any nits into this house." *That did it!* I was only nine, but the implied criticism of my mum was too much and I was having none of it!

"Hey, don't call mi mam like that," I retaliated angrily, "she's better than you are and she looks after us better than your brother does!"

"Watch your lip, you cheeky young beggar, you're nowt else," Beatie replied. "Speak when you're spoken to!"

"I'm not being cheeky and I'm not a beggar. It's you who's being rude, calling mi mam names."

"Right, that's it, wait till we see your dad, then you'll be forrit!" Beatie rapped. "You won't be so cocky then."

"I'm not bothered, you can tell him what you want. Anyroad, I'll tell him myself what you've bin saying about mi mam." At this Beatie and her family realised that I'd fully understood everything they'd been talking about, and tried to play down the situation.

"Now come on, our John, don't take on so, we didn't really mean anything wrong. Anyroad, sit yourself down, lad, and have a nice piece o' cake and a glass o' pop." But it was too late, the damage was done. They'd run down mi mam and I didn't want any more to do with them.

"No thank you, I don't want anything off you. Anyroad, I'm not your John and I don't want to be. I'm going now and I won't come back to your house ever again."

Beatie tried making amends. "Now come on lad, let's be friends ... we don't want this to get out of hand, do we?"

"Don't fret yourself, Aunt Beatie, I won't say anything to mi mam, I wouldn't want to hurt her feelings, she's been hurt enough already. I won't be coming again, but I'll still talk to you if I see you in the street," I said respectfully, adding food for thought: "That's the way mi mam has brought us up." At that, I turned and left; sadly I never went there again.

Another time I went to Blackpool with our Barry and Barbara. I'd scrimped and saved every bit of spending money until I had enough to go to Blackpool on the train as it was a dream of mine to see this magical place. I'd heard tales from Dad that his eldest sister, my Aunt Annie, had a large hotel in the heart of town and I'd planned for ages to go there on my own account. I didn't mention it to Mum because I was afraid she wouldn't let me go, but my younger brother and sister still got wind of my plan and pestered me to take them along.

"But I've only got enough money to pay for mi fare and a butty when I get there," I said, trying my best to put them off.

"Oh go on, our John," pleaded Barry, "we won't need to buy anything cos we'll be able to go to Aunt Annie's hotel and she'll give us somet to eat."

"U-um, I suppose you're right, but I still don't have enough to buy your train tickets." As it happened, our Jimmy was listening and he always had a little put to one side from doing odd jobs and errands for the neighbours. Despite his fiery temper, he was generous to a fault and regularly treated his younger siblings to a penny drink at the toffee shop. On this occasion he went a bit further, and gave us enough to buy two more return tickets. It was all he had, but he wasn't bothered.

"Oh it's reight," he said, "I can always mek some more money collecting jam jars and taking bottles back to the Labour Club."

"But what about you," I asked, "don't you want to come?"

"No, I'll be all reight playing soldiers upstairs with mi dried peas. I'd rather do that than owt else."

"Right, thanks our kid," I said, turning to Barry and Barbara. "Come on then, you two, we'd best get going afore mi mam gets home."

We caught the train, landing in Blackpool about one o'clock, and after asking directions, we finally arrived at Aunt Annie's hotel two hours later. It was the first time in my life I'd ever seen her and I wasn't too sure what to expect. On knocking on the door we were received by a maid who showed us into the hallway. Within a minute, Aunt Annie made herself known and she wasn't very pleased. It was obvious by the stern look on her face that she felt put out by our sudden appearance.

"What the flippin 'eck do you think you're playing at," she barked, "don't you realise I have a busy schedule … I haven't got time to mess about with you lot!"

"So this is my Aunt Annie, is it?" I thought. 'U-um, she's not what I thought she'd be like."

She interrupted my thoughts by asking bluntly, "Anyroad, what does your mother think she's playing at, sending you over here without letting me know?"

"Mi mam doesn't know we're here," I replied indignantly, "it was my idea to bring mi brother and sister."

"Oh was it now? Well you can bloomin' well turn round now and take 'em back to where you came from!"

"Come on," I said to Barry and Barbara who were both showing their obvious disappointment, "let's go, we're not staying where we're not wanted."

"But I'm hungry!" groaned Barbara, "I haven't had anything to eat since breakfast and I only had some cornflakes then."

"So am I," Barry said, rubbing his tummy, "and I'm thirsty as well!"

"Listen here, both of you, I'm hungry as well," I moaned, loud enough for Aunt Annie to hear, "but it makes no difference ... we'll make do till we get back home."

"All right that'll do," put in Aunt Annie, "you can stop for ten minutes. I'll make you a cup o' tea and some biscuits, but then you'll have to go. Like I said afore, I haven't time to mess about with you!"

I felt like telling her to shove it, but I demurred for Barry and Barbara's sake. After our little snack, we made our way to North Station and caught the five o'clock train back to Burnley. That was my first experience of Aunt Annie and Blackpool; we never went to her hotel again. On arriving home Mum scolded us for going without her consent and then asked how we'd gone on. She was obviously displeased at the outcome, adding further friction to the relationship between her and Dad's sisters. Dad tried to play down the situation, pointing out that Annie was right in some respects.

"Bloomin' 'eck, Winnie, you've got to see it from her point of view," he stressed, "she's got a business to run and you must admit she didn't know they were coming."

"Never mind that!" Mum snapped, "I know it must have been inconvenient for her, but for crying out loud, Jack, she could have made them some dinner before they set off back home."

"Ar-rgh, you've no idea what it's like to run a business," he moaned, "our Annie ...."

"Never mind your Annie," Mum cut in, "you always side with your sisters no matter what! Can't you just see our side of things for once in your life? Bloomin' 'eck Jack, she knew they'd travelled all that way ... couldn't she have offered them the hand of friendship?"

"Well," he responded, mellowing a little, "maybe she should have made 'em a meal, I'll go along with that."

"There's no maybe about it," Mum barked, "it's the first time your Annie's ever seen any of 'em. Surely she could have gone out of her way under the circumstances!"

"Yeah, I suppose you're right," Dad mumbled, not wanting to get into an argument about it.

"Oh 'eck," I murmured feeling guilty, "I hope I haven't created more ill-feeling between Mam and Dad's sisters."

The final incident that determined my way of thinking was when I went to a Christmas party at my Aunt Lily's house. Aunt Lily was stone deaf, following a childhood illness. This was the first time I'd ever been invited to her house, whereas my cousins had been there many times. In spite of wanting to go to the party, I was a little tentative, as I wondered what sort of reception I would get. When I reached the house a few of my cousins were already there in the front room frolicking about. I felt out of place but when they started playing Monopoly I became intrigued.

I'd never seen this game before and found it much more interesting than snakes and ladders ... especially when I saw the banker dealing out the fake money, I asked if I could join in.

"No, it's too late ... we've already started," grunted one of them. I didn't know how to play the game, but I knew this wasn't true.

"No you haven't ... nobody's shook a dice yet," I protested.

"Aye all reight then," moaned another, "you can join in, but no spoiling our fun!"

The game got under way and the activity started to build up. Before long I got excited, becoming a little boisterous and an argument ensued between us. Aunt Lily came stomping into the room to see what all the noise was and, without asking what the quarrel was about, she clouted me around the earhole.

"Now that'll do," she rapped, "behave yourself and let the others play properly. They were invited here before you!" I wasn't hurt physically, but that remark finally convinced me that neither my siblings nor I were welcome there.

"That's it," I muttered to myself, "I'm not stopping where I'm not wanted!" I turned heel and went to the lobby to put on my coat.

"And where do you think you're going, then?" asked Aunt Lily, annoyed at me.

"I'm going home, Aunt Lil ... I don't want to stop at your party."

"Don't be so touchy," she bawled, "now get your coat off and get back in there and enjoy yourself."

"U-um, some hopes," I muttered under my breath.

"What's that you just said?" she rapped. "Look at me when you're talking to me ... you know I'm deaf!"

I was aware of her affliction, and I felt sorry for her, but in my mind, that didn't excuse her for what she'd just said and done.

"No, I'm sorry Aunt Lil, I'm going home. I don't want to stay any longer." She tried to stop me leaving but to no avail ... I was determined to go, and go I did.

As I walked home past the cotton mills I reflected on the situation and what I was going to tell Mum. Once again, I didn't want to cause Mum further grief or widen the chasm that already existed between her and her sisters-in-law.

"No," I thought to myself, "there's enough animosity between them without me making it worse."

"Hello our John," said Mum on seeing me, "what are you doing home so soon from the party?"

Being discreet, I told a white lie. "I felt a bit sick, Mam, and I wanted to come home. Anyroad, there were loads o' mince pies and you know I don't like them." Mind you, I suffered for it ... by teatime I was absolutely starving. To make matters worse, I got a right rollicking later when Dad got home.

"You ungrateful little wimp, you're nowt else ... that's the last time you ever get invited to any parties. Our Lily told me how you turned your nose up at everything they offered you, you faddy little bugger! Anyroad, what have you got to say for yourself?"

"Nowt Dad ... I just didn't want anything."

"Oh you didn't want anything did you not? Well just cop this for good measure," he growled giving me another clout across the head.

Still, I wasn't for telling the true story. I didn't want Mum hurting any more.

A few days later when I was out with Dad on the rag-cart, we happened to be in the Croft area.

"Right, our John, we'll just call at our Lily's for a sandwich and a brew. Aye, and while we're there you can apologise for upsetting her t'other day."

" But Dad, I …!"

"No buts, lad … you'll do as you're told!"

I reluctantly followed Dad into Aunt Lily's house but adamantly refused to eat or drink anything.

"All right, you awkward little sod, maybe you don't want owt but there's one thing for sure," bellowed Dad, "you're gonna apologise to your Aunt Lily afore we leave this house!"

I resolutely stood my ground. I just put my head down, hunched up my shoulders and said nothing. Dad raised his hand to hit me again, but then Aunt Lily intervened.

"No Jack, don't hit him … it doesn't matter, let it go." It wasn't so much what she'd said as the way she'd said it. Dad sensed there was more to it than met the eye.

"What's up, our Lily … is there something you haven't told me?"

"No no, it's just that I don't want to get the lad into trouble."

"It's a bit late for that … now, just tell me again exactly what happened."

"Well, they were all arguing in t'other room, so I went in and clouted him."

"Aye, and what were they arguing about?"

"Well, I don't really know," she replied, nervously, "I never asked."

"Hey, hang on a minute … did you clout any o' t'other kids?"

"Well no, I …"

"Oh, come off it, our Lily. I'm beginning to see our John's side o' things now … no wonder he left the flamin' party!"

Turning to me, Dad said: "Right lad, now you can give me your version of events."

Reluctantly, I told him what had happened.

"Right, our Lily," quipped Dad, "I wanted our John to apologise to you, but now I think shoe's on t'other foot."

"It doesn't matter, Dad … honest!" I tried to protest.

"Aye it does lad, and I think I owe thi an apology too for clouting you the way I did," he stressed and then made it clear that he understood my mode of thinking. "By 'eck lad I'll tell thi what it is … I'm proud o' you, trying to keep it all from your mam an' all." Talking to me like this, Dad made me feel good, a feeling that was enhanced when he added, "I'm sorry for clouting you our John and to make amends I'm gonna give you a tanner today instead of thre'pence."

My eye's lit up and even more so when my Aunt Lily came in with some cream buns and a glass of pop. From that moment, I grew rather fond of Aunt Lily.

On the way home, Dad mentioned the incident once more. "You acted very wise for your years, our John, keeping it from your mam the way you did, and I think it's best left that way." We were both in agreement about that.

5

MISS GORDON

Time passed by and then came the day that everyone dreaded ... moving into Miss Gordon's class. She was the renowned 'Dragon Lady' a reputation handed down to us by the older children. Miss Gordon had a short, boyish crop of dark, straight hair, streaked with grey, giving it a salt-and-pepper effect. Her pointed nose and ruddy complexion blended with her little beady eyes, giving her a wizened look. She was about five foot four tall with a slender frame but she was still a daunting figure as she peered frosty faced over her jam-jar spectacles. In her shrill, piercing voice, she made it quite clear, from the start, that she would not tolerate any nonsense whatsoever. However, it must be said she was given good reason to assert her authority on the very first day.

Everyone was stood by his or her assigned desk, awaiting the command to sit down. I was stood in-between Ronnie Hopkinson and Bobby Cheetham.

"Bloomin' 'eck Johnny," whispered Ronnie, "it doesn't look like we're gonna get away wi' much in this class, does it?"

"Aye I think you could be right there, Ronnie," I muttered through the side of my mouth for fear of being heard.

"See who dares to stand longest after she's tel't us all to sit down," dared Ronnie adding, "pass it on to Bobby." Feeling edgy, I nudged Bobby, giving him the message, this time using the other side of my mouth.

"You what?" replied Bobby, "I can't hear thi." Just then the chalk duster came flying through the air, hitting Bobby on his left cheek.

Miss Gordon's autocratic manner had now changed to anger. "You insolent boy, come out here this minute ... what have I just said about talking in class?"

"But Miss, I ...."

"Never mind excuses ... come out here now!"

Bobby made his way to the front of the class, but not before glaring at me, teething, "I'll get thi for this Cowheel ... it's your fault!"

"Right then," bellowed Miss Gordon, "what's your name?"

Bobby gave her a bemused look and answered, "But Miss, you know my name ... I was in Miss Drennan's class last year."

"Don't be impertinent, boy ... just answer the question!"

"Bobby Cheetham," said Bobby, through tight lips.

Bobby Cheetham what?" she asked, indignantly.

Bobby paused a little before replying, "Bobby Cheetham nothing else ... I haven't got another name."

"U-umph, you stupid boy ... how do you address me, then?"

"Oh, by 'Miss Gordon', Miss."

"Right then, now I'll ask you again ... what's your name?"

By now, Bobby had got the message, 'Bobby Cheetham, Miss,'" he replied, with a smile, feeling pleased with himself.

"And you can take that smirk off your face, I won't tolerate that sort of nonsense in my class."

Once again Bobby tried protesting, "But Miss ...."

His pleas fell on deaf ears, as Miss Gordon deftly picked up the bamboo cane; she was determined to use Bobby as an example to stamp her authority on the class. She swished the cane a couple of times before ordering Bobby to hold out his hand. He tentatively held it out but nervously kept drawing it back.

"Keep it still, boy," she rapped, "or you'll receive two instead of one!" Bobby's face winced and turned a distinct red as the cane came down on the four fingers of his left hand.

As he returned to his seat he clamped his bottom lip with his top teeth and curled up his top lip hissing, "Right Cowheel ... in the schoolyard at playtime!"

This playground fight was just one of our many squabbles, but on this occasion we were caught by one of the nuns and had to report to Miss Gordon. We both walked sheepishly into the classroom, and on seeing us she was furious ... especially with Bobby.

"Well well," she pointed out, "it's you again, you impudent boy! Obviously one stroke of the cane was not sufficient to make you behave properly ... this time, my boy, you're going to get one on each hand!"

Bobby knew it was hopeless to protest, but then I jumped to his defence. "But Miss, it wasn't his fault ... I started it." I wasn't being heroic ... the way I saw it, I was going to get the cane anyway; besides, Bobby had already had the cane on my behalf.

"Oh yes, and what happened then?" she rapped.

"Well I jumped on his back and he was only tryin' to get me off."

"Right," she said turning to Bobby, "under the circumstances you can go, but mark my word boy, any more fighting and you're for it ... understand?"

"Yes Miss, it won't happen again, I promise," muttered Bobby, backing edgily out of the classroom. I had to stay and I got the same punishment that Bobby had received previously. Just one stroke of the cane, but it was enough to bring tears to my eyes.

Bobby and I became bosom friends thereafter, getting up to all kinds of mischief; neither of us ever became a favourite of Miss Gordon. But I must admit, despite getting the cane on a few occasions, I became quite fond of the headmistress.

My change of heart came about during the reading session. Every afternoon we all had to read quietly to ourselves for about an hour ... I was reading the story of Saint George and the Dragon and I loved it. Whereas most of the other children hated this lesson, I actually looked forward to it. Once I got my nose stuck into the book I became completely enthralled. Miss Gordon noticed how engrossed I was and, to my embarrassment, she sang out my praises to the class.

One day she actually peered over my shoulder, commenting, "I'm very pleased with you John, your reading skills have come on a treat. Mind you, you must take after your mother ... she's a wonderful writer."

"U-um," I thought, "I might have been chastised on a few occasions, but only when I deserved it ... she might be strict but at least she's fair. Yeah, she encourages me with mi reading and sums and she praises me when I do well.

Perhaps she has a soft spot for me. Anyroad, no matter what t'others think, I like her."

The first hour of each day was taken up by religious instruction, which entailed reciting passages from the Catechism, parrot fashion. The twins, Nora and Teresa, were always well versed in these matters, as were certain other members of the class. But lots of boys got bored, mumbling under their breath making a mockery of the recitals and especially 'Decades of the Rosary':

> Hail Mary full of grace,
> Wore broken clogs and fell on her face!

The girls, being much more serious, would reprimand them. One girl happened to say to Bobby, "A-ah, that's a great big sin, you'll have to go to confession on Saturday and confess to Father Hartley what you've bin saying."

"E-eh there's no need for that," Bobby teased, "I'll just say three 'Hail Mary's, an 'Our Father' and an 'Act of Contrition' afore I go to bed tonight … I'll be all reight then."

"I'm gonna tell Miss Gordon over you … then you're forrit," she responded.

"Please yoursel' you tell-tale tit," he mocked followed by,

> Tell-tale tit,
> Your tounge'll split,
> And all the little dogs'll have a little bit.

"Oh shurrup you!" she snapped, "I'm not bothered what you call me."

"Woo-oo, temper temper, mind your halo doesn't slip!" Bobby sneered. "Anyroad, if I went to confession that's all the priest would tell me to say."

"A-ah, you're bad you are … you'll go to hell for ever and ever!"

The girl's efforts were fruitless. Bobby just jeered, "Yeah, yeah, yeah … and I suppose you'll go to heaven on a broomstick!"

*   *   *

I liked arithmetic, but found one aspect of it quite difficult: multiplication using double figures or more. Miss Gordon introduced this new topic, but despite going over it several times, I couldn't grasp the fundamentals of it. One day I was really struggling with a problem and turned to Bobby Cheetham.

"I'll never do this Bobby, I don't get it … how do you multiply 45 by 23?" Bobby had grasped it very quickly and eagerly showed me the method.

"Well just put the 23 under the 45 like you would if you were adding up."

"Yeah, I know that … but then what?"

"It's easy, first you multiply the 5 by the 3 … what's that?"

"That's 15 … now what?"

"Well just write down 5 and put the 1 up onto the line next to the 4."

"Yeah … go on."

"Multiply the 4 by 3 and then add the 1 that you've put onto the line … that meks it 135."

"Right, I can get that far but I don't know what to do next."

"Oh that's easy," replied Bobby, feeling pleased with himself, "all you do now is multiply the 45 by the 2 using same method but this time you have to move the number one step o'er to the left."

"Aye, and then what?" I asked, still nonplussed.

"Well, all you have to do now is add up both o' them numbers and you've got the answer."

On doing this, it clicked. I too had now grasped it.

"Great, Bobby, I've got it … the penny's dropped at last." It was strange that Miss Gordon, with all her knowledge and expertise, had not been able to get through to me, whereas a bit of friendliness from my mate did the trick.

* * *

Around this time, I started to get interested in girls. The local 'Sweetheart' of St Thomas's was a girl called Sally Kelly. At the time there was a song that went:

Oh … the boys are all mad about Nelly,
The daughter of Officer Kelly,
And it's all day long they bring
Flowers all dripping with dew,
So … let's join in the chorus of Ne-el-ly Kelly,
I…I … lo-ove you!

All the boys chanted the song in unison, replacing the name Nelly with 'Sally'.

As it happened, there was another girl in the school with the same surname: Moya Kelly. On first setting eyes on Moya, I was smitten … all thoughts of Miss Quinn quickly vanished … this was the real thing. Moya was a little younger than me, and, like Miss Quinn, she had the most gorgeous dark hair, with natural waves. I so much wanted to talk to her in the schoolyard during playtime, but I was too shy and could never get up the courage.

Alas, the nearest I ever came to being her boyfriend was at the Saturday matinee at the Temp, better known as 'The Bug and Scratch'. We were sat next to each other watching *Flash Gordon and the Clay Men* and I bought her a bag of crisps, spending my last thre'pence. But my little ploy didn't work – she wasn't interested; it was as though I didn't exist. Ironically, Moya started to go out with a friend of mine shortly after that ... Bobby Cheetham.

"Mind you," I kept telling myself, "Bobby has got the advantage over me cos he lives on Finsley Gate, the same as Moya."

Poor me, what a shame. The first two loves of my life, both unrequited!

*   *   *

Mum always greeted us with a warm meal when we came home from school and would have a warm meal ready. Doing a part-time cleaning job for a wealthy lady fitted in well with her busy timetable and tea was usually served about 5pm. The extensions on the wooden table would be pulled out, ensuring a place for everyone. The meals were sparse, but Mum knew that we'd all had at least one good meal: the school dinner. One fad she had was that she always brewed up in a large teapot, putting plenty of sugar in. She strongly believed that sugar was good for keeping our energy levels high. Sugar was on ration but no matter, Mum would send me across to a neighbour's house with a packet of Brook Bond tea to swap for a two-pound bag of Tate and Lyle sugar. The teapot didn't blend in well with the drinking vessels – jam-jars, some still with the golliwog label on them.

"Oh, I'm fed up o' drinking outta jam-jars," Mary would complain, "when I get bigger and have some money I'm gonna go down town and buy some proper cups."

I didn't like milk in my tea, so the boiling water was forever cracking the jam-jars and also, I kept burning my mouth on the rim of the hot glass.

Maureen's complaint was different again: "Oh no, Mum … you've gone and put a load o' senna pods in the teapot again!"

This was another of Mum's fads. "Hey, never you mind about that, get it drunk … it's good for keeping your bowels open."

"Keeping 'em open," quipped Jimmy, "by 'eck, Mum, the amount you keep putting in the teapot … we should have cleanest bowels in Burnley."

"No, I'm sorry Mam," Maureen would protest, "I can't drink it with senna pods in it … I can't stand the smell, never mind the taste."

* * *

A major craze amongst the lads at the time was collecting fag cards in the schoolyard and around the streets. These were only discarded cigarette packets but no matter, a lad was never happier than when he had a handful. Most kids were poor and never had any money, but, they could always swap the fag cards for other stuff from their more fortunate mates. Park Drive, Woodbine, Player's Navy Cut and Capstan Full Strength packets were very common; Rough Rider and Passing Cloud were much rarer, and therefore more collectable. The most sought-after card by all and sundry was a Royalty and every lad wanted to add this precious commodity to his collection.

The fag cards were found under seats in the pictures, on buses or even in the gutter. The Ribble Garage was situated on Trafalgar close to Gresham Place and there were some large waste bins just inside the main entrance. Lads would forage through the bins finding many of the common fag cards and sometimes if they were lucky ... a 'Miss Blanche'!

Lads could be seen playing 'faggies' on every street corner. A card was stood up against the wall and two boys would kneel down on the flag edge and alternately flick cards at it. Many cards would finish up on the floor and the boy who knocked down the target would happily scoop up the lot. Mind you, the lads wouldn't play with the rare fag cards, as these were far more valuable and were used as a form of collateral, readily exchangeable for other things.

I became very skilful at the game and so never went short of tuck. However, there was one lad called Jack Lofthouse, who was even better at the game than I was. Jack didn't go to St Thomas's School, but he lived on Rowley Street, just below the railway. I spent many hours on that street trying to triumph over Jack, but I nearly always ended up the loser. Jack was older than me and a bit of a tearaway, but I liked him and looked up to him. We frequently got into mischief, often doing very dangerous things.

Many a time I would be walking along Trafalgar and I'd hear a voice shout, "All reight Cowheel, how d'you fancy your chances today?" On turning, I would discover Jack.

"Aye, all reight Lofty ... but less o' the Cowheel!"

"Aye and less o' the Lofty afore I clips thi round the lug'ole!"

It was all friendly rivalry and we both took it in good part. Mind you, as well as being a good fag packet player,

Jack was also a very good fighter ... not many lads tangled with him.

During one session I lost about fifty cards to Jack and felt rather dejected.

"Well, what can ya expect?" teased Jack, "You Albion Street wallies don't stand a cat in hell's chance playin' against us Rowley Street kids."

"Don't kid yourself ... I'll win some more at school tomorrow and I'll be back here after I've had mi tea," I retaliated.

"Oh aye, and where are you gonna get some fag packets from to play with in the first place?"

"Don't worry, Lofty, I'll think o' somet."

Some kids would go to any lengths and risk life and limb to obtain rare fag cards, and Jack was one of these. He was a few years older than me and tended to lead me into mischief, and I followed enthusiastically. On this particular day, as I was walking off rather disheartened after my heavy loss, he shouted after me.

"How would you like a sack full o' brand new fag cards, John ... aye, and rare ones at that?"

"Oh yeah, sure, Lofty... and what's the catch?"

"No catch, I've been told there's thousands of 'em just waiting to be picked up in the Paper Mill."

"Aye, I believe so," I replied, my spirit rekindled, "there's bin tales going round the school yard about it."

"Well, whaddaya say ... are you gam" o' what?"

"What, now?"

"Aye, why not, it'll be goin' dark in about half an hour ... we should be able to sneak in th'back way along the Swift River."

"Aye, all reight Jack, but have you got owt to carry 'em in?"

"Yeah, I think there's a couple o' sacks in the coal 'ole."

"Just one thing Jack ... before we go, you've got to agree to split everything fifty-fifty when we get back."

"Yeah, all reight, fair enough, I promise thi... come on then, let's go!"

Off we set towards the railway viaduct, which ran by the side of Ashfield Road. We stealthily made our way past Clifton Lodge and down by the side of the Paper Mill via an old ginny track until we reached some steel railings overlooking the Swift River. Being quite nimble, we easily scaled the railings and climbed down a steep wall until we were on a narrow cobbled bank at one side of the fast-flowing river. By now it was quite dark, but the moon was emitting a little light as we scrambled along cautiously, keeping near to the wall, finally reaching the main entrance to the mill. There were two ways into the mill: a natural way across a bridge from the factory yard or by scaling the bridge from the far side of the Swift River, which lay directly under the main entrance. To avoid being seen by workmen, we had to take the latter path. To reach the entrance we had to climb a high wall and then more steel railings. Once inside the mill we dived for cover behind a large stack of paper bales. There were books, comics, magazines and lots of other things but we were only interested in one-thing: fag packets. We'd rooted through various bales for about twenty minutes, then Jack let out a shout of sheer delight.

"Quick John, come here! See what I've found!" I couldn't believe it ... there were stacks of 'Airmail' cigarette cards, all in pristine condition.

"Bloomin' 'eck Jack, what a good do ... them's one o' the rarest fag packets and they're all brand spanking new!"

"Sh-shh, be quiet afore anybody hears thi! Anyroad, hold one o' them sacks open so I can fill it up." Within minutes we'd filled both sacks and were on our way back along the bank of the Swift River and for the next few days Jack and I were the envy of our schoolmates. We certainly didn't go short of tuck for a while after that!

On one occasion, when raiding the mill, it had been raining and the Swift River had risen, flooding the banks to within a foot of the wall. Jack and I stealthily made our way to the bridge and managed to gain entrance to the mill. Whilst filling the sacks we heard footsteps, and were forced to hide behind some large bales. Three men came and started moving some of the bales about. Two hours passed before we got the chance to escape, making our way to the bridge. However, there was a shock awaiting us; the heavens had opened and the river had overflowed its banks. We couldn't walk over the bridge to the other side, as the office and the watchman's hut were there in the main yard.

"We'll have to crawl across that pipe, John, it's th'only way outta here," suggested Jack. On looking down I could see a steel pipe about twelve inches in diameter, which ran alongside the bridge, spanning the river.

"Flippin 'eck Jack, I hope I don't fall off. I know I'm a good swimmer but I don't fancy goin' in that raging water."

"Arg-gh, you'll be all reight … anyroad, we don't have much option, do we?"

After climbing down we both inched across the pipe on our bellies, finally reaching the other side where there was a narrow ginnel that led onto Ashfield Road.

"What a good do," said Jack, "let's go!" We ran off as fast as our legs would carry us and didn't stop till we reached Trafalgar.

We raided the Paper Mill a few times after that but our little escapades came to a temporary halt because lots of other lads started to do the same thing. Consequently, the mill owners got wind of what was going on and took preventative measures, putting up barbed wire on top of the bridge and around the pipe. But Jack wasn't to be put off; he'd had a taste of the good life and wanted more. Come what may, he was determined to find another way into the mill.

Consequently, he came up with a scheme – one that was fraught with danger. I was with our Jimmy at the time.

"I don't know about you, John," said Jack, "but I'm gonna raid the Paper Mill again tonight."

"But how are you gonna do that, Jack … we only tried last week and you know we couldn't get past that barbed wire."

"Yeah, I know that but I've fathomed out another way o' gettin' in there."

"Aye, and how's that then?" I asked.

"Well, we can get in by side o' the lodge and o'er the roof."

"O'er the roof … you must be joking! To get into the main part o' the mill we'd have to cross from one roof to t'other over a steel girder and there's shredding machines below it. And anyroad, what d'you mean … we can get in there?"

"Well, you'll be coming with me, won't ya?"

"No, will I bloomin' 'eck as like! No way!"

"Oh come on, what's up withee? We've shinned o'er that pipe that runs o'er the Swift River loads o' times."

"Yeah, I know we have but that ain't nowhere near as high as that girder and there's no flipping shredders underneath it!"

"Please yourself, but you'll not get any fag packets off me if you don't come."

"I'll come with thi if you want Jack," interrupted our Jimmy, "our John's freightened to death of his own shadow."

"Whaddaya talking about?" I grunted, becoming slightly annoyed, "I've raided the Paper Mill loads o' times more than you have."

"Oh aye, but you've never gone o'er the roof afore, have you?"

I thought about it for a minute before greed got the better of me. I couldn't bear the thought of our Jimmy out-doing me, so I foolishly agreed to go with them.

We made our way to Clifton Lodge prior to scaling the factory wall. The roof was constructed like a saw blade similar to the ones on a cotton mill with north-facing windows. We jumped from one set of sloping slates to another, but then came the dangerous part … crossing over the girder, which was about nine inches wide and eighteen inches deep. The gap in-between the buildings was only six feet across, but when I looked down, I could see a glass roof with paper-shredding machines underneath. It was terrifying! I was used to racing along the backyard walls at breakneck speed and jumping over the gates, but this was different; very different. My heart sank, thumping wildly and I temporarily froze on the spot. But it didn't seem to bother our Jimmy or Jack as they balanced across the girder like trapeze artists. I had come this far and didn't like backing out for fear of ridicule. I knew I was being foolish but I eventually got up the nerve to follow them cautiously straddling the steel girder on my backside, gripping the top flange tightly.

On entering the building through a skylight we found ourselves in a different part of the mill.

"You look o'er yonder Johnny while me and Jimmy rout through these here bales," said Jack. 'Give us a shout if you find anything."

"Reighto Jack, but keep your voice down, somebody might hear you."

I tentatively made my way across the floor and climbed in amongst the mountainous stacks of bales. I was still reeling from the effects of crossing over on the girder and my hands shook nervously as I fumbled about looking for any signs of fag packets. The shaking stopped, however, when I noticed a silver object that seemed to beckon me.

"It can't be what I think it is," I thought, as a feeling of excitement passed down my spine, "surely it's not a Royalty?"

But to my sheer delight, it was. It was a Royalty, exactly what the name implies: 'The king of all cards', the most prestigious and sought-after fag packet ever. I couldn't believe my eyes as I stared at the sacred card in the palm of my hand, unblemished in mint condition. I pinched myself to make sure I wasn't dreaming ... I just couldn't believe my luck. Coming back to reality, I realised that where there was one there may be more. I eagerly rummaged deeper into the bale. My excitement grew to fever pitch as I found another fifteen. I just couldn't put them into the sack; I put them in my pocket.

"There's no way I'm sharing these wi' Jack and our Jimmy," I thought, as greed once again overtook me, "these are mine!" I convinced myself that I wasn't doing anything wrong. "Yeah, fair do's," I smirked, "finders keepers."

Besides the Royalties, there were lots of other rare cards.

"Jack ... Jimmy," I shouted, forgetting the advice I'd previously given Jack, "come over here quick, there's millions o' good uns in these bales.

"Flamin' 'eck I don't believe it," Jack blurted out. "Let's get our bags filled and get out of here quick!" Filling the sacks was the easy part; the hard bit was going back the way we'd come, this time burdened down with the loot.

This proved even more difficult than I'd anticipated, because when we climbed back onto the roof through the skylight it was dark and had been raining. Hence, the slates were slippy, leaving us no option but to make our way back from bay to bay, sliding down the slates on our backsides. By the time we reached the girder our pants were soaking wet. But now came the precarious task of crossing over the steel support, which was also slippy underfoot from the downpour.

A shiver went down my spine as I knelt down onto my hands and knees and grasped the top flange of the reinforced steel joist. The building was now lit up and as I looked down I could see men working the shredding machines – a fearsome sight. As I cautiously edged myself inch by inch across the fearful divide, Jack became impatient.

"Come on Johnny, you soft bugger … get a move on, we want to get out of here!"

I didn't answer; I was too scared. In fact, I momentarily froze with fear. Our Jimmy joined in with Jack, throwing out similar remarks until I gradually reached the other side. I paused a moment, then sighed with relief for the very thought of falling through the glass roof to a horrible death made the hackles on my neck stand up like the quills of a porcupine.

Jack was the next to follow, but unlike me, he made it seem easy. Despite the damp, he fearlessly walked across the divide without any bother.

Then came our Jimmy's turn. He was almost across when our little scam nearly ended in disaster! He stumbled a little and on trying to regain his balance, he dropped his sack.

"Blast it!" he cursed, "All that work for nowt!" Nevertheless, on looking down he could see the sack was lying on top of the glass roof. It was only about two feet down, so he decided to try and retrieve it.

"Come on, our Jimmy, leave it, it's not worth it!" I pleaded, becoming agitated.

"No way ... I didn't come here for nowt, I'm not leaving without them faggies."

"It doesn't matter, Jimmy, there's enough in my sack for both of us," I pleaded all the more, "just leave 'em, it's too dangerous." My plea fell on deaf ears ... Jimmy was fearless. He got down and placed his foot on the bottom flange of the girder, and then, holding on with one hand, he tried reaching out with the other. But no matter how he tried he just couldn't reach the sack ... it eluded him by about six inches.

"Can ya find me a stick with a nail in it, our John? I'd be able to hook it if I had one."

"Oh sure, Jimmy, there's bloomin' hundreds of 'em lying about up here."

"All reight don't get fly. Just have a look about, there might be somet." I looked, but to no avail. We had no option but to leave the sack where it was.

"Bloomin' 'eck, I could bloody well kick myself," Jimmy kept repeating as we made our way home, "I'm a dozy swine, aren't I?"

"Never mind, Jimmy, look on bright side," said Jack, "we've still got plenty o' good fag packets and a good tale to tell all our mates."

"Aye we have haven't we and ..." Jimmy stopped in mid-sentence, and cracked up into a fit of laughter.

"What are you laughing at, Jimmy ... what's up?" I asked, puzzled.

Jimmy couldn't stop chuckling. "Well it's just struck me, and I think it's really funny. Whatta them fellas in the Paper Mill gonna think when they see that sack o' fag packets on top o' the glass roof?" He roared with laughter again,

"They'll be wondering for ever an' a day how the hell it got up there!"

Jack and I laughed along with him. "Yeah, you're reight there, Jimmy," said Jack, "eh, it's bin a good night, an'it?"

All three of us were happy. Needless to say, we never raided the Paper Mill again ... at least, I didn't. In all probability, Jack or our Jimmy went back with some gadget or other to retrieve the sack of fag cards. Anyway I wasn't bothered. I still had my secret treasure: the precious Royalties.

I was a show-off and, like Jack said, it was a good yarn to tell in the schoolyard. After I'd finished telling my tale, Bobby Cheetham laughed and as usual came out with a funny comment that raised a few laughs.

"Bloomin' 'eck Johnny ... I'll bet you were cut up about that, ha ha!"

Somebody else went a bit further. There was a small notice board in the cloakroom area and at playtime quite a few girls had gathered around it and were laughing hysterically.

"Whatta they laughing about?" asked Bobby.

"I don't know," I answered, "let's go and have a look." Some other lads, whose curiosity had been aroused, came along too.

Bobby was the first to look at the board and immediately roared in laughter, as did the other lads when they saw it. I just smiled at first, but then even I had to laugh – not quite as loudly as the others, as the joke was on me. But I had to admit, I saw the funny side.

Somebody had written on the notice board:

SPECIAL OFFER
Chopped Cowheel
3 fag packets per 1lb.
Can be obtained from the Paper Mill.

I never did find out who the culprit was. But I strongly suspect it was Bobby.

* * *

I was always the outdoor type and loved camping along with my mates Ronnie Hopkinson and Kenny Clayton. We often went to Hurstwood, a popular picnic area on the outskirts of Burnley, and pitched our tent down by the riverside. We only had a small tent and a make-do ground sheet, but this didn't put us off. We'd usually set off Saturday afternoon and return back home Sunday evening. One weekend Barry asked if he could come along with us.

"U-um, I don't know, our Barry … what about your asthma?"

"Oh I'll be all right. I haven't had an attack for ages."

"Yeah I know that, but don't forget, it gets really cold at night in a tent."

"Oh come on, our John, let me come. I've never been camping afore."

"Aye, all reight then, but you'll have to get stuck in like the rest of us."

Barry's eyes displayed his obvious delight. "Great, I'll just go and tell mi mam so she knows where I am."

Before setting off on our little adventure, I handed him a rucksack. "Here, you can carry that for starters and don't forget what I said about keeping up with the rest of us." So off we went arriving at our destination around three o'clock. It was a nice day, with brilliant sunshine, so it was still quite warm.

"I'm going for a swim," said Ronnie, "is anybody else coming?"

"I'm gam," replied Kenny, "especially down near that little waterfall, where the water's deeper."

"Me too," I said, "how about you, our Barry?"

"Yeah, why not? I'd love to." All four of us splashed about in the running water, thoroughly enjoying ourselves.

"Hey this is great," yelled Barry as he doused his head under the waterfall, "have we any soap so I can wash mi hair?"

"Whaddaya going on about? It's not the bloomin' Ritz!" joked Ronnie. All four of us laughed; we were having a great time. Afterwards, we got down to the nitty-gritty of making something to eat. This is where Barry came into his own, collecting some kindling, with which he got a fire going. He was also more adept than the rest of us when it came to cooking.

"Hey, your Barry's doing all reight John," said Ronnie, "we'll have to let him come again sometime."

We all got settled around the fire and laughed the night away. Taking everything into account it had been a really good day … we felt like cowboys out on the range after a day's round up.

"Reight lads, time for a bit of shuteye," quipped Kenny in his best cowboy accent, "another hard day tomorrow."

"We'll all have to kip together, our Barry," I said, "you can sleep in the middle wi' Kenny … it'll be warmer."

"Aye, all reight our John, I couldn't care less where I sleep … I've really enjoyed misel today; it's bin really good."

We talked a little while longer before gradually drifting off. Everything was fine until about four o'clock in the morning, when Barry woke me, tugging at my shirtsleeve. At first I couldn't make out what he was trying to say, but then I realised that my younger brother was struggling for his breath.

"I ... I ... ca-n't bre-a-the, our John, I ... ca-n't ...!"

He was having an Asthmatic attack and I realised the gravity of the situation. I'd seen Barry like this many times before, and knew that I had to do something quickly. I wasn't versed in first aid, but knew instinctively that I had to get Barry sat upright to help his breathing.

"Right our Barry," I reassured him, "whatever you do, don't panic ... I'll get you home somehow!" After helping him to get dressed, I decided we had no option but to make the long walk home. By now, Ronnie and Kenny were stirring and I told them what was happening.

"There's nowt any of you can do about it, so you may as well go back to sleep. I'll see you when I get back." The sun was just coming up as Barry and I stepped outside the tent and the early morning dew was glistening on the grass.

"Put this around your shoulders, our kid," I said, draping a blanket around him. Barry offered no resistance; he was only too grateful. Besides, by this time he could hardly speak.

"Come on, our Barry, we'd best get going. We've a long trek back." He could only walk slowly and kept stopping to catch his breath, and so it took about one hour to reach the village of Worsethorne and another ninety minutes to get to Brunshaw Road. It was about seven o'clock as we passed Turf Moor Football Field, when I heard a voice from behind us.

"And where d'you two think you're going at this time o' the morning dressed like that?" someone growled in a deep, gruff voice. I turned to see a rather stern-looking policeman, whose face was full of suspicion.

"We're going home. Mi brother's not well, and he needs some medicine," I answered.

"Oh yeah, sure. And where would that be, then?" After explaining the situation, the constable became very sympathetic to our plight.

"Right lads, come with me and I'll get thi sorted out." At that, he went to the nearest police telephone box and within minutes there was a police squad car on the scene.

"Right lads, we'd best get thi up to t'hospital right away."

"Oh it doesn't matter, officer. If you take us home, mi mam'll know what to do," I told him.

"U-um, I don't know about that … It'd be going against mi better judgement."

"Honest, officer, it'll be all right," I assured him, "mi mam's done it loads o' times afore!"

So the policeman took us home to Albion Street, but he insisted on staying until he could see that everything was all right. It didn't take long, Mum was ever so efficient, giving Barry the necessary medication and nursing care. Within minutes he was feeling much better and his breathing became easier.

Mum, who was always so correct in her speech, then spoke in a way which surprised me. "Righto lad, get this warm drink inside thi and then get thasel upstairs into a warm bed afore you catches your death o' cold … tha'll be as reet as rain afore dinner time."

"Bloomin' 'eck, Mam," I chuckled, "I've never heard you talk like that afore … it sounds really funny coming from you."

"Yeah, well I'm tired, aren't I? Anyway, it just goes to show that anything rubs off after a while, doesn't it?"

Mum then turned to the policeman. "Thank you, officer, for all your help, I'm very grateful. I don't know what we would do without the police force."

"Think nothing of it, madam," the policeman replied, touching his helmet, "I'm only too glad to be of service and happy that the young lad's all right. Anyroad, now that things are in order I'll be on my way."

I was happy now, knowing that our Barry was all right, and I felt rather peckish. I had some cornflakes, a nice pot of tea and a fry-up before setting off back to Hurstwood.

"Where are you going, our John," Mum asked, "surely you're not going back to Hurstwood, are you?"

"I sure am Mam. I told Ronnie and Kenny I'd be back to let them know how we went on."

"Aye, go on then, on your way, there's no stopping you," she muttered.

Barry recovered all right and over the years he did go camping again. But only with organised groups such as the Police Youth Club – never again with me!

* * *

I never had any money, but armed with a few fag packets I was always assured of some tuck. One of my mates, Desmond Lee, always came to school with sixpence, which was enough to buy a packet of dates at the corner shop on Whittham Street. I loved this exotic fruit and would gladly exchange ten faggies for a handful, feeling quite confident that I would soon replace the much sought-after fag packets.

Mind you, even though I was skilful at the game I didn't always win, as some of the other lads were very competitive. One of these was Tommy Neville and he generally gave me a good run for my faggies. However, one day, luck was on my side. I couldn't go wrong and by the end of playtime I'd skinned Tommy of every fag packet he had.

Feeling rather despondent, Tommy tried wrangling with me. "Come on Cowheel, lend us a few fag cards and gimme a chance to win some back."

"You must be joking, Nev, I'd be playing for mi own faggies!" I noticed the dejected look on his face and remembered how I'd felt when Jack Lofthouse had skinned me. "I'll tell thi what, Nev ... have you owt to swap?"

"Aye all reight Cowheel," he replied, fumbling in his pocket, "how about this?"

I couldn't believe it. There, in Tommy's hand, was a little white mouse. Wham ... instantly I was interested!

"Right, Nev ... how many faggies forrit?"

Tommy was a crafty so-and-so. He immediately noticed my enthusiasm, "Well, you can have it for sixty fag cards, but I want some rare ones as well."

I realised my impetuousness had cost me, so I went into haggling mode. "I'll tell thi what, Nev, I'll give you fifty forrit, and that includes twenty brand new Airmail."

Tommy couldn't resist, and so the deal was made ... I was now the proud owner of a little white mouse.

I couldn't wait to get home to show my brothers and sisters. "Don't tell mi mam," I told them. "She'll go mad if she thinks there's a mouse in t'house." Mary became excited as she saw the little mouse run along my arm.

"Oh can I have it, our kid ... I promise you I'll look after it."

"No way!" I responded, "I want to keep it for myself. I'll have loads o' fun with it. Anyroad, I'll be able to look after it better than you ... I've already got it a little cage to sleep in."

Mary tried her best to get round me, but to no avail. Nonetheless, she'd made her mind up to have the little mouse … at least for a little while, anyway.

Next morning I couldn't wait to go to school to show off my new pet. But to my horror, when I went to pick it up, the cage door was open – it had gone!

"Hey, who's got mi mouse," I yelled, "somebody's whipped it!" My mind flashed back to the previous day. "Come on, our Mary, you've got it, haven't you?"

"Have I 'eck as like," she snorted, "the bloomin' cat'll have et'n it!"

"Oh don't say that, it can't have," I cried anxiously, "I put the cage reight on top o' the sideboard afore I went to bed last night."

"Well that's no good is it you silly sod … the cat can easily climb up there!"

"Oh no!" I thought, feeling really deflated at losing the little creature, and really bad for being so thoughtless as to let it come to harm. My self-esteem was to return later that day, though, when I realised that Mary had conned me. She had taken my pet and, after putting it in a shoebox, hidden it in a safe place. Being crafty, she'd sewn a pocket with a buttonhole to the inside of her blouse. After placing the little mouse therein, she made her way to school.

She was the centre of attention amongst the girls in the schoolyard as she let the mouse run from the palm of her hand, up the sleeve of her cardigan and out onto her neck. She was unafraid of the little thing whilst most of the girls screeched loudly as it scurried along.

I paid no attention to the noise, because the girls were forever screeching about nothing, but all the same, Mary's little scam came to light shortly after entering the classroom.

Halfway through Catechism, the lesson was disrupted by giggling from the girls' corner, as the mouse had got out of the pocket and was once again running within Mary's clothing. Wanting to show off, Mary pulled funny faces and exaggerated her shoulder movements, making the girls laugh hysterically.

Miss Gordon restored order by bringing the bamboo cane down onto her desk and bellowing loudly, "Quiet!" Silence descended on the class immediately and a semblance of order was restored. "Mary Cowell, what are you playing at?" rapped Miss Gordon. "What's going on?"

"Nothing Miss," replied Mary, acting innocently. "I've just got an itchy back and I'm trying to scratch it." By now the mouse had run down her sleeve and she had it grasped firmly in her hand. It was obvious to Miss Gordon that Mary was holding something.

"Never mind nothing, come out here at once and show me what you've got in your hand ... I won't have you disrupting the class!"

Under the circumstances most girls would have wet themselves, but Mary, although anxious, was actually pleased.

"Oh 'eck, I'm dead," she muttered under her breath, as she made her way gingerly towards the headmistress, "she'll kill me when she finds out what I've got." But her anxiety was offset by the thought that she'd look good in front of her classmates.

"Right, Mary Cowell," said Miss Gordon, sternly, 'I'll ask you just one more time ... what have you got in your hand?"

Mary bent her head as she felt Miss Gordon's eyes boring down into her, but still remained defiant. Looking up from beneath her furrowed eyebrows, she made a gesture by a barely perceptible movement of her shoulders and repeated, "Nothing Miss. I haven't got anything!"

It was plain to see that Miss Gordon was fast losing her patience, as her voice raised a decibel. "You impudent, stupid girl! Now, open your hand this minute!"

Mary chuckled involuntarily, unable to suppress a giggle.

"You insolent girl ... open your hand I say!" snarled Miss Gordon, now completely losing some control.

Mary said no more, but amusing thoughts went through her head: "Right Miss Gordon, you asked for it ... on your head be it!" By placing her left hand over her right and cupping them together, she managed to take hold of the little mouse's tail in-between her right thumb and forefinger. Then, to the delight of the class, she held out her arm, dangling the little mouse in front of the headmistress. At the sight of it, Miss Gordon let out an ear-splitting yell as she dropped the Catechism to the floor.

"A-ar-rgh," she screamed, backing away from Mary, "get away from me and take that horrible creature out of my classroom this minute, you awful little girl!"

Mary, amused by the look of horror on Miss Gordon's face, prolonged the situation by letting go of the mouse's tail, allowing it to land on the headmistress's desk. As it scurried along the desktop, Miss Gordon stiffened and backed up against the wall with outstretched arms and open fingers.

Hardly able to speak, she pleaded through gritted teeth, "O-oh catch it quick and take the nasty thing away!" The tiny mouse seemed to sense her fear as it crouched at the end of the desk, sniffing the air with its nostrils and looking up at her with little red eyes. The movements of its whiskers were enough to make Miss Gordon freeze as though she was being held up at gunpoint.

Mary was enjoying the moment more and more, as by now, the classroom was in raptures; she had become a celebrity. She purposely fumbled, allowing the little mouse a final dash across the desktop before picking it up.

"Right, have you got it now?" asked Miss Gordon, sighing with relief.

"Yes Miss, it's here ..."

"No no, don't show me ... just take the horrible thing away out of my sight and don't come back until you've got rid of it!" Mary happily took her leave, sniggering a little as she passed by my desk.

"I'll get you for this," I mouthed, through clenched teeth, "I'm warning thi ... you'd best look after mi mouse or I'll murder you!"

Mary wasn't bothered – just the opposite, in fact. She was able to skive off school for the rest of the morning to take the mouse home.

"Great!" she muttered to herself, "I've got outta doin' the Catechism and a boring arithmetic lesson."

However she didn't get away with it scot-free; she had to return to school that afternoon to face Miss Gordon's wrath. And mine.

6

THE ELEVEN-PLUS
EXAMINATION

The final year at St Thomas's was in Miss M. Gordon's class
– she was the niece of Miss Gordon. My favourite lesson
was mental arithmetic. One morning, Miss M. Gordon
handed out slips of paper with the numbers one to twenty
printed on them.

Tapping her desk with a ruler, she addressed the class.
"Right everybody, I'm going to give you some problems,
which I want you to work out in your head. I won't be
writing anything down on the blackboard, so listen
carefully. Once you've figured out the answer, write it down
against the appropriate number."

"Please Miss, can we have some scrap paper to work it
out?" asked Ronnie.

"No Ronald, that's the whole point of the exercise. You
have to work it out in your head and just write down the
answer. That's why it's called mental arithmetic."

"Bloomin' 'eck, that'll be hard, won't it Miss?"

"Try not to worry about it," she reassured him. "I'll start off with easy questions and gradually build up to harder ones. Now, get your pens ready." You could have heard a pin drop as all the class waited in anticipation. "Right first question ... 7 times 3 take away 11."

"U-um that's not too bad," I thought, as I wrote 10 against the first number.

"Second question ... 18 take away 7, then multiply by 7."

Once again I found it quite easy. Mind you, the problems became more difficult when objects were involved.

"If you bought 3 pounds of apples at 5d a pound and a loaf of bread for 4d ... how much change would you have left out of 2 shillings?"

"That's one and thre'pence for t'apples," I thought, "plus 4d for t'loaf ... that's 1s/7d. Tek that away fro' t'two bob ... yeah, 5d." I chuckled a little to myself. "U-um, I think I'm gonna like this here mental arithmetic."

I did appear to have a natural ability at this topic, nearly always attaining a 20-20 score, but our Mary, who sat just in front of me, really struggled, obtaining very poor marks. On the other hand, she was very good at English, both composition and grammar, whereas I found these subjects very difficult. When it came to filling in choice words to spaces in a sentence, I was hopeless. For example:

I WENT – THE PICTURES WITH MY – FRIENDS BUT WE ARRIVED – LATE. The choice words, of course, were:

TO, TWO, and TOO.

The way I saw it ... the space in between 'WENT" and 'THE" was smaller than the other two spaces so that must be TO. But now I couldn't fathom out which of the other two words to use, because the spaces appeared the same and besides, both TWO and TOO were three-letter words. I had no alternative but to make a wild guess at it. Consequently, I came up with many wrong answers, whereas Mary always fared very well.

Sobeit. Mary and I got our heads together in order to solve the problem.

"Right our Mary, when it's mental arithmetic I'll give you the answers and when it's English grammar you can give 'em to me." Subsequently, during various tests, a lot of whispering went on from one desk to another. Other times, I craned my neck to see what she had written on a scrap of paper.

Our little scam worked, both of us attaining better marks in our weaker subjects. However, it worked so well, we ended up being too clever for our own good ... Miss M. Gordon saw through our little ploy and made an example of us in front of the whole class.

Unaware of what was to come, I swelled with pride as she announced, "Very good, John Cowell, your English marks have greatly improved this week." But I was quickly deflated by her next remark. "It seems strange, in fact miraculous, that Mary's marks in mental arithmetic have also suddenly improved." At this, all the class started laughing.

"Stop that ... stop it at once!" she rapped. "This is no laughing matter, I won't tolerate cheating in my class ... is that understood?" Both Mary and I were ordered to the front of the class, where we received a severe whacking on each hand. We were then separated, each having to sit at opposite sides of the class.

My English grammar gradually improved, but mental arithmetic remained my favourite subject. I obtained a puzzle book and would set little problems for my friends during playtime.

I had a favourite conundrum and one day asked Ronnie to solve it:

"If a man an' half earned a guinea an' half in a day an' half ... how much money would one man earn in a day?"

"But you can't have half a man," smirked Ronnie.

"All right, a man and a boy if you like ... come on Ronnie, stop muckin' about, you know what I mean."

"Yeah, I know what you mean all reight. I were only kidding. Anyroad, it's easy: a guinea."

"No that's not it, you're wrong."

"Whaddaya talkin' about ... it must be. If a man and half earns a guinea and half then a man must earn a guinea."

"Yeah, he earns a guinea all right, but in a day and half ... I said a day."

"Oh aye, I see what you mean." He thought about it for a while and made a few stabs at it before saying, "All right then, I give up ... how much?"

"Fourteen shillings."

"Fourteen shillings ... how the flippin' 'eck do you mek that out?"

"Well, do you agree that a man earns a guinea in a day and half?"

"Yeah."

"Right then, there's three half-days in a day and half ... do you agree on that?"

"U-um ... go on."

"Well, all we have to do now is divide twenty-one shillings by three, which gives us seven shillings. This means that if he earns seven shillings in half a day, then he must earn fourteen shillings in a full day."

"Aye all reight clever clogs, you've proved your point. Now I've got a riddle for thi. Are you ready?"

"Yeah all right ... go on then," I said.

"Right, I've got a photograph here of one person. Now listen to what I'm gonna say and then you have to tell me what relation this person is to me."

"Right Ronnie I'm listening. Fire away."

"Reighto, here goes .... 'Brothers and sisters have I none, but this man's father is my father's son.' Now like I said afore ... what relation is this person to me?"

I pondered for a while before answering, "It's you, yourself."

"No. No it's not," replied Ronnie, with a smirk.

"It has to be, cos you've no brothers and sisters and you said 'my father's son'."

"Yeah, but I didn't say this man is my father's son ... I said this man's father is my father's son."

"Bloomin' 'eck Ronnie, the mind boggles tryin' to work that one out ... who is it, then?"

"Well, it's a bit complicated," gloated Ronnie, "but here goes. I have no brothers and sisters so I'm definitely my father's son ... are you with it so far?"

"Yeah righto ... carry on."

"So according to the riddle, I am this man's father ... therefore the man in the photo is my son."

"Oh aye, is that right?" I said jokingly, "Well all I can say Ronnie is you don't look that old!"

This is how life was in those days. We all liked to crack jokes, but at the end of the day exams had to be passed and it was in this final year at St Thomas's that we had to prepare ourselves for the eleven-plus prior to moving up into senior school. It was Miss M. Gordon's responsibility to encourage us with our studying. However, hardly anyone took it seriously and the frolicking and tomfoolery continued.

*   *   *

Sunday ... the day of rest. Dad made sure all his kids went to church in the morning and would have a hearty breakfast of bacon, egg, beans and fried bread waiting for us on our return.

Jimmy was always ravenous. "Pass me the brown sauce will you ... I love bacon butties wi' loads of HP on 'em," he would say, impatient to gobble up all that was laid before him

Mum was usually allowed a lie-in, but she always knew what the sermon at mass was each week. To keep us on our toes she would ask one of us at random what the Gospel was about ... this particular morning she asked Barry.

"Oh it was about a man having two sons and one went away for a long time without telling anybody where he was going."

"Oh yes, Barry, go on ... tell me more."

"Oh well, to tell you the truth, Mum I didn't get it cos, instead of being mad at him, when he got back home, his dad killed a cow and then they had a big party. The other son, who'd been there all the time, was mad cos he said they'd never ever done owt like that for him."

"That's very good, our Barry," said Mum, "you've more or less got the gist of the story ... I'll just enlighten you a little." She then went on to explain the meaning of the parable.

Mary was always on her guard in case Mum asked her questions, because many a time she'd skive off church, pocketing the collection money for a penny drink later on in the week.

"A-ah, that's a really big sin, our Mary!" Barry would say seriously. "If you die before going to confession next Saturday you'll go to hell!"

"Oh yeah our Barry, and even if I go to confession … d'you think I'm gonna tell the priest I kept his flippin' penny … some hopes!"

She was crafty. So as not to get caught out by Mam's probing questions, she always covered her tracks, asking one or other of us what the sermon had been about. One Sunday morning, shortly after the mouse incident, I dropped her right in it.

"What was the sermon about this morning, our John?" she quizzed me the moment she spotted me coming home from church.

"Oh it was about the master giving each of his three servants a bag of gold to look after whilst he went away on business. The first two servants invested the gold well and were praised on the master's return. But the third servant got told off cos he'd buried his gold in the ground."

"Yeah, I know the one," said Mary, highly delighted, "I'll be all right now if Mum asks me." Little did she know that the sermon had been 'The feeding of the five thousand'!

Mary fell for it, hook, line and sinker. When the truth came to light, she got a right good hiding. Mum also dragged her to the priest's house making her own up to everything.

"There were no need for that, our John," she moaned bitterly afterwards, "you got me into a load o' trouble."

"Well it serves you right, our Mary," I scoffed. "I were only gettin' mi own back o'er mi mouse!"

One thing that everyone looked forward to on Sunday morning was reading the *News of the World* newspaper. Mum liked doing the crossword and used to send it away every week in the hope of winning a thousand pounds. She never did, although one time she did win a writing competition for an article she wrote about a poor lonely old lady who had a very bad skin complaint and whose only companion was a very old dog. The title of the story was 'The loneliest person'. The prize, a prestigious television set fully licensed and maintained free for five years, didn't go to Mum, but to the old lady about whom the story was written. This pleased Mum, for it made her happy to have been able to bring some happiness into the old lady's life.

Dad was more into the football results and league tables. And, of course, reading the many scandals that filled the pages. However, he got the shock of his life one morning when Mary asked out of the blue, "Mam ... what does 'intimate' mean?"

"You what!" Dad bawled out, nearly falling off his chair, "Whattaya doing reading that paper?"

"Well you read it, Dad. Why can't I?"

"Never mind, 'why can't I', you cheeky young bugger! Give it me here right now. And don't let me catch thi reading it again!"

* * *

Mum was always fair, treating us all in the same way. Having said this, she was also strict and her word was law ... if she asked one of us to do something, it had to be done. She tried to share the chores and errands equally amongst us. No matter, she didn't always get it right.

"Oh 'eck we've run out of bread," I remember her saying to me once. "Just run on to Dick Smith's and get a loaf, our John."

"A-ah Mam, I went this morning – it's our Barry's turn!"

"Oh you went this morning, did you? Well, I've just asked you to go again, so you can bloomin' well go again right now!"

"U-umph, flippin' 'eck, it's not fair," I complained bitterly.

"Oh it's not fair, is it not? If you give me any back chat I'll make you go again every time we need something for the rest of the week." I knew not to argue further. She never made idle threats and certainly meant what she said, so I did as she bid.

The gas mantle was a constant nuisance in our house. It hung very low from the ceiling and was forever being broken by someone's head, creating a great long flame. It also got broken many times by sudden gusts of wind created by the back door slamming as someone opened the front door. This meant switching off the gas fitting, leaving the house in darkness except for the light emitted from the fire. The mantles only cost pennies, but Mum never had enough money to keep any spares.

"Nip round to Nora's back door our Jimmy for a new mantle and be quick about it," Mum asked him one day. Jimmy was too wily to grumble. He just took the money, muttering one or two things under his breath. The house was in darkness while we awaited his return.

One chore we all hated was emptying the slop buckets from each bedroom. These had to be carried from upstairs, through the living room and into the cellar via the stone steps and then emptied down the lavatory. Many a time they would be almost full to the brim, with the contents swishing about and spilling all over the place.

"Right, our Mary," Mum would shout, "mop that lot up with some disinfectant." A daily ritual in our house for whoever happened to be closest to the mop and bucket.

It wasn't very nice having to use a bucket, but it was the lesser of two evils. Having to go to the lavatory in the middle of the night and sit in the dank, dark air-raid shelter was enough to put the 'willies' up the hardiest of men. The thought of having to go downstairs and then down the outside stone steps into that cold dark place was, to say the least, frightening!

It wasn't only during the night either. In winter, as the nights drew in, the girls would be frightened of venturing out into the dark. One evening, one of the girls complained she was too scared to go to the lavatory.

"Oh I daren't go down there on my own … will somebody stand on guard at the top o' the steps for me?"

"You'll be all right," said Mum, "I'll get one of the lads to watch out for you."

"Oh, but what about the light Mam? It's pitch-black in that shelter!"

"You'll just have to roll up part of the *Burnley Express* and use it as a torch."

"It's too windy, Mam. Every time I do that it always blows out before I get there."

"Not if you go through cellar it won't."

"O-oh no, Mam, you know I'm scared to death o' that cellar … it's even darker than th'air-raid shelter!"

"All right, I'll go to the bottom of the cellar steps with you and our John can stand at the top of the outside steps."

"Flamin' 'eck," I whined, "nobody ever does it for me!"

"That'll do our John!" warned Mum.

By the time she got to the lavatory, the paper was almost burnt through and she moaned that the flame was dwindling.

"You'll have to use some of the lavvy paper that's hung on the nail our kid," I shouted, "that's what I do!"

*   *   *

Every July during Wake's weeks, when all the factories shut down for two weeks' holiday, Dad used to put his horse Peggy out to pasture in a small field. He really did have a way with horses and was a great believer that they needed a break, just like humans. At the end of the fortnight he would go and collect her and she would come running happily to the fence as soon as she saw him. One particular morning, he asked Barry and me to go with him to give him a hand.

"How come, Dad, you've never asked us to come before?" I asked.

"Ah well, this time she's in the field with two other horses, so she won't be as keen to lose her freedom."

"Oh right, Dad, but can we ride her back to the stable?" asked Barry.

He agreed and so the three of us set off. As soon as we reached the field, Dad gave a loud whistle. Peggy lifted her head and saw him all right, but instead of coming like she usually did she bolted off in the opposite direction.

"There, what did I tell you, I knew what she'd do," he said, pointing to the far side of the field, "it's always the same in a situation like this. Can you see them other horses that she's with o'er in yon corner?"

"Aye, I can Dad," said Barry, "and they seem to be really enjoying themselves."

"You're reight there, lad, they've got used to their freedom in th'open air."

"E-eh, just look at 'em frolicking about, kicking their hind legs into th'air Dad," I chuckled, amused by their playfulness.

"Yeah, Peggy's enjoying herself all reight," put in Dad, "but I'm afraid playtime's o'er … it's time now to go in there and collect her." This wasn't so easy. As soon as we approached Peggy, all three horses set off at the gallop together.

"Right lads, there's only one thing for it now," said Dad.

"What's that, Dad?" asked Barry.

"Well, take a stick each and go and stand where I tell you."

"Oh 'eck, I've a feeling I'm not going to like this, our John," said Barry.

"No, me neither," I replied.

Dad could see the concerned look on our faces. "Don't fret about it, you get over to that end of the field, our Barry, and you stand near that corner o'er yonder, our John."

"Oh aye, and what do we do then?" I asked.

"Well, I'm gonna approach the horses and when they start running towards you, I want you both to start waving them sticks about and drive 'em into that far corner where the field narrows a bit. When they're there we'll all close in on 'em and I'll do th'rest."

"You must be joking, Dad – they'll trample on us!" I protested.

"No they won't, trust me. If you do what I say, I'll have Peggy in no time." After reassuring us, Dad walked towards the horses and as soon as he got near to them they set off at the gallop again. The moment I saw them heading my way, I took fright and bolted for the nearest fence.

Dad was furious and really bawled me out. "Why didn't you do what I told you and stand your ground like our Barry did?"

"Cos I was freightened o' getting trampled on, Dad, them blooming horses were galloping straight at me!"

"Come on lad, like I said … they'll not run thi down. Trust me, I know all about horses."

"Yeah, you know that Dad, and I know it … but do them flaming horses know it?" I said, quivering from head to toe.

"Look, our John, listen to me, I've dealt with horses all mi life … I wouldn't let you do it if I thought you'd get hurt."

"All right Dad, I'll do it, but I'm telling you now – I'm scared!"

"You'll be all reight lad, you'll be all reight. Don't worry about it."

This time I did stand my ground. I was shaking like a leaf, but I held out. As the horses thundered towards me, I could feel the thud of their hoofs pounding the ground. After a few moments I had reached the point of no return … it was too late to run, they were almost upon me! With no alternative left I started to wave the stick in the air and Barry did the same from where he was standing. To my amazement and relief, the horses did exactly as Dad had said they would. They headed for the confined space in the corner where Dad was waiting and he did the rest. Within minutes he had the bridal on Peggy and quietly guided her out of the field.

"Bloomin' 'eck Dad, I've got to put mi hand up, you were right … but it were still scary."

"I can imagine it were, our John. I've got to admit, there was one point there when I saw them galloping towards you that I got a little bit concerned myself!"

"Oh thank you very much Dad – now you tell us!"

"Anyroad lads, you did yourselves proud, thanks a lot. You can take turns now at riding Peggy back to the stable. You've earned it."

As I rode Peggy from the field, she proudly raised her head and whinnied as though saying goodbye to her comrades.

*　*　*

Every Good Friday a festival was held down Pendle Bottoms, a local beauty spot in the vicinity of Pendle Hill, and Dad went there with his horse and trap to sell buggy rides to the excited children. One year, Jimmy and I asked if we could go with him.

"Aye, you can if you want, but don't expect any free rides."

"Whattaya mean, Dad? We're talking about helping you so that you can go for a drink in the pub."

"Oh aye, there's a fat chance o' that, I'm hoping to be busy all day. Anyroad, you can come if you want, but think on what I said."

It was a pleasant sunny day and we arrived there about 10am. Already crowds of people were beginning to emerge on the scene. Dad set up his pitch outside the pub and it wasn't long before a few kids were queuing up for a ride. The trap seated eight children and by midday, Dad had done about seven trips.

"Right lads," he said, "I'm going in the pub now for a drink … I'm dying o' thirst."

"That's all right," I said, "I'll tek over while you're in there." Dad had no qualms about this, as he knew I could handle Peggy, so he handed over the reins to me.

"Aye all reight then, but I'll keep slipping out now and agen to check on things and to collect the brass."

"You'll be all right there, Dad," said Jimmy, "I'll look after the money whilst John teks care of t'horse."

That was it; both Jimmy and I thoroughly enjoyed the rest of the afternoon. After a while, Jimmy took the reins, letting me handle the money. Every now and then Dad kept popping out of the pub to bring us both a glass of lemonade each and to keep check. Each time Jimmy handed him a handful of money.

"Bloomin' 'eck," he said with a big grin on his face, "I should have thought o' this afore, shouldn't I ... what a good do!" Nonetheless, he was still aware that Peggy needed a rest and so ordered us to stop for a forty-five-minute break. After the interval, lots of kids were queuing up around the buggy again raring to go, clamouring for more. Things carried on much as before and we took handfuls of money. At the end of the day everybody had enjoyed it. To make it even better, Dad gave Jimmy and me half a crown each.

* * *

One morning I looked out of the front bedroom window and to my surprise there was a lorry parked straight facing on the other side of the street. As I poked my head out of the window I saw a man delivering bundles of wood from door to door.

"That's funny," I thought, "I'm sure I saw a child's head move behind the steering wheel in the cab." Sure enough, at that moment, a little lad's head bobbed up in the driver's seat and then the horn started to blast.

"Bloomin' 'eck!" I spluttered, "That's dangerous, leaving a little lad in the wagon on his own ... I'd best go and check it." I scampered downstairs but as I got to the lobby I could see through the open door that the wagon was moving slowly.

"Bloody hell, the little lad must have taken t'hand-brake off!" I cried out loudly.

I raced through the lobby, but by the time I reached outside the wagon was careering out of control down the steep street. All I could do was watch in horror, hoping that the young boy would be all right. The wagon careered in a straight line until it hit the flatness of Trafalgar, where it veered left and crashed into the factory wall, taking part of the factory gates with it. Luckily, there were no other kids playing on the street and it didn't collide with any traffic on the main thoroughfare. I was the first to arrive on the spot and, to my delight, the little boy was no worse for wear, though he was certainly shaken up.

Tears rolled down the youngster's cheeks. "Mi daddy'll kill me for brekkin' his wagon!" he sobbed.

"Don't worry about it, cock," I reassured him, knowing that his dad would be only to pleased that he was all right, "I think he'll let you off this time. Mind thi, you'll have to promise not to mess about in any big wagons agen."

I was quite touched by the young lad's reply. "Oh I promise thi ... I won't e'er do it agen, mister ... honest!"

*   *   *

Trafalgar was a very poor area, yet, most people seemed to be happy there. Despite living in deprivation and having to endure appalling conditions, the resilience and fortitude of the people were second to none. The inhabitants rallied together when the situation demanded it and the community spirit was very close knit. During these austere times, one shopkeeper profited more than any other: the pawnbroker. Various pawnbrokers' shops established themselves in different areas of the town. There was a pawnshop on Trafalgar at the corner of Lord Street near to the Alhambra Picture House and one Monday morning, Mum asked me to take some oddments there. One of the neighbours, Mrs Thompson, who happened to be in our house, stopped me before I got to the front door and started to talk to me in her broad Lancashire dialect.

"E-eh I'm glad I've copped thi lad," she whispered, "dusta think tha cud tek a few items to the pop shop for me while tha's at it?"

"Yeah, course I will, Mrs Thompson," I replied politely.

"Reight cock, wilta just come with me o'er to my house to collect 'em?"

"Yeah, righto."

"Here you are, lad," she said cautiously, handing me a gold watch and chain, "now think on tha doesn't mention this to anyone ... mi husband'd kill me if he found out, cos it's a family heirloom. The reason I daren't go myself is I'm freightened of anybody seeing me."

"Yeah I understand Mrs Thompson and I promise you," I said crossing my heart, "I won't tell a soul."

"Good," she muttered, routing through her purse, "there's a tanner here for your trouble. Mind thi, I want you to barter wi' yon fellow in that pop shop and get as much as tha can."

"Leave it with me, Mrs Thompson, I've bin there a few times and I have a good idea on the goin' rate."

"Aye, I know tha has Johnny Cowell, some of the neighbours have telt mi about thi."

"U-um what a good do," I chuckled to myself as I left the house, "a tanner just for going to t'other end o' Trafalgar."

When I reached the shop there were already two elderly chaps and a woman in there, all skint, wanting to pawn various items.

"How much wilta give me for popping this," asked the first man, handing over a brown paper parcel, which contained a pinstripe suit.

"After scrutinising the suit the pawnbroker answered with a straight face, "Well, the most I can let you have is eleven shillings ... I'm being generous, mind!"

"Eleven bob? Tha's being generous all reight," sniggered the bloke, "on the reight bloody side!"

"Well that's my offer. Take it or leave it."

"Aye all reight I'll tek it, but first … what will it cost me to redeem it?"

"That depends, sir. Do you want it hung or wrapped?"

"How dusta mean, hung or wrapped?" asked the fellow, scratching his head.

"Well, if you want it hung on a coat hanger and placed in a wardrobe, so as to keep it nice and trim, the pledge price is one and thre'pence for the first three months and a tanner for any other month after that."

"Oh aye, and what's the other method, then?"

"Well then I'll just put it under the counter wrapped as it is now amongst some other parcels," said the pawnbroker, going on to stress, "where it may become a little crumpled."

"Never mind about it getting crumpled … what will the pledge cost me?"

"Well, that'll be a shilling for the first three months and thre'pence a month thereafter."

"A bob!" he moaned, "that's daylight robbery!"

"That's my charge sir," the pawnbroker replied smugly, "and like I said before … take it or leave it!"

"I'll tek it, I'll tek it … I don't have much option, do I?"

"Thank you sir," the pawnbroker smiled. He took the parcel, placed it under the counter and gave the poor man his money, along with a redemption ticket.

The woman, a thin-faced lady in her late forties and wearing a dark shawl over her shoulders, handed over a small gold ring.

"How much dusta think tha could let me have for this?" she mumbled with bated breath. Once again the pawnbroker scrutinised the gold ring, this time using an eyepiece, which fitted snugly into his right eye.

After what seemed an age he answered with the same smugness as he had done with his previous customer, "U-um, the best I can do for you is five shillings and sixpence."

"Five and six," she cried out, "but that's my wedding ring, I've had it for nearly twenty-five years … it's worth a lot more than that!"

"It may be worth more than that to you dear, for sentimental reasons, but this is a business I'm running, not a charity. Anyway, that's my price … take it …."

"… I know," she cut in sharply, 'tek it or leave it'! Cut the yuk and just give mi the money and mi ticket!"

The next gentleman was treated in much the same manner. He pawned a brand new pair of boots that he'd probably just procured from a mail-order catalogue.

Then came my turn.

"Right," he said after going through the same rigmarole, "fifteen shillings for the watch and chain."

"Fifteen bob … you must be joking!" I echoed, "It's worth a lot more than that and you know it … you've got some for sale in the window for three quid and they're not as good as this one."

"That's my price, take …!"

"All reight," I bluffed, "I'll leave it and tek it to that pop shop on Parliament Street!"

Even though I was only a young lad he took me seriously, because I'd frequented the shop quite a lot of late.

"Go on then, twenty-one shillings, but that's definitely my last offer."

"U-um," I thought, "a guinea, that seems about right. Yeah righto," I agreed, handing him the watch and chain. I then went into the bartering mode for my mam's articles.

I got back to Mrs Thompson's house and she greeted me cheerfully as I handed her the money, along with the ticket.

"Eh tha's a grand lad, Johnny Cowell … y'wanna a cuppa tay?"

"Oh yes please, Mrs Thompson … thank you very much."

"And I suppose tha'd like a piece o' cake to go with it, eh, seeing as tha's a growing lad?" She paused for a moment, looking at me with her wizened eyes, then asked, "Anyroad, wilta do me a favour, young Johnny Cowell?"

"Yeah course I will, Mrs Thompson … what is it?"

"Well, I'd like thi to hold on to this ticket for me for chance mi husband finds it. He'd murder me if he thought I'd popped owt … y'know what I mean, lad."

"But how will you be able to redeem it?" I asked, rather naively.

"Not to worry thysen. If tha comes across here after school on Friday I'll have enough money for thi to get it back for me. And don't fret thysel', I'll give thi another tanner for your trouble."

"Righto, Mrs Thompson, I'll do it for you, but thre'pence'll be enough."

"Tha's on, Johnny Cowell, tha's on … let this be our little secret!" Sure enough, true to her word she redeemed the watch and chain the following Friday. But it wasn't long before she required my services again. In fact, after that I made many more trips to and from the pawnbroker's with that gold watch and chain. A friendship developed between Mrs Thompson and me and our little secret remained safe over the years. I liked this lady and it wasn't just because of the thre'pence … she always came out with a cup of tea and biscuits. I also liked the different funny expressions that she used to come out with. One day she reminisced a little with me about her life.

"E-eh dusta know lad, I might not have much money but I still count mi blessings. When I'm feeling down in the dumps I just thinks o' poor Nellie Higgins and her family who live across the back ... poor woman, she's as poor as a church mouse! Aye, mi heart goes out to her, especially when I sees them lads of hers with their breeches' arse hangin' out ... e-eh, the poor little mites! I've seen her many o' time traipsing down them stone steps to t'petty wi' nowt on her feet ... she can't even afford a decent pair o' clogs. Aye, and there's plenty more in the same boat as her. I might be poor, but my Alf's a good husband, who works every hour that God sends. It were only t'other day that I got onto him and I were agate that he's doing too much but he won't tek any notice o' me. Mind thi, we're still living fro' hand to mouth but it don't matter cos we more than mek up forrit with all the love we show each other."

It was obvious by the way she carried on that she was a God-fearing woman.

"Mind thi, I don't take owt for granted. I might not go to church every Sunday but I allus puts misen in God's hands afore I goes to sleep. I thank Him every night for giving me mi health and strength to look after misen and for having a good husband. Once I've done that I drops off to sleep cos there's nowt nobody can do about it." She paused for a moment before adding, "E-eh lad ... if I didn't have God in mi life I don't know what I'd do."

"Where does Alf work," I asked, becoming intrigued with her tales.

"Oh, he's a tackler in one o' weaving sheds and a bloomin' good un at that. He works his socks off to keep them looms running. He were only agate last night, 'I've gotta keep 'em running, luv … them weavers are on piece work and the more they earn, the more I earn.' He don't mek much but, bless him … he comes homes Friday dinnertime and tips up every penny."

I had to smile as amusing thoughts ran through my head, "That's where I come in all ready willing and able to carry out my little service."

"Aye, and that's when I call upon thee lad, to redeem mi goods fro' pop shop," she said, as if reading my thoughts.

"What time does Alf start work?" I asked. I actually knew the answer to this, because I slept in the front bedroom. I was awakened every morning around seven o'clock by the sound of weavers making their way to the mill. At this time a crescendo of clog sounds always built up as the workers went clattering down the street, going clip clop, clip clop! But the reason for the question was because I wanted to glean even more fascinating tales from this interesting woman.

"He starts at seven o'clock lad, but he doesn't need to leave t'house till five to seven, cos he only has to go to Thompson's mill at bottom o' the street. Mind thi, he gets up at six o'clock when Joe Fletcher, the knocker-up, taps on the bedroom window with his long stick."

"But you don't need a knocker-up, Mrs Thompson," I countered, "there's always a couple o' colliers coming down the street at that time making their way to the pit."

"Aye I'm aware o' that, but Alf allus says that tha can't rely on that. He were only agate t'other day, 'What if they didn't turn out one day … I'd be in a reight stuck if I were late for work. Anyroad, tha can allus rely on old Joe Fletcher … he's the best knocker-up in Burnley.' There were nowt I could say about that, were they lad?"

"No I suppose not," I responded, "but one thing puzzles me, Mrs Thompson … Joe Fletcher must have to knock the miners up at five o'clock or even sooner?"

"Yeah that's reight, lad," she said, nodding her head in agreement.

"Well, what I'd like to know is … who knocks Joe Fletcher up? I've always wondered who gets the knocker-upper up?"

"Go on, y'daft ha'porth!" she responded, with a hearty laugh.

"Righto, Mrs Thompson," I said, after draining the last drop of tea, "I'll be on my way now. Thank you very much for the brew … I'll see you on Monday if you need me."

This woman's sense of humour and special qualities intrigued me. I liked the way she went about tackling life's problems. A particular incident that springs to mind was about the window cleaner.

One day after returning from the pawnbroker's she asked me to sit down. "Here you are lad," she said handing me a brew and one of her scrumptious scones, "get this down thi … tha deserves it."

She was pleasant but something was different … she wasn't her usual bubbly self. I couldn't pinpoint why so I broached her about it.

"Is something wrong Mrs Thompson … you look a little down in the dumps?"

"By gum John lad … does it show that much?"

"Not really … it's just that you don't seem quite as chirpy as you usually do."

"Bloomin' 'eck lad … tha misses nowt. To tell truth there is some't bothering me but I don't want to burden thi with mi troubles."

"Oh that's all right," I replied curiously, "I don't mind … honest!"

"Aye all reight lad I'll tell thi. What it is … it's that bloomin' window cleaner o' mine."

"What's happened to him?"

"Oh nowt's happened to him … it's what he's bin up to what's bothering me."

"Why … what's he done?"

"Well," she said shrugging her shoulders and gritting her teeth a little, "it's not so much what he's done, it's more about what he's not bin doin' … I'm sure he's bin robbin' me for ages. Ya see … I go down town every Thursday afternoon to do the buying in and that's when he comes to clean the windows."

"Oh aye … and don't you think he's been cleaning yours then?"

"Tha's on the reight track …. he's been cleanin' mi downstairs' windows but I'm bloomin' sure he doesn't allus do the ones upstairs." Her face tensed a little betraying a sign of anger. "I think the lazy swine's been too idle to climb the ladder!"

"It's not like you to let things slide," I enthused. "Have you tackled him about it?"

"Not yet," she replied pouting her lips, "but I'm gonna do when he comes to collect his brass. As a matter of fact I'm expecting him anytime now."

She'd hardly finished speaking when there was a knock on the door followed by the sound of footsteps in the lobby. A moment later the window cleaner entered the living room to collect his money. Mrs Thompson didn't mess about and got straight to the point.

"I'm only giving thi half pay this week cos tha's never cleaned mi upstairs windows," she grimaced pointing her finger at him.

"Now that'll do Mrs Thompson!" he rapped. "Are you calling me a thief?"

"I'm not calling thi a thief but I'm telling thi straight ... tha's ne'er cleaned 'em!"

"And I'm telling thi straight I have ... and I want my brass."

"All reight then ... if you cleaned 'em, how come there's still some marks on the glass that were there afore I went down town?"

"Now come off it," he scoffed. "With all the smoke and grime from the factory chimneys around here ... them marks could have been made since I left."

Mrs Thompson argued her point a while longer but to no avail ... he wouldn't be swayed and insisted that she pay up. Reluctantly she handed over the full amount ... however, she wasn't happy about it. After he left the house she didn't dwell on it too much, but muttered something about catching him out.

"Take heed John lad ... that fella's a rogue and one o' these days he'll get his comeuppance."

True to her word she did catch him out and fortunately I was there to witness the event ... it was a joy to behold to see her in action.

It was about a month later when she put her little plan into play.

Once again I was in her house enjoying all the fringe benefits after returning from my trip to the pawnshop. "D'you remember me tackling the window cleaner t'other week about mi upstairs windows?" she asked with a cheeky grin on her face.

"I do that Mrs Thompson. How could I forget, you certainly didn't mince words."

"Ah well, what it is ... I'm gonna tackle him agen today about the same thing. The reason I'm telling thi is cos I want you as a witness. He'll be here any minute now but when he comes I don't want thi to say a word. Just keep your lug'oles open and say nowt, and happen tha'll learn somet. He bloomin' well thinks he's the best flamin' window cleaner in the 'Northern Union' but I'm gonna knock him down a peg or two."

I was half way through my brew when there was a knock on the front door.

"Hey up," she said, "here he is … action stations, don't forget what I just tell'd thi."

"Don't worry, I'm gonna enjoy this," I thought as the window cleaner's footsteps got closer.

He entered the living room in his usual glib manner.

"Good afternoon Mrs Thompson," he quipped, "a nice day isn't it?"

"Aye it is," she replied followed by, "I suppose tha's come for tha brass?"

"Of course I've come for mi money," he said cockily," I've cleaned your windows so now I want paying."

"Oh tha's cleaned mi windows have you? Well I'm telling thi straight you robbin' bugger … tha's ne'er cleaned the ones upstairs!"

"Now that'll do, don't start that again … we've gone o'er this ground afore!"

"Aye we have and were goin o'er it agen cos I'm telling thi to your face … tha's ne'er cleaned 'em!"

"And I'm telling thi I have!" he rapped. "Now give me mi money!"

"So you want your brass d'you?" she said slow and deliberately with a wry smile on her face."

"Of course I want mi bloody brass!" he replied with a puzzled look. "What the flaming 'eck d'you think I'm here for?"

"All reight then," she said, the wry smile changing to a snigger, "If tha wants it then put your flamin' ladder up agen mi front bedroom window sill."

"What are you talking about?" he queried uneasily.

"I'll tell thi what I'm talkin' about," she grimaced. "On Thursday afternoon afore I went down town I put your money inside an envelope with your name on'it and left it on the window sill upstairs." She pondered for a moment before saying coolly, "And d'you know something ... it's still sat there like cheese at for'pence. Now what d'you think about that you robbin' swine!"

Realising he had been caught out he just stood there aghast. He didn't say anything at first and then started to splutter.

"Oh that's right, I remember now ... I was going to ..."

"Never mind," she rapped cutting him short, "lying through your teeth trying to worm out of it won't help thi now, tha's not as clever as tha thinks, in fact, tha's neither use nor ornament ... tha's bin rumbled." Her voice then became more serious. "Tha's bin pullin' the wool o'er my eyes for long enough ... aye and probably lots of other poor unsuspecting folk. Then tha's got the audacity to walk in here as bold as brass demanding pennies that we've had to work our fingers to the bone for. Now then, what have you got to say for thesen?'

He took a step back, then stood there and said nothing.

"Right ... no wonder thas got nowt to say. Now I'm gonna tell thi a thing or two. First of all ... tha can clean all my windows for nowt for the next two months. If tha doesn't I'll tell all your customers what tha's been up to, and whilst I am at it I'm in two minds to report thi to't cop shop."

Having no choice he reluctantly went about his assignment under the watchful eye of Mrs Thompson. She didn't sack him, in fact he was to remain her window cleaner for many years to come, but never again got up to his old tricks. On numerous occasions after that, Mrs Thompson and I would chuckle about it over a brew.

* * *

Mrs Thompson wasn't my only customer; lots of other neighbours, who were in a similar predicament to her, got in touch with me and were only too willing to use my services. The pawnbroker got used to my haggling ways and so I always got the going rate for my customers.

Mr Jenkins, a retired weaver who lived on his own in dire circumstances, stopped me one day.

"Young Johnny Cowell, wilta tek these to pop shop for me to see if tha can get owt forr'em?" he asked, handing me a pair of well-worn shoes that he'd highly polished.

"Well, I'll see what I can do for you, Mr Jenkins, but I can't promise anything."

The pawnbroker must have been in a good mood that day because he actually offered two shillings. Mr Jenkins was delighted – it was enough to get him a bite to eat.

"Eh, thank you very much, cock ... here's tuppence for your trouble!"

"No, it doesn't matter, Mr Jenkins ... I were goin' there anyroad for somebody else." It was a white lie, but what else could I have done? I didn't have the heart to take that two pence off him. "No," I thought, as I left his house, "the poor bloke looks like he hasn't got two ha'pennies to rub together." As it turned out, I got an even better deal for him later on.

"Johnny Cowell, canya redeem mi shoes for me?" he asked, about a week later.

"Yeah, course I can Mr Jenkins," I said, taking the redemption ticket from his hand.

I handed over the ticket to the pawnbroker and he disappeared into the back of the shop. After what seemed an age, he came back to the counter, scratching his head.

"I can't seem to find them," he said, "the ticket must have fallen off the box and I think it's got mixed up with a load of others that have never been redeemed."

"Oh 'eck!" I answered, acting naively, "what can we do about it, then?"

"Well, can you nip round the counter and come into the back of the shop to see if you can spot them?" It was the first time I'd ever been invited to go through into this mysterious room, and what a surprise I got ... it was like Aladdin's cave. At the back of the shop, there were lots of tea chests filled with children's toys, including dolls of all shapes and sizes. One doll was lying about on the floor like a discarded marionette. There was wooden shelving all around the room from floor to ceiling and each shelf was cram-packed full with little parcels. Three large sideboards with large drawers took up most of the floor space. In one corner there was a tall stack of boxes full of shoes.

"They must be amongst that lot," muttered the pawnbroker, "there's nowhere else they can be."

"None of these have any tickets on 'em," I pointed out, "how come?"

"Ah well, they've all gone past their redemption date ... so they'll be going on sale when I've time to sort 'em out."

"That'll do me," I chuckled inwardly, using all my willpower to suppress a giggle. I knew Mr Jenkins took size nines and I didn't think for one minute that he'd object to getting back a better pair of shoes than the ones he'd pawned. After routing through the boxes for a short time, I came across a pair that had hardly been worn. "Great," I thought, "he'll be dead chuffed wi' these."

But that was the easy part. Convincing the pawnbroker that these were Mr Jenkins's shoes was slightly more difficult.

"No, it couldn't have been these, they're nearly brand new," he said, "I'd have allowed more than two bob for them."

"Maybe not but they were very similar to these," I insisted.

"Aye, as maybe but you still can't have them. I'll tell you what, go in the back room again and have another look."

"Yeah, reighto," I agreed, making my way through to the stockpile, "but we'll have to sort something out, cos Mr Jenkins needs 'em for tonight." Unbeknown to the pawnbroker, I'd already spotted Mr Jenkins's shoes, but I was all geared up to get him this quality pair. "Besides," I said to myself, "it'll mek a nice change from the bloomin' pawnbroker profiteering off somebody's back." After about ten minutes I reminded the shopkeeper again that Mr Jenkins needed the shoes immediately.

Reluctantly, after a few grunts and groans, he agreed to the transaction. "Aye, all right, I don't like it but I don't seem to have much option."

"Superb," I gloated as I ran along Trafalgar, "Mr Jenkins'll be o'er the moon with these!"

"By gum lad, tha's done well," he said, highly delighted, "I've never had a pair o' shoes of this quality afore."

The funny part about it was that he pawned them a few times after that and got an average of half a crown each time!"

*   *   *

The weeks passed quickly and before I knew it, it was time to go back to school. The ordeal that some kids had been dreading for ages finally arrived: the eleven-plus examination! Miss M. Gordon was kept very busy in the classroom, preparing us all for this important event. Only the chosen few took the exam seriously – most of the children took it for granted that they would be going to St Mary's Senior School the next term, just as their older peers had done before them. On the morning of the test I went into the examination room feeling quite relaxed, because I wasn't bothered one way or the other whether I passed or not.

"There's one thing for sure," I told myself. "I certainly don't want to go to the Grammar School."

We all sat down at our appointed desks, where the papers had already been carefully laid face-down. The headmistress, Miss Gordon, gave out all the routine instructions on what to do during the test. Miss M. Gordon, along with two nuns, overlooked the proceedings, making sure everyone adhered to the rules.

"Right everybody," Miss Gordon announced. "The morning test that you have to undertake is your arithmetic paper. If you need anything at all during the test, whether it is paper or anything else, then you must hold your hand up and someone will attend to your needs. The same applies if you want to go to the toilet ... understand?"

"Yes Miss Gordon," echoed the entire class.

"Right then," she advised in an uncharacteristically soothing voice, "you can turn your papers over now and I'll give you five minutes to scrutinise them before you get down to writing."

On reading the paper I was a little surprised to find the questions quite easy and I'd soon finished, with plenty of time to check my answers. I found the afternoon paper much more difficult – then again, English never was my favourite subject.

"Oh well," I thought, "I'll just have to make a stab at some o' the questions and guess what the answers are!"

Then came the day of reckoning ... the results!"

"Right, children," said Miss Gordon, "first of all, I'm going to read out all the names of those who have passed for Grammar School." No one was surprised to hear certain names called out, but then came the roll call for those who'd passed for Towneley Technical High School. This time a few eyebrows were raised ... including mine.

"I'm pleased to say that three boys have passed for Towneley," she announced. "Alan Carter, Alan Green and," she faltered for a second before announcing, "John Cowell!"

"Whoo-oh," went up a mocking chorus around the class, "who's a clever boy, then?"

"That'll do!" rapped Miss M. Gordon, restoring a semblance of order.

"I can't blame 'em for taking the mickey," I mumbled to myself, "I'd have done the same if Ronnie or Bobby had passed."

"Bloomin' 'eck, our John, haven't you done well," said our Mary, "mi mam won't half be pleased."

"Aye I suppose so, our kid, but I'm not sure I am ... I want to go to St Mary's with all mi mates."

When I got home, Mum knew about it because Mary had already told her.

"Well, I'm right proud of you, our John, we've finally got a scholar in the family."

"Thanks Mam, but all the same, if you don't mind, I'd rather go to St Mary's."

"That's up to you, lad, it's your life. I've got to say, though, that you'll have far more opportunities to improve your education if you go to Towneley."

"I'm not bothered about that Mam, cos I want to go working down the pit when I leave school."

"Oh don't say that," interrupted my older sister Maureen, all excited for me, "you'll never get this opportunity again, our John ... you must go to Towneley, it's got a really good reputation."

I tried telling her how I felt, but Maureen wouldn't listen ... she was really enthusiastic about Towneley and anxious for my future prospects.

"But our Maureen," I protested, "I want to ...."

"I know what you're going to say, our John. You want to be with your mates, but believe me our kid, they won't stay with you all your life. Please go to Towneley, our John, because if you don't like it you can always pack it in later on and go to St Mary's. I'll tell you what ... you've got six weeks off school now, so promise me you'll think about it."

"Aye, all right, our Maureen I promise." I knew she was sincere, only wanting what she thought was right for me. Maureen had always cared for me, along with my other brothers and sisters, and had always had our best interests at heart. I wasn't sure what to do, but I knew she was making sense ... so I eventually succumbed to her wishes.

7

TOWNELEY

I'll always remember the first morning I set off for Towneley School dressed in the school uniform. Our Maureen was full of pride as I donned my short grey pants, black shoes, school cap and my maroon blazer with a badge depicting Towneley Park Gates.

"Go on, our John," enthused Maureen, "you can do it, I know you can."

"U-umph, I don't know so much, our Maureen," I said, nervously. "I wish I were going to St Mary's with all mi mates."

"Oh, I know how you feel, our kid, but you've a lot better chance of doing well at Towneley than St Mary's."

"Aye, I suppose you're reight ... I only wish I had as much confidence as you do, our kid."

I walked down Albion Street full of foreboding ... I didn't fancy the prospect of facing the unknown. When I reached Maggie Astin's house, I glanced back over my shoulder to see Maureen eagerly waving me off.

"You'll be all right, our John," she shouted cheerfully, trying to reassure me, "you can do it … I've got loads o' faith in you."

When I reached the school, my worst fears were confirmed … I felt totally out of place. The school had a much stricter regime than St Thomas's and everything about it seemed regimental. Even the school bell was triggered off by an electrical system, unlike the traditional hand ringing at St Thomas's. As it rang, we all lined up in single files and then systematically marched into a large assembly hall. All the schoolmasters were sat on a stage behind a long wooden table with the headmaster, Mr Lancaster, sat in the middle of the group. After formalities were dispensed with, Mr Lancaster gave a long speech, which left no doubt in everyone's mind that he wouldn't tolerate any nonsense.

It wasn't the regimental aspect that bothered me so much as the fact that I had no friends. Also, everywhere I went the other pupils seemed to tower above me; I felt quite small and intimidated. After the initial ceremony, we were allocated our form teacher and classroom. All first-year students were graded A B or C, according to their exam results … I was graded B, and I felt happier about this.

"U-um, at least I don't have to compete with the brainy ones," I said to myself.

Another thing that made me unhappy was that the word soon spread amongst my peers that my dad was a ragman and that he'd been to prison.

"Oh no," I thought, "I'm gonna have to go through all the same rigmarole that I had to at St Thomas's." Some of the lads were all right, but others were bullyboys, especially with me being so little. During my years at Towneley I hardly grew. I was the smallest in the class and I still wore short pants. Because of my size, I got nicknamed 'Bimbo', after a popular song in the charts at the time. Just like at junior school I got into many fights and the worst thing was that I lost most of them. Still, I gave a good account of myself, so the taunting began to dwindle.

I gradually made a new friend called Peter Neary, who lived in the Able Street area on the other side of town to Trafalgar. We became bosom buddies and this helped me to settle down a little. But most of the time I still longed to be with all my other friends at St Mary's.

One teacher I liked was the art teacher, Mr Barton. But the irony of it was that I missed a lot of his classes, because I had to attend a clinic every Thursday afternoon for speech training. I'd attended the clinic during my last two years at St Thomas's Junior School because I couldn't pronounce my R's, and although the lady in charge of my training was very nice, with infinite patience, it was slow progress. This was a constant worry to Mum, because one kid or another was always ridiculing me, especially so because my best friend was called Ronnie, which I pronounced 'Wonnie'. This had got me into many scrapes at St Thomas's School and the problem seemed to have followed me to Towneley. One incident that I won't forget in a hurry concerned a big lad called Steven, who had the same affliction as me. It caused a ruction one day as we were getting dressed in the pavilion after a game of football.

"That were a good game, I weally enjoyed it ... did you?" Steven asked me.

"Yeah I did," I replied, "it were weally good."

Without any warning, he took a swing at me and called me a 'fly little git'! I immediately reacted, but got the worst of it because he wasn't just a good footballer ... he was a good fighter too. Luckily for me, one of the teachers stopped the fight.

"What's going on here?" bawled the sports master as he towered over us, "I won't allow fighting in here. Now tell me … what started it?"

"Well sir," stammered Steven, "he were in the wong … he was taking the mickey cos I can't pronounce my R's wight."

A little smile crept to the corner of the teacher's mouth. He was aware of my affliction and obviously found the situation rather funny.

"Oh … u-um, I see," he muttered, not really knowing what to say, "I think, Steven, there is something you should know."

After being told about my speech impairment, Steven was a little embarrassed at first, but then saw the funny side and started to laugh. He held out his hand and apologised. I was only too glad to accept his apology … I didn't fancy being on the wrong side of this strapping lad! We both ended up laughing and were on friendly terms thereafter.

Within a year, the dedicated training of the speech therapist had its desired effect and I never had trouble pronouncing my R's again.

*　　*　　*

We had lots of homework to do at Towneley, but because Dad didn't help me with this aspect of my school life I became very unsettled. Indeed, rather than encourage me to study, he did the opposite. Night after night he made his disapproval quite clear as I tried to do my homework on the end of the sideboard.

"What are you doing, cluttering up the sideboard with all them books, our John," he rapped, "what have I told thi about bringing schoolwork into t'home? You should do that at school afore you come home."

"But Dad," I protested, "I can't ... we're not allowed. Anyroad, all mi classmates get homework that they've got to do at home."

"I'm not bothered about anybody else, I don't want thi to bring any into this house."

"Bloomin' 'eck Dad, I'm struggling with this French as it is ... I'll get in bother if I don't hand it in tomorrow."

"French," he yelled, "what d'you need to learn all them foreign languages for anyroad, you're never gonna use 'em?"

I constantly tried to get my point across but to no avail. Things didn't change much, and this affected my studies; consequently, I lost interest and this became apparent in my results.

The French teacher was called Mr Fox and he didn't like me very much. But that was understandable – my results were appalling ... in the Christmas exams I got a paltry three per cent. He was also the geography teacher and I didn't fare any better in this topic either. I think Dad's attitude rubbed off onto me: the way I saw it, I would never leave Burnley, so what was the point of learning a foreign language or the whereabouts of this or that particular country. Mr Fox's displeasure was self-evident as he severely scolded me.

As the years passed, my results didn't improve. It wasn't only these two topics that I did badly at either; my favourite subject suffered too: mathematics. I couldn't understand why other lads in the class, whom I knew were no better than me at this subject, got much higher marks than I did for their homework. I didn't realise that their parents must have been encouraging them, and maybe helping them with their studies. The maths teacher also happened to be the deputy headmaster, Mr Redhead, and he really took me to task because of my poor marks. He even ridiculed me in front of the class, much to the pleasure of my classmates.

However, one thing that I did like about Towneley was that it had a great big gymnasium, geared up with wall bars, vaulting horses, balance beams, climbing ropes and other equipment.

The teacher in charge of physical training was called Mr Saul. He wasn't very tall and had a slim physique. But despite his appearance, he was in peak condition. He could easily walk the length of the gymnasium on his hands and he excelled on every piece of apparatus in the large hall. He quite impressed me with his vigour and enthusiasm in everything he did.

"He's only small," I thought, "but it doesn't seem to bother him ... he really looks like he can handle himself."

Mr Saul was a pleasant, easy-going man, but asserted his authority and instilled discipline into the class when necessary. This became evident one day when a very big lad refused to do as he was told and started getting stroppy. However, it didn't last long; Mr Saul sorted him out in no time at all and put him in his place.

I liked this man and from then on took a definite interest in gymnastics.

*　*　*

Despite being singled out by many kids at Towneley I still loved going out on the rag-cart with Dad, and especially looking after Peggy, our horse. So during the school holidays I spent most of my leisure time with Dad.

"Come along with me, our John," he'd say, "and I'll teach thi the tricks o' trade … you're better off learning the ropes from an early age. Aye, you never know, you'll be able to tek o'er from me when I'm past it."

However, Dad had an ulterior motive. Every morning he'd send me off to the stable to feed Peggy and muck out the stable. After dressing her in all her working regalia, I'd harness her to the cart and then proudly drive her to our house. I loved taking the reins and driving Peggy through the many cobbled streets.

This suited Dad, as it gave him ample time to have a brew and a bite to eat before setting off for work. But nevertheless, he always showed his approval.

"Eh thanks cock, you're a grand lad and doing a great job." However, Mum wasn't so approving.

"Never mind he's doing a great job!" she'd snap at him. "You mean he's giving you another hour in bed!"

"But Mam!" I always protested, "I like going with Dad on the cart and I love looking after Peggy … honest!" It was true; I was never prouder than when I was driving the cart through the streets or riding Peggy bareback when taking her to the blacksmith's to be re-shod. I felt like one of my favourite movie characters – Hoppalong Cassidy, Johnny MacBrown or Roy Rogers – as Peggy trotted along.

Dad mainly dealt in scrap iron, but he sometimes went out 'ragging' and this could be quite lucrative too.

As he guided Peggy through the many backstreets he shouted in a drawled-out voice, "Rag-bone … rag-bone, any old rags for donkey stones!"

Often people come to the backyard gate and hand over a bundle of rags and other items. It was my job to hand out a white stone or yellow stone, whichever they preferred.

Others simply left the bundle on the backyard wall and I would exchange these for a donkey stone. I always left them a white stone unless they'd specifically left a note requesting a yellow one. Most women preferred white ones and would donkey stone the whole of their front step every day. The yellow stone was sometimes used to touch up the front corner of the step. The lady of the house was never prouder than when the doorstep gleamed bright and whiter than anyone else's. Woe betide her husband, or anyone for that matter, who happened to stand on it after it had just been done.

One sunny day a funny incident happened as we were working the backstreets of Trafalgar. I felt quite chuffed, as Dad let me steer Peggy through the many cobbled streets. I always loved taking charge of the horse and cart, but even more so in my own territory.

"Stop at the next backstreet in between the Ribble Garage and Gresham Place, our John," said Dad, "we might as well start here."

"Whoa Peggy … that's a good girl!" I said, exaggerating my voice so as to draw attention to myself from two passing lads.

"Reight, our John," mumbled Dad as he backed Peggy up the backstreet, "get the bag o' donkey stones and let's get cracking! "Rag-bone … rag-bone …!"

He usually backed the cart about halfway up the backstreet, but on this occasion he couldn't, as some workmen had been digging there.

"Watch out, Dad," I warned him as I walked in front, "there's a great big hole in the backstreet and there's a load of stone cobbles all over the place."

"Aye I know, I can see 'em, I'm not blind yet tha knows. Anyroad, don't hang about, our John, pick up them bundles o' rags and leave 'em a donkey stone." There were three bundles of rags, some old dresses and two donkey jackets. By the time we got back to the cart I'd gathered a sack full of rags.

"Get another sack from the back o' the cart our John," said Dad, "and sort out the woollens from t'other rags."

"Why's that, Dad?"

"Why? Because I get paid a lot more for woollens than I do for cotton rags … that's why!" he rapped, impatiently.

"All reight, Dad, I only asked. I'll know in't future."

"That'll do – I want none of your lip!"

We carried on working the backstreets of Patten Street, Albion Street, Rowley Street and Whitaker Street. We didn't stop for a brew at our house because Mum didn't approve; she didn't like the stigma attached to the rag-cart. By the time we reached Sandygate there was a mountainous heap of rags on the cart.

"U-um, we've done well, our John," grinned Dad, feeling pleased with himself. "We might as well make tracks for Reader's Rag-shop down Sandygate."

We were just turning right at Sandygate Junction by the side of Sandygate Youth Club when we heard some blokes shouting frantically from the other side of the road.

"What the bloody hell aya playin' at?" bellowed one, in an angry voice. "Tha's gone and nicked our jackets!"

As it happened they were council workers, who were replacing damaged drains on Gresham Place backstreet.

"Oh 'eck," I thought, "them donkey jackets musta been theirs!"

"Flamin' Emma, man!" exclaimed one of the men. "We'd only been away two minutes having a brew … what the bloody hell d'you think you're playin' at?"

Luckily, Dad sorted it out amicably. After explaining what had happened, we all had a good laugh about it. Mind you, Dad wasn't too happy about having to unload half the cart to find the right sack.

"Never mind, eh," he laughed afterwards, "it's still bin a good day, hasn't it our John?"

"Yeah it has Dad," I agreed, "and it'll be a good tale to tell t'others when we get home."

There were many such funny incidents that came about whilst I was working with Dad, and that's why I liked it. I also enjoyed going with him to the many weaving sheds where he made deals with the different managers to collect scrap iron.

But one aspect that I didn't like happened every time he'd weighed in some scrap iron. Just around the corner from Reader's Scrapyard was Dad's favourite pub – the Salford Hotel. Ironically, Peggy went into automatic pilot after the cart left the scrapyard: without being prompted, she'd pull the cart the short distance and always stop outside the pub.

"Oh no, Dad," I moaned, "you're not going in there again, are you? You'll be ages."

"Eh cock, don't knock it!" he replied critically. "This is where I mek a few deals ... lots o' them factory owners go in here and I've got to keep 'em buttered up. Like I keep telling you, our John ... you've got to speculate to accumulate."

"Speculate to accumulate, Dad?" I replied. "That's your favourite saying, but I can't see how it works in this pub."

"Whaddaya talkin' about, lad ... how d'you mean?"

"Well, every time I peep in through the door you seem to be throwing your money away buying drinks all around the pub for a load of boozers."

"See, there you go again, you don't know what you're talkin' about ... I have a lot of good connections in there."

"All right, maybe some of 'em are mill owners who you make deals with, but most of 'em are just drunkards."

"Aye that may be so, but I've got to appear generous to keep up appearances. D'you know what I mean?"

"Yeah, all reight Dad, but if you can spend so freely on them, how come it always causes ructions at home when mi mam asks you for some housekeeping money?"

"All reight our John, that'll do!" he rapped. "You're geddin a bit near the bone now. I don't want any cheek off thi!"

"U-um, all right, Dad … but promise you won't be so long this time."

"Yeah, reight lad … I promise, I promise."

Promise or not, Dad was full of false assurances. He meant what he said when he said it … but I knew that once inside the pub he would take some shifting.

Consequently, I prepared myself for a long wait. I hated it, but I had nobody to blame but myself … I always went with Dad of my own choosing. On the other hand, Peggy loved the respite she got from these hold-ups. During these situations I stroked her forehead and talked to her for hours on end.

"Yeah, Peggy, you enjoy it when we get here, don't you? Aye," I'd laugh, "you know where to come all right when we leave Reader's Scrapyard."

Peggy would whinny in response, nodding her head as if she understood every word I was saying. I became very fond of her and her of me – especially with me feeding and looking after her. Even so, she loved Dad best, and made that quite clear by whinnying happily the moment he came out of the pub.

I could always tell whether Dad had made a good deal by the look on his face. This particular day he came out of the pub sporting a broad smile.

"What did I tell thi lad, I've just med a cracking deal with one o' them 'boozers', as you put it. It'll tek me two days next week to pick up all the scrap iron from his mill. And," he added, chuckling to himself, "I got it for a song. Like I said afore, our John, it's not what you know in business, it's who you know ... it's what you call wheels within wheels. So think on – don't knock it in future."

"Yeah, reighto Dad," I replied, having to agree with him on this occasion. "I put mi hand up."

Nevertheless, most days he'd come staggering out of the pub, hardly able to stand up.

"Oh no," I'd say to myself, "it looks like I'm gonna have to tek him home again afore I tek Peggy back to the stable." I'd help him onto the cart and then take him as far as Albion Street. I always dropped him outside the Trafalgar pub and pointed him in the right direction. This gave him a little time to sober up as he tottered up Albion Street. Once he'd reached Maggie Astin's house, I'd jump on the cart and head for the stable. Mind you, I'm sure that Peggy could have got back there on her own – she certainly knew the way. She used to make me laugh as she trotted along Healeywood Road and turned into Marlborough Street. The stable was situated at the end of Rumley Road, which ran parallel on the topside to Marlborough Street. To reach Rumley Road, Peggy had to first negotiate a short, steep street, which ran from Marlborough Street to Rumley Road. When she got within fifty yards of the short street, Peggy would pick up speed to give herself a good run up the steep incline. Once she had reached the level on Rumley Road she would then settle back into a gentle walk.

*　　*　　*

As a lad, I really enjoyed swimming. Dad had taken me to the Central Swimming Baths at a very early age and I'd taken to the water from the word go. Mary was also a great swimmer and swam for the town team, but she couldn't beat me. If she could have, I'd never have lived it down!

One particular incident sticks out in my mind. It was a scorcher of a day, with brilliant sunshine. Loads of little kids were on the front street, poking at the gas-tar in-between the cobbles. I was pondering on how I used to do exactly the same thing when I was a little lad.

"U-um," I smiled, "many's the time I've had a good hiding for doing that."

Just then, Jack Lofthouse interrupted my thoughts, shouting from the bottom of the street, "All reight Johnny, it's a cracking day to go for a swim ... what d'you think?"

"You're not kidding, Jack," I replied enthusiastically, "I'd love to go swimming, but I ain't got any trunks."

"What do we need trunks for? How about goin' swimming in that water tank on the top o' Trafalgar Mill?"

"U-um I don't know, Jack, we'd be in real bother if we got caught up there."

"Oh come on ... don't be so bloomin' soft. Anyroad, when has that ever stopped us from doing owt afore?"

I never could resist Jack's persuasive ways and anyway, the thought of the cool water tempted me. "Aye all reight then," I shouted down the street, "I'm gam if you are."

So off we went. The first part, getting into the loft space of the mill, was easy – we'd done it many times before, just for the fun of it. The second part was much more difficult and dangerous. It meant having to scramble up onto the roof, and then climb a steel ladder, which was fixed to the walls of the tall, square tower. But on reaching the top, our reward was great. The tank was full and the water just seemed to be beckoning us to jump in. Both of us stripped down to our pants and dived in. We both thoroughly enjoyed ourselves floating about on our backs, soaking up the afternoon sun. By now we had become complacent, all fear of being discovered forgotten … we actually got cocky, and that was our undoing. We both climbed up onto the Trafalgar side of the water tank and started to show off by shouting down at passing lads.

"Hey down there! Why don't you come up here for a swim, it's bloomin' great!" It didn't take long for a crowd of eager lads to gather below and start shouting excitedly back up at us.

As it happened, a lady was just coming out of the Co-op and she was horrified to see our legs dangling over the sides of the tall tower. Without hesitation, she crossed over Trafalgar, went inside the police telephone box at the side of the footbridge, and called for the fire brigade.

Within minutes the brigade arrived and the telescopic ladder was soon in action, reaching up towards us. Jack attempted to climb back down the steel ladder, but a fireman bellowed up to him through a loudspeaker, warning him not to.

By now the crowd had swollen, including lots of adults. All the attention we were receiving from the cheering kids made us feel good … even important. However, our pleasure was short-lived … we were both taken to the Police Station, where we got severely reprimanded. That wasn't the end of the matter, either … we both got a good hiding when we got back home. It didn't put us off though – Jack and I enjoyed many more similar escapades together.

* * *

Like me, most of the local kids enjoyed swimming. Many went to the Gannow, North Street or Padiham Baths, where they had diving boards, although in the summer months they frequented the Nelson Open Air Swimming Pool. Other favourite places were Hacking Boat Ferry, near Whalley and the 'Sheepdip' near to Hapton Valley Colliery. This was a deep basin in the riverbed overlooked by a high rock. Kids dived off the high platform into the murky depths, missing underwater rocks by inches. Our Mary was a right daredevil, regularly doing the dangerous stunt to show off to her mates. But this came to an abrupt halt one day when a lad was badly hurt, needing about thirty stitches to a deep gash in his forehead.

Despite warnings, many kids would go for a dip in the canal, known locally as the 'Cut' and come out of the over-polluted water stinking of factory waste or decomposing dead dogs.

Water always had a strange attraction, drawing kids to it whether for swimming or fishing. Around Burnley, official outdoor swimming places were non-existent. This was the main reason why kids chose to swim in the Cut, the Sheep-dip, the mill towers and other murky places. Lowerhouse Lodge was a particularly notorious place. It was a dangerous spot where many a child had drowned, but this didn't deter other kids. They wanted to swim and swim they would, despite the consequences.

Another murky site for a dip was Clifton Lodge – in fact, it was downright filthy. A rubbish tip surrounded the lodge, where lots of kids would forage for fag packets and comics. They didn't often swim in this dirty water, but many ventured onto it using make-do rafts or anything else floatable.

One day, our Jimmy and his mate Victor Thompson made a raft from an old backyard gate, which they'd reinforced with old wooden joists from a demolition site. As they set off for the lodge carrying the raft they saw me on Trafalgar and invited me along.

"D'you want to come with us, our kid?" asked Jimmy. "We're gonna sail this on Clifton Lodge." Unwittingly I went along, trusting them both implicitly.

As it happened, Mum had just bought me a new pair of pants. "Now think on, our John," she'd warned me, "make sure you change your pants before you go playing out." Of course, once Jimmy and Victor asked me to join them, it never entered my mind to get changed.

On reaching the lodge, we launched the makeshift raft and then attempted to board it. Victor was the first to embark and I followed. It became evident that it wouldn't take any more weight, as it floated precariously on top of the water. We'd attached a long rope to the raft and Jimmy's task was to pull us into the shore in case of any trouble. To cast off, Victor shoved against the bank with a pole, creating a pushing motion and moving the raft outwards into the lodge. We thoroughly enjoyed ourselves out in the middle, but eventually came the time to be pulled back to the shore.

"All reight, Jimmy," bellowed Victor, "we've had enough … pull us back in!"

"Reighto, Vic, here goes." Without further ado, he picked up the rope and started pulling.

"Whoa, hang on a bit Jimmy … the ropes got tangled under one o' the joists!" shouted Victor.

Jimmy didn't hear, or at least he didn't seem to … he just kept on pulling. The raft started to tilt a little and both of us tried shifting our weight to rectify it. This added to the problem, causing the raft to tilt to the other side. Victor lost his balance and plunged into the filthy water and I went tumbling in after him. There wasn't any danger of drowning – we were both good swimmers – but that wasn't the problem.

"Oh no," I moaned on reaching the bank, "mi mam'll go mad when I get home! I've ruined mi best pants!" Victor, concerned that he too would be in bother, conjured up a story.

"Listen John, if we go home like this we're forrit. We'll both get a good hiding. But if we say that you fell in and I dived in to rescue you, we might get away with it."

"I can't see that, Vic ... mi mam's not daft and she knows I'm a good swimmer."

"Yeah I know, but if I say that I thought you'd hurt yourself and you were struggling ... she might believe that."

"Aye, all right," I agreed, "I suppose owt's worth trying."

I didn't have a lot of confidence in our scam, but to my surprise, it worked. Both parents fell for it ... in fact, Victor was treated like a hero. His dad even thought of going to the *Burnley Express* for a write-up and some kind of commendation. It's just as well that the truth never came to light; we'd have both got a commendation all right – right around the earhole!

* * *

One day I did something very stupid that almost cost me my life, and all because of a silly dare. Many a lad had done it before me and, being cocksure that I could easily do it, I accepted the challenge ... to swim through the Gannow Tunnel.

"It's only about a quarter of a mile," I thought, "I should be able to swim that far. Yeah why not ... I can easily swim thirty-six lengths of the Gannow Baths, so I should be able to make it through the tunnel without any trouble."

In order to carry out the swim, two lads needed to stand on guard, one at each end of the tunnel to ward off any canal barges. I dived into the murky water and set off into the darkness of the grimy tunnel full of confidence. It was a scorcher of a day, but what I hadn't taken into account was the temperature of the water inside the tunnel … it was absolutely freezing. After about two hundred yards I was chilled to the bone and began to realise my foolishness … the little speck of light ahead was much smaller than the one behind me.

"Oh blow this for a tale, I'm going back … sod the bet," I mumbled. But suddenly I became frightened, aware now of my predicament and the danger I was in. Bizarre thoughts started to go through my head: "What if a barge comes through … that's my lot. Oh, and I hope there's no rats in here … I never gave them a thought before I set off."

Then, to make matters worse … I got cramp. I tried swimming back towards the light but had to stop and cling onto the nicks in between the large stones forming the tunnel sides. There was a small lip jutting out, but it was nigh impossible to cling onto it, as it was full of slime, making it slippy.

"I'll have to rest," I thought, "I'll stand on the bottom." That didn't work either, because the water was too deep. In my stricken state I swallowed some water, almost choking. In a way this brought me to my senses, making me take control of the situation.

"Come on John lad, you can do it," I encouraged myself, "don't panic, whatever you do!" I then added a little prayer: *"Please God, help me in my plight, let me get out of this tunnel and I promise You I'll never do owt like this ever again."*

I couldn't swim properly but I managed to float on my back and moved slowly along by paddling with my hands. Eventually, after what seemed like hours, I made it through the tunnel and back to safety. Luckily, I was none the worse for my experience – indeed, I was a lot wiser ... I never, ever attempted anything so foolish again.

*　　*　　*

Bonfire night was one time the neighbourhood kids looked forward to with great eagerness. The main priority for the lads was collecting wood for the street fire. We were all determined to have the best bonfire in the district, so went to great lengths, collecting the wood from wherever we could, including wooden boxes from the market stalls and old furniture off the tip. Many a time we'd finish up fighting with the kids from King Street after raiding their stockpile of wood, or vice versa. Some of us used old rusty saws to cut branches from trees in Piccadilly Gardens, and if we were lucky we obtained some logs from the timber yard on Stanley Street.

We all enjoyed the run-up to bonfire night, as this gave us the opportunity to go singing from door to door and earn some money to buy fireworks. Another way to make money was to take out a Guy Fawkes and stand outside shops or pubs.

On one occasion, Barbara, Barry and Rose Clarke wanted to do this, but they didn't have a Guy.

"I'll tell you what, Barbara," said Rose, "you dress up in some old clothes and me and Barry'll go with you."

"Yeah, all right," Barbara agreed, "but I'm not gonna walk through the town centre in tatty clothes."

"It doesn't matter," said Barry, "we've no need to go down town … we can stand outside that photographer's window that's on Manchester Road at th'end of Trafalgar."

"Good idea," said Rose, "there's loads o' people around there all the time."

Off they went and were faring quite well, making about two shillings in just a short time. "This is great," enthused Rose, "we'll be rich if we stay here for another hour." However, their little scheme came to an end when they were told to move on by a passing policeman.

"Come on you two young uns, you can't stay here blockin' the pavement," he said, "take your Guy and be on your way." He got the shock of his life when Barbara got up and started following them.

"That were great, weren't it," quipped Rose, "did you see the look on that bobby's face?"

"Yeah, it were really funny," laughed Barry, "I can't wait to get home to tell t'others."

But it was a different story and not so funny when David Whittaker, Kenny Clayton and I decided to do the same.

"You're best dressing up, Kenny, you'll mek the best Guy," said David. "Whaddaya think, John?"

"Hey, never mind I'll mek the best Guy," rapped Kenny, "why don't one of you do it?"

"No, David's right, Kenny," I said, "you'll definitely be the best."

After a bit of deliberation, Kenny agreed, but with conditions, "Aye all reight, I suppose so … but we're splitting money three ways."

"Oh yeah," replied David, "that's only fair."

So after our little discussion, Kenny got dressed up in some rags. He really looked the part.

"Bloomin' 'eck Kenny, you look great," said David, "especially with all that straw stickin' outta that rag cap. Come on, let's get going … we should mek a bomb!" Sure enough, Kenny raised a few eyebrows and laughs from passers-by as we walked along Trafalgar.

"Reighto Kenny," said David, handing him a mask, "now for the final touch. Afore you sit down, put this on."

That did it. I burst out laughing, "E-eh, I'll tell thi what, Kenny, you're the best Guy I've ever seen!"

It didn't take long before the pennies started rolling in, as grown-ups commented on what a good job we had made of the Guy. Everything was going great until three teenage bullyboys interfered. They were big lads, about seventeen years of age, all dressed up to go dancing. I spotted them first coming down Manchester Road.

"Keep still, Kenny, there's three men coming," I mumbled, "they're just walking past th'Education Office now."

As they drew closer, David approached them, "Please have ya got a penny for the Guy, mister?"

"A penny for the bleedin' guy?" snarled the first one, "How about givin me somet for a pint, you cheeky little swine!" Then something very sinister happened!

"How about a bit o' football practice," joked the second one, "let's see if we can kick the flamin' Guy's head off." Without further coaxing he took a run and kicked poor Kenny in the face. Another one was going to do the same until he saw Kenny stand up, crying.

"Flamin' Nora, it's not a Guy," said one of them, panic-stricken, "it's a real lad!" On realising their mistake, rather than care for the injured boy, the cowardly youths went scampering down Manchester Road. Luckily, Kenny wasn't badly injured, but he had a cut lip and a great big bruise on his right cheek. It wasn't funny at the time, but we had a good laugh about it later – at least it gave us something to talk about.

On bonfire night, there was always a friendly rivalry between the Cowell's bonfire and the Wilkinson's further up the backstreet. And, as the night drew to a close, both parties would congregate together on an air-raid shelter, telling ghost stories whilst eating roast potatoes from the bonfire. "Eh, that were a good night, weren't it?" we would all agree. "It's great is bonfire night … roll on next year."

* * *

I never stayed in bed late and usually got up before any of the others. I always lit the fire and the best way to get the fire started was to use a metal blower, which was placed across the opening of the fireplace, creating a sucking effect from the chimney. We didn't have one, so I'd stand the shovel on the fire-grate and then place a sheet of newspaper over it, which had the same effect as a blower. This was a tricky job because I had to be very vigilant, otherwise the newspaper would catch fire. Once the fire got going, the old cast-iron fireplace retained a lot of heat, which radiated into the room, making it nice and cosy. Coal was the main fuel for keeping the fire burning but it was on ration and also expensive. To subsidise it, many people queued for hours on end at the gas depot on Parker Lane for cinders. Cinders only cost sixpence a bag, but despite the price, many folk couldn't afford it and were reduced to picking coal off the railway. This was strictly against the law, but it was the lesser of two evils – be law abiding and cold, or a law-breaker and warm. It was often a topic of conversation:

"Bloomin' 'eck Burt, aya not freightened o' geddin caught on the railway? You're forrit if tha gets nicked?"

"Aye, course I am, but what choice have I got? I either pick the coal or we freeze to death in our house!"

I made a small truck from a discarded crate and some old pram wheels, which came in handy for carrying a bag of cinders. It worked out great and it got me to thinking. "U-um, I'll ask Mrs King and some o' t'other neighbours if they want any cinders bringing. Yeah, why not … it'll be a bit of extra brass." Before long I had a few willing customers.

Despite the long queues, I only used to carry one bag at a time, because the first half of the return journey home was uphill. It wasn't too bad pushing it up Finsley Gate, but once I turned the corner into Manchester Road, the gradient became much steeper. I always had a rest outside the Canal Tavern before pushing it over the steepest part … the Canal Bridge.

It was on this part of the journey that I spotted young Rose Clarke one day, who lived at number 18, two doors higher up than I did on Albion Street. She was attempting to carry two bags of cinders at once on an old, makeshift trolley. Consequently, it had broken down.

"Bloomin' 'eck, Rose, what are you tryin' to do, kill yourself o' what?"

"Ha, ha," she sneered, "it's not bloomin' funny, Johnny Cowell … I've bin here for ages."

"Yeah, I can believe it, I'm surprised you've got this far."

"Oh well," replied Rose, "a bloke shoved it to here for me, but when it broke down he had to go."

"Broken down, the flamin' trolley's comin' apart… who made it, anyroad?"

"Mi dad made it … anyway, what difference does it make, are you gonna help me o' what?"

"Yeah, all reight Rose, but we'll have to unload them cinders off your trolley first and try and mend it. I have some rope on mi truck that may do the trick." The axles had buckled on Rose's truck, but by using the rope I managed to hold it together a little better.

"I'll tell you what I'll do Rose, I'll just load one o' the bags on it for now and shove it o'er the bridge as far as Trafalgar and then come back for t'other."

"But somebody might pinch it if you leave it unattended."

"Maybe, but have you got any better ideas?" Rose just shrugged her shoulders, implying she hadn't.

"Right then, just guard t'other bag and mi truck while I push it up there." When I got back we both set off pushing our own load, but poor Rose had to give up.

"I'm sorry, Johnny, I can't push it up this steep part o'er the bridge."

"All reight, Rose I'll give you a lift, but how the bloomin' 'eck did you hope to shove it with two bags on it?"

"I don't know … but mi dad said I had to fetch two."

"Your flippin' Dad! That's not fair …why didn't he come and fetch 'em himself?"

"Well, he said that t'other kids have to do it, so why shouldn't I."

"Oh yeah, lots of t'other kids do it, but mostly lads – it's bloomin' hard work. Just hang on till I've shoved my truck o'er the bridge and then I'll come back for yours." Once we'd reached Trafalgar we placed the other bag on top of Rose's trolley and set off again. The going was much easier now, as it was slightly downhill. All went well until we reached the main doors of the Ribble Garage.

"Oh no," groaned Rose, "the flamin' trolley's collapsed again!"

"Not to worry, Rose, we're nearly home," I said, "I'll just tie the rope a bit tighter." But when I attempted to do so, I realised it was hopeless. "It's no good, Rose, the axle's broken completely in half."

"Oh 'eck, what am I gonna do now?" she moaned.

To make matters worse, a bloke came out of the Ribble Garage, shouting, "What the flamin' 'eck's going on here? Get them bleeding bags outta the way now ... there's a bus waiting to leave the depot!"

"All reight, keep your hair on, we haven't done it on purpose," I barked.

"Hey, I don't want any lip either ... just get 'em outta road!"

"Oh blow this for a tale" I moaned, "I look well getting shouted at when I'm trying to help you, Rose. I'll tell you what ... I'll get home wi' my bag o' cinders and I'll tell your dad to come and collect yours."

"But he'll go mad if he has to come out," said Rose.

"Well he's no right to, he should have fetched 'em himself in the first place ... especially when he wanted two bags."

It turned out better for Rose in the long run, because although her dad roasted her, she didn't have to fetch any more cinders after that. As for me, as soon as I'd had a bite to eat I set off for another load.

*   *   *

Young Rose Clarke was in between our Barry and Barbara's age and they used to play together. Like other children they were curious and used to get up to mischief and on one occasion their curiosity frightened our Barbara so much that she had recurring nightmares for a while after.

One Sunday afternoon my dad was in the Trafalgar Pub playing cards with Walter Clarke, young Rose's dad, and his Uncle Tommy, better known as Nobby Clarke. Dad looked across the table and noticed that Tommy was clutching his chest and wincing. He nodded at Tommy but didn't get a response.

"Hey, Walt, I think there's somet wrong with your uncle Tommy."

"Leave it Barney, he's probably had one o'er the odds ... the old bugger can't take his ale anymore."

"I don't think so Walt, he's only had three halves ... I've seen him drink ten pints afore today."

"Aye maybe but that were in his heyday ... two pints is his limit nowadays."

All the same, Dad didn't like the way Tommy was snorting and wheezing. "You don't look so good Tommy. Are you in pain?" he asked.

"I am that, Barney," Tommy managed to splutter in between grunts. I feel really poorly ... I ca ... ca-an't breathe."

By now Walter had become concerned. "Blimey, Uncle Tommy, tha's turned as white as a sheet." Taking hold of Tommy's arm he turned to Dad, "Bloomin' 'eck Barney, he's sweating like a pig and feels really clammy all over ... I don't like the look of this."

"Neither do I," said Dad, "we'd best get him home quickly ... I think he's having a heart attack."

"Right," said Walter, "you take one arm and I'll take t'other."

Joining hands together, Dad and Walter chaired Tommy up the steep street to his home. When they reached the front door they gently eased him down and asked if he could walk into the house. Very slowly, Tommy removed his arms from around their necks, but as soon as his feet touched the floor his knees buckled under him and once again Dad and Walter had to take the full weight of his body. To carry him through the lobby, Dad took his arms whilst Walter held his legs, finally managing to sit him down in the armchair.

"There, we've got you home now Uncle Tommy," said Walter stroking his hand, "you should be all right now."

But Tommy didn't hear Walter's words ... he'd gone!

It all happened so quickly and Rose, Walter's wife, who had just prepared dinner mumbled, "Well that's a bugger, it's Sunday ... how are we gonna get hold of th'undertaker, they don't work weekends."

"That's a fine thing to say woman," rapped Walter, "my Uncle Tommy's just died and all you're worried about is what we're gonna do!"

Dad defused the situation by saying, "Hang on a minute Walt ... leave the lass alone, she's in shock! I've got an idea ... go and see Alice King next door, she's had plenty of dealings with this kind of thing afore."

Alice was a very kind lady, well known for helping out neighbours in distress. She was experienced in this kind of situation, as she had been called upon many times before to prepare a dead body for the undertaker. She was very obliging, immediately coming to their assistance. Dad and Walter discreetly left the scene.

"Is there anything I can do to assist you, Alice?" asked Rose.

"Well yes, there is Rose, you can nip down to the police telephone box at the bottom of the street to call the doctor so that he can confirm Tommy's death."

"What do we have to do that for?" asked Rose. "He's dead all right, anybody can see that."

"That may be so," replied Alice, "but it's standard practice ... I can't do a thing until he's been seen by the doctor."

The doctor had left and Alice started to undress Tommy when our Barry, Barbara and young Rose Clarke entered the house ... Alice quickly ushered them out.

Young Rose complained tearfully, "Ar-rgh it's not fair, mi grandad's died and I want to see him."

"All right young Rose, I know how you feel," said Alice soothingly, "but you can't come in just yet cos you're far too young to see what's goin' on. Just go out and play whilst I attend to him and perhaps your mam'll let you see him later."

In the meantime I'd heard of Tommy's death on the grapevine andwas sat on our front doorstep, watching our Barry, Barbara and young Rose as they played hopscotch and other street games. After a while they appeared fidgety and came and sat at the side of me.

"I'm sorry to hear about your grandad," I said to Rose.

"Yeah, so am I," she replied, "they won't even let me see him."

"I'm sure they will later on Rose," I assured her, "just you wait and see."

Just then Alice came out of Rose's house. The three youngsters immediately sprang to their feet and approached her.

"Can we go in to see him now Mrs King ... please?" asked young Rose. "Is he ready?"

"No you can't," Alice replied, "I haven't finished yet, and even then you won't be able to see him for quite a while. Anyroad, have any of you youngsters got any pennies on you?"

"No," said Barry, "but mi mam'll have some cos she uses 'em for the gas metre."

After Alice had gone Barbara asked, "What does she want pennies for?"

"Ah well," said Rose taking a deep breathe, "she wants 'em to put o'er my grandad's eyes to keep 'em closed ... she did it to my Aunt Mollie when she died."

"U-ugh, that sounds awful ... will his eyes not shut if she doesn't put pennies on 'em?" asked Barbara.

"It might sound awful but my mam says they always do it," replied Rose.

"U-ugh, just think how scary it would be if you saw a dead body staring at you," said Barry.

"Trust you to come up with that one Barry," said Rose. "Anyroad, have you ever seen a dead body?"

"Yeah, I saw Mrs Taylor when she died last year."

"I haven't," said Barbara, all intrigued, "what's it like?"

"D'you really want to know?" asked Rose. "Cos if you do I'll take you in once they've taken him into the front-room ... no moaning mind!"

"I won't moan ... honest!" said Barbara.

"How d'you know they'll put him in the front-room, Rose?" asked Barry.

"Because that's where they put my Aunt Molly.

About half an hour later Mrs King left Rose's house and went into her own.

"Good," said Rose, "she's finished. We can sneak in now." By now it had gone dark but a little light emitted from the gaslight in the front room as they crept up the lobby. Barry pushed opened the door and to their alarm Tommy was lying on a bed under the window with a large towel covering his midriff ... they had never seen him look so clean. A white cotton rag was tied around his head and chin to keep his mouth closed and pennies were placed on his eyes.

The front door opened causing the gas light to flicker, making Barbara scream out loud as she ran down the lobby right into the arms of Mrs King, who was carrying a white sheet to cover Tommy with.

"Right young Barbara," Alice said, "I know what you've been up to ... serves you right for being so nosy."

Barbara went home with her tail between her legs wishing she'd never seen the dead body whereas Barry and young Rose said a little prayer for Tommy after Alice had placed the sheet over him.

Alice organised a collection and the neighbours donated what they could to buy flowers and I, along with Rose and the others, went from door to door collecting jam jars and milk bottles, raising a little money for the collection.

On the day of the funeral neighbours closed both their upstairs curtains and their downstairs curtains, then paid their respects by standing on their front steps as the funeral procession made its way up Albion Street.

*   *   *

By my fourth year at Towneley School I had still hardly grown and the nick-name Bimbo stuck to me. Because of my size and the way I handled horses Dad mentioned that he thought I would make a good jockey.

"That may be so, Dad, but I want to go working down the pit," I replied, unconvinced.

"Working down the pit! You don't know what you're letting yourself in for, lad ... you'd be a lot better off training to be a jockey."

"Aye, maybe I would, Dad. I'll have to think about it."

I did think about it and I became quite keen on the idea. But then, when I broached the subject with Dad, he brushed the scheme aside as fruitless."

"But Dad," I stressed, "it were your idea in the first place!"

"Yeah, I know it were, but I've had second thoughts about it. You're only little, our John, but I think you're a bit too stocky. You needs to be quite slim to be a jockey."

"P-ph!" I pouted, "Thanks a lot Dad. First you build me up and now you shoot me down in flames."

"Sorry lad, I just don't want you geddin your hopes built up. That's why I'm tellin' you."

That was all very well, but my hopes were already raised. I hadn't been enthusiastic at first, but the more I'd thought about it, the more the idea appealed to me, and I was determined to do something about it. I felt let down and, being frustrated, I went about things in the wrong way.

"It's not fair," I moaned to myself, "nobody takes me serious. Even the careers teacher scoffs at me when I tell him what I want to do."

I brooded on it for a while and then decided to play truant. I knew there were some stables over in Gisburn, a little village a few miles on the other side of Nelson.

"U-um," I thought, "if I ask the headmaster for a day off to apply for a job, he'll probably think I'm stupid. But he'll think differently if I get the job."

The next morning, I left the house as though I was making my way to school, but instead of catching the Towneley bus, I caught the one heading for Nelson. From there, I hitchhiked it the rest of the way to Gisburn. I visited a riding stable but it wasn't geared up to training apprentice jockeys and the owner regarded me suspiciously. He was a rather smart, well-built country gentleman, who wore a deerstalker hat and sported a handlebar moustache. He asked me what I wanted in a very posh voice, but his manner was offensive.

"Now come on, boy, what do you take me for," he barked after listening to me, "what do you really want?"

"What do you mean?" I asked. "I wanna be a jockey, like I've just told you."

"Go on, get off this property before I throw you off!" he growled, pointing to the gate.

"All reight, I'm going," I grunted, "keep your hair on ... I didn't want the job anyroad."

"That'll do ... I don't want any cheek, you scruffy urchin, or I'll wallop you! And shut the gate behind you!"

I didn't give any more backchat, as he really was a big bloke – and aggressive with it.

But as I closed the gate, I couldn't resist a sarcastic parting shot: "Thank you for your hospitality!"

"Go on, get away you little runt," he rapped, "and don't let me see you around here again!"

I was a little disappointed as I made my way to Nelson, on the back of an open-back wagon. But I didn't dwell on it too long.

"A-ah well John lad," I mused, "it looks like you're going down the pit after all."

That was the beginning and the end of my career as a jockey. But the incident had repercussions, as I found out to my displeasure the next day when I got to school. Mr Lancaster, the headmaster, summoned me to his study and asked me why I had not attended school the previous day. I didn't have a letter from Mum excusing me, as I hadn't dared to ask her for one. I'd been on the verge of asking her to write one for me before leaving for school, but I'd had second thoughts about it.

"No, she'll bloomin' kill me if I tell her where I went," I thought, "and there's no chance of her giving me an excuse-me note. I don't have much option ... I'll have to take my chances without one." On reflection, I should have told her rather than face the wrath of Mr Lancaster.

"You what!" he bawled when I told him what had happened. "You mean to say you were playing truant?"

"We-ell no, not really," I stammered nervously, "I – I didn't think I were ... I – I thought ...!"

"Never mind what you thought!" he roared, cutting me off in mid-sentence. "You were absent without permission, and that's truancy in my book!"

"But Mr Lancaster, I – I ...!"

He cut me short again. 'I don't want any excuses," he snarled, now yielding a bamboo cane in his hand. "You've broken one of the cardinal rules of the school. Now bend over that chair and grab hold of the bottom rail!"

"But Sir, I – I ...!"

"Bend over that chair now!"

What happened next was to remain with me for the rest of my life.

I reluctantly crouched over the chair, just half-bending and fidgeting about.

"Bend over I say," he growled through clenched teeth, "and clutch the bottom rail!"

"Oh well," I thought, "I might as well get it over with ... I've had the cane afore."

I may have psychologically prepared myself for the idea of a caning, but I wasn't prepared for the excruciating pain I felt as the cane landed hard and heavy on my buttocks.

"O-o-oh-h!" I screeched, dancing around, clutching my backside with both hands. But my wailing had no effect on the headmaster.

"Bend over the chair!" he ordered, unmoved by my reaction.

For the second time I tentatively bent over.

"Get hold of that bottom rail!" he repeated, in an icy voice.

Once again the bamboo cane came crashing down onto my rear end with an almighty force, landing in the exact same spot.

"O-o-oh-h!" I screeched again, as I danced on the spot. He was still unmoved.

"Bend over that chair!" he repeated, in a cool and calculated voice.

"But sir," I pleaded, "Please ... please ... it won't happen agai-"

"No, it won't happen again ... not in my school!" he rapped, uncharacteristically betraying his impatience by gently tapping the palm of his left hand with the cane. "Now do what I say ... get over that chair!"

"Who-o-osh!" sounded the cane as it came down once more onto my throbbing buttocks. I'd received many a whacking from the schoolmasters, but I had never felt pain like this in my life before. By now the tears were streaming down my face.

"Get over that chair," came the dreaded order, "and grab hold of the bottom rail!"

"I can't take another," I whimpered pleadingly, "please sir ... please don't cane me again!"

"Get over that chair now, you insolent boy!" he demanded, completely devoid of compassion.

For the fourth time the fearsome cane struck home in the same spot, inflicting the most agonising, sickly pain.

"I can't take any more, I just can't," I thought to myself as nausea started to overcome me, "and anyway, I don't think it's fair. I don't think I've done anything so bad as to warrant this."

I tried to stem the flow of tears, looking up at him with pleading eyes. But I didn't utter another word, as I felt it would only fall on deaf ears. I stood there quiet and ashen faced, feeling as though my spirit was broken. He weighed me up for a while, seeming to sense that I'd had enough.

"Please God … no more," I sobbed inwardly, "please don't let him hit me any more!"

My silent prayer was answered. "Right boy," he rapped, "now go and sit in that chair facing my desk!" I did as I was ordered, and sat tentatively down on the wooden seat. After seating himself down opposite me, he began to give me a lecture.

"Right John Cowell," he said sternly, "I'm not going to beat about the bush, because you've gone right down in my estimation." He picked up a file, which was lying on the desk in front of him. "Do you know what this is?" he asked me.

"No sir," I replied meekly."

"This is your personal file, and it's strange really because I was only looking through it at the beginning of the week and I've been in touch with a factory enquiring about a job that, in my opinion, would suit you fine."

"Oh, thank you sir," I muttered, with bated breath.

"Don't thank me, boy," he said soberly, "because after this incident I've lost complete trust in your reliability."

"But sir!"

"Quiet! Speak when you're spoken to and listen to what I have to say. When you leave this room I am going to contact the firm again and cancel the application. No, I don't think I can entrust you with the job, I no longer have confidence in you … my reputation and that of the school is at stake here."

I asked him what the job was, but he wouldn't tell me. To this day I often wonder what that job might have been.

"You don't deserve to know," he replied coldly, as he placed my file back into the drawer of his desk, "let that be part of your punishment."

I felt deep down that all was not fair. "Right Mr Lancaster," I thought, "I've always respected you because even though you're strict, I've always found you to be fair. But now I don't think so any more. You've already punished me, why punish me a second time? You should have either taken the job opportunity away from me or caned me ... not both." But I didn't voice my opinion, as I felt vulnerable and afraid that I might receive more of what I'd just had.

"So what are you thinking of doing now," he asked, interrupting my thoughts, "have you looked for anything?"

"Yes sir," I replied grudgingly, "I've applied to Bank Hall Colliery and they informed me I can start after the Easter holidays if I pass the medical."

"Oh yes ... and what was all that nonsense about training to be a jockey, then?"

"I don't know sir," I mumbled. I really wanted to say that he wouldn't have thought it was nonsense if I'd got the job.

"Right, on your way," he said pointing to the door, "and let this be a lesson to you."

I left the room feeling rather dejected. I'd never been happy at Towneley, but this incident made me want to leave the place as quickly as I could.

"Yes, it's been a lesson all right, Mr Lancaster," I mumbled to myself as I walked along the corridor, "more than you'll ever know ... I'll think twice before owning up to anything ever again."

THE YOUNG MINER

April 1954 was a time that I had longed for ... I was fifteen and it was time to leave school. On my first day as a trainee miner I strutted off down Albion Street with my bait box under my arm, full of enthusiasm, reflecting on the time that my Uncle Jimmy had done the same all those years ago in Bacup. In spite of Mum's tales of the terrible accident and young Jimmy's death, I wasn't to be put off. I'd always fancied working down the mine, ever since being a small boy, and this was my big day.

Mum was obviously concerned about me, but I reassured her. "Don't worry, Mam, everything will be all right ... you'll see."

When I first entered into the coal-mining industry, I had to undergo a vigorous sixteen-week course along with a lot of other young lads. I reported to Bank Hall colliery to commence my training. Bank Hall was the main pit in the Burnley area, and by far the biggest. The sixteen weeks' training was divided into two sections, which meant studying eight weeks at college and working eight weeks down the pit. However, the course was arranged so that one alternated weekly between college and pit. To my disappointment, my first week was to be spent at college.

"Oh bloomin' 'eck," I moaned, "back to school already. I thought I'd left that behind me."

The college was just a small building in the Croft area of town situated near Parker Lane. I found myself in a classroom of twenty-five lads from poor backgrounds. I soon settled down, as I already knew two of them – Bobby Cheetham and Freddy Man, who lived on Trafalgar. Everyone was as disgruntled as me about the situation, but as we were all in the same boat, or rather classroom, we accepted our plight. I was still only four feet nine inches tall, and the smallest in the group. Certain bullyboys in the class tended to pick on me and taunt me, but not for long ... they soon found out that, despite my size, I could handle myself. Mind you, I was helped out by my friend Freddy Man, who was about seventeen. Freddy was a really strong lad and took me under his wing.

Another lad, who was seventeen and quite a big lad, picked on me a lot, and I was no match for him. Freddy, who didn't like what he saw, eventually stepped in on my behalf and soon sorted him out. With hardly any effort he got hold of the lad by the throat and pinned him up against a wall. "What have I told thi about pickin' on John?" he growled. "If you don't leave him alone I'll rip your head off!"

"Bloody hell Fred, you can't be stickin' up for that little brat all the time," grimaced the lad, "you're not his flamin' chaperone!"

"No, maybe not, but you're older and much bigger than he is so leave him be ... right?" The lad knew better than to mess about with Fred, so that was the end of the matter.

After that little escapade, things settled down and most of us became quite friendly with each other.

*   *   *

On the second week I was very excited, as I knew I would be working at the pit. Once again I reported to the reception area at Bank Hall where I met up with the same group that I'd been in class with the previous week.

We were all given overalls, boots, kneepads, a belt and a safety helmet, which had a special fitting to hold a miner's lamp. Being so small and kitted out like a miner, I looked quite funny to say the least. We were split up into five groups, each group being supervised by an ex-coalface worker.

Each team leader in turn addressed the young apprentices. "Right lads, let's get one thing straight from the start. I'm the gaffa and if you do owt wrong you'll answer to me ... understand?"

All five ex-colliers were mean-looking men, with blue scars on their faces – a legacy of working on the coalface.

There was no opposition, as we all answered in unity: "Yeah ... righto."

The first group cheered loudly when they were informed they were going down Bank Hall. Three groups were sent to other local pits, Hapton Valley, Clifton and Reedley. The fifth group wasn't quite so happy because they had been picked to work on the pit-top. I was in this group and sorely disappointed ... my day of going underground seemed to be eluding me.

"Still, not to worry John," said Bobby Cheetham nudging me, "our day will come."

The first thing I noticed was how large the tubs were … in fact, they were more like railway wagons.

"Bloomin' 'eck!" I commented. "What are them? I thought tubs were a lot smaller than that!"

"Eh, them're not called tubs, young fella," replied the gaffa, "them's mine-cars. We stopped usin' tubs a while back now. Mind you, they still use tubs at a lot o' the smaller pits."

The day was not altogether fruitless; we worked ardently, filling large mine-cars with wooden props, bricks, girders and other materials that were needed by the colliers underground. In-between time, the boss explained the workings of the pit and the importance of keeping supplies going.

On Tuesday we were taken to Clifton Pit on the back of a NCB coal wagon, but yet again I didn't get to go down the mine. This time I had to work in the screens, where the coal was separated from the shale. Rubble was conveyed onto large steel shaker pans with holes in them, sieving the slack from the cobs. The pans were not fully efficient and it was the job of me and my mates to lift large lumps of shale and place them onto another pan. It was a heavy job, so by the end of the shift I was quite tired.

Finally, the day came when I got to go down the mine. It was quite daunting, because we had been subject to a lot of scaremongering from the more experienced colliers.

"Do you know, lad," they'd quip, "it's 500 yards to the bottom o' the pit … that's about three times deeper than height o' Blackpool Tower! Aye, and the bloomin' cage drops like a stone till you're nearly at the bottom. Mind you

... there's nowt to worry about, cos it only takes about three seconds."

On reaching the cage, all the trainees, including me, had butterflies in their stomachs, but didn't like backing out for fear of being mocked. Sure enough, the cage did drop very fast, leaving our stomachs in our mouths. But after the initial shock it wasn't so bad ... in fact, we soon began to look forward to the thrill of it.

Once we were underground, we found lots of long, winding tunnels running throughout the mine. To reach some of the coalfaces we had to walk about two miles through these tunnels. The nearer we got to the coalfaces, the dustier it became.

In order to cut down absenteeism, the wage was calculated on a bonus system. My daily pay was eleven shillings and one penny. If I completed five days, I received an extra day's pay, making my gross pay £3-6s-6d. I couldn't wait to receive my first wage packet, but when I did I got quite a shock. I was on an emergency tax code and my total stoppages, including the insurance stamp, were a staggering five shillings ... leaving a net pay of £3-1s-6d.

After tipping up to Mum, she gave me ten shillings spending money and we came to an agreement that should I work overtime I would share the extra with her.

The first thing I did on receiving my ten shillings was to go straight down to Fitzpatrick's bike shop and buy myself a bike on hire purchase. It cost £15-15s, and I had to put down nine shillings as a deposit and pay nine shillings a week for thirty-four weeks. However, by doing extra part-time jobs, I managed to pay off the debt in twenty weeks.

* * *

The sixteen-week training period soon passed, and then I went to the pit of my choice ... Thorney-Bank Colliery in Hapton. Mum used to give me a shout at quarter to six in the morning, and after a hearty breakfast I would leave at quarter past six to catch the Accrington bus, close to the Mitre Junction. Just as I was leaving the house, Mum would give Mary a shout, as she was now working at Barden Mill as a weaver.

Unlike Bank Hall, Thorney-Bank was a drift mine, without a shaft. The entrance was via a great big tunnel at the mouth of the mine that inserted itself into Hameldon Hill, which was situated in-between Hapton and Accrington. The pit top was like a railway siding, with about four sets of railway lines with points, enabling carriages to interchange. Being a modern pit, Thorney-Bank only had a few small tubs, but the majority were mine-cars similar to the ones at Bank Hall. These were connected together in the same way as railway wagons and pulled along by a locomotive engine, commonly known as the 'Loco'. As the mine-cars came out of the pit full of coal and shale, they were shunted over a turntable that automatically tipped the contents of each one onto a conveyer belt. This in turn ran up steeply to a very large screening plant, which was much more sophisticated than the one at Clifton Colliery.

At the new pit I was allocated a clean locker and a dirty locker. Shower units separated the two locker sections and it was forbidden, after coming out of the pit, to return to the clean section before having a shower. Once kitted out in my working gear, I made my way to the lamp-room. Along with two of my mates, I stood out like a new pin from the more mature colliers, who were strapping special batteries to their belts and fixing miner's lamps into their helmets. A rather stout, official-looking man approached us trainees and started giving out a few facts.

"Right you young uns ...right from start, I want to point out who I am and just what my job is. My name's George Riley, and I'm the safety officer. And I want to make it quite clear from the word go that I won't stand for any monkey business of any kind. If I catch any of you riding conveyor belts, jumping onto the back of any of the moving mine-cars or anything else untoward, it'll be instant dismissal ... understand?"

"Yeah we understand," muttered all three of us, not having much choice.

The safety officer then turned his attention to me.

"What's your name, young fella, and what made you come working at the pit, then?"

"John Cowell and I'm here because I've always wanted to work down the mine since I was a little boy."

"A little boy? You're not much bigger than a little boy now," he grunted.

That irritated me – even more so because many of the miners burst out laughing, including my two mates. I was fuming!

"He might well be my gaffa," I thought, "but that doesn't give him the right to take the mickey outta me." I paused for a minute before replying, "Excuse me ... you may well be the safety officer, but I think you're out of order. How would you like it if I started making personal comments about your belly?"

"Well, you cheeky young bugger, you're nowt else and on your first day!" he rapped.

"Serves you right, George," laughed one of the colliers, "you asked for that ... give the young lad credit for stickin' up for himself." The safety officer frowned a little, but luckily didn't hold it against me.

"Right John, there's two checks here," he said, reasserting his authority, "now listen whilst I explain what they're for." Firstly he handed me a triangular metal check with the number 200 stamped on it. "This is your personal number," he stressed, "and you must keep this particular check on your person at all times whilst in the pit for identification purposes." He then handed over a round disc with the same number stamped on it. "This one is for job allocation, which will be explained more thoroughly once you get into the pit."

After the instructions and advice, I was taken to another room and introduced to a mature collier. The man's name was John William Worseley and throughout his working life his nickname had always been 'John Bill'. When starting at a new pit, it was the custom to be supervised for the first four weeks by an experienced collier. In my case, my destiny was to be under the scrutiny of John William Worseley.

"Naythen, John Bill," said the safety officer, "this here young lad's gonna be under your care for the next twenty working days, so think on you show him the ropes and teach him properly."

"Yeah reight-o', George ... leave the young lad wi' me. I'll take him under mi wing."

"Aye, think on you do, and no teaching him any o' the wrong things, eh?" At that, George Riley handed a slip of paper to the collier. "Take special care o' this, John Bill ... it's an authorisation slip giving you full responsibility o'er the young lad."

Whilst reading the slip of paper, John Bill paused for a minute then burst out laughing. "I don't believe it," he said, chuckling all the more. "I don't believe it."

"Come on, John Bill," interjected one of the other colliers, "let us all in on the joke."

"Well, all the years that I've worked here I've been labelled wi' the nickname 'John Bill' … I feel as if I've just become a dad."

"How d'you mean? What's so funny?" enthused more colliers, now crowding around, all wanting to be in on the joke.

"Well believe it o' not … this little fellow is called John William Cowell."

At that, quite a lot of colliers started laughing. "Eh bloody hell … you mean to say we've got a young John Bill now!"

I didn't know whether to be mad or pleased. At least I seemed to be accepted. One thing for sure … the nickname 'Young John Bill' was to stick with me throughout my working life at Thorney-Bank.

After the initiation, my overlooker, John Bill senior, guided me to the entrance of the mine. The tunnel was about ten feet high and ten feet across and the roof was supported by steel girder-type rings. These were placed about four feet apart. Unlike Bank Hall, it wasn't dusty but there was a lot of water seeping in from the hillside above. Running throughout the tunnel was a single-rail track laid on wooden sleepers about three feet apart. The men had no trouble straddling the sleepers, but with my short legs, I found myself jumping from sleeper to sleeper rather than walking. After about half a mile, I heard the sound of the loco.

"Get yourself into one o' these here cubbyholes, Young John Bill, afore you get run o'er," shouted one of the miners.

As it happened, there were cubbyholes about every hundred yards for this kind of situation. We all waited patiently whilst the loco passed dragging about twelve mine-cars. After walking approximately one mile, we arrived at a very large cave-like opening, which was about 200 yards long, twenty feet high and twenty feet wide. It was unsupported, as it had been driven out of solid rock. The single-track line formed into a double track and this is where all the empty mine-cars were exchanged for full ones. This large expansion was known as 'the Landing' and it was here where many job allocations took place. Being a main section of the pit, it was well lit up. It was also the place where all the materials, which had been carried on the mine-cars, were unloaded and stacked prior to being transported to the coalfaces. The firemen's station was also situated here and it was the nucleus of the pit. The firemen, who acted as underground foremen, planned the day's activities and were responsible for the day-to-day running of the pit. The Landing was also the main loading point where the mine-cars were filled with coal from the various coalfaces.

There were a few firemen at the Landing, each one in charge of a coalface. I watched with interest as the colliers handed over their round metal tags, then made their way through adjacent tunnels to their respective coalface. After the dispersion of all the colliers, the firemen then allocated jobs to all the other pit workers.

"Reight, Young John Bill, afore we start," said my senior, "I'll take you to the fireman's cabin to explain how things work." When we got there a fireman was just hanging the round discs on specially designated hooks. "Naythen lad, can you tell me what he's doing that for?"

"Well, I think it's something to do with the allocation o' the men," I replied. "George Riley said something like that."

"Very good lad," interrupted one of the firemen, "but do you realise the importance of it?"

"Well, it's so that you can tell what everybody's doing … I've heard that every hook represents a job."

"Aye, you're reight there, but there's somet else that's really important … it's so we can pinpoint where everybody is. Not only that, but afore you knock off at th'end o' the shift, you have to pick up your check from here."

"Why do you have to do that, then?" I enquired.

"Good question, cock," said the fireman, impressed by my enthusiasm. "Well, it serves two purposes. One, nobody can leave the pit without me knowing about it. And two, you've to hand your check o'er to the lamp-chap in the lamproom, who then books your time and also knows you're out of the pit. Having to check out like this has a safety aspect attached to it."

"How's that, then?" I asked.

"Well, if somebody happened to get hurt while working on his own and he couldn't move, we'd know something was wrong cos his check would still be hanging here at th'end of the shift … we'd then send out a search party to go an' look for him."

"U-mm, what a good idea … simple but effective," I replied.

Turning his attention more closely to me, the fireman now started to weigh me up. "By 'eck lad, you're only a little un for workin' down the pit." Then, stroking his chin, he added. "U-umph, I can't see you being much use as a tackle lad, but I suppose you'll be all right working on a belt end." That did it! During the sixteen weeks' training I'd noticed men tending conveyor belt ends and had shivered at the thought of how boring it must be to just sit there all day with nothing else to do except watch in case the main belt stopped.

Once again I was on the defensive. "Excuse me, I might only be small but I'm very strong and I'm not frightened of hard work. Besides, I want to be a tackle lad."

"Blimey, that's telling me," he responded, a little taken aback. "I can see, young fellow, from th'onset that you'll stick up for yourself. All reight, fair enough, you'll get your chance."

Turning back to John Bill senior, the fireman more or less repeated the same words that the safety officer had said. "Right John Bill, tek Young John Bill under your wing and show him the ropes."

After handing over our checks I set off with my boss for number 4 coalface. We strolled along at a steady pace as he pointed out various aspects of the mine to me.

I asked him why the men in charge were called firemen.

"A-ah well, one o' the firemen's jobs is to fire the coal by packing pre-drilled holes on the coalface with explosives and then using special detonators … hence the name 'fireman'. They also carry a special lamp on their belts called a Davey Lamp, which they use for testing for firedamp, a very explosive gas. They've got to do this test every time afore they fire the coal in case there's bin a build up o' gas … otherwise there could be an explosion. In th'olden days they used to keep canaries down the pit in a cage and these'd flake over at slightest sign of any gas."

"He-ey, that were a shame weren't it – the poor birds?" I chipped in.

"Poor birds mi arse … that were better than the colliers copping it, weren't it?"

"Yeah, I suppose so, but anyroad … how does the Davey Lamp work, then?"

"Good question, lad. Well for a start, a very clever bloke by the name o' Davey invented it. It's a very special lamp, as it actually has a naked flame. You know only too well by what they taught thi in training school that no naked flame, matches or anything inflammable can be brought into the pit. Well, the Davey Lamp is so well designed that the flame is rendered harmless. The naked flame is encased in such a way by special thick glass and gauze that it cannot come in contact with the gas. When testing for gas the fireman turns out his own cap lamp and then turns down the naked flame of the Davey Lamp so there's just a small flame. The lamp is then slowly lifted to the highest point of the coalface and if there's any gas lingering about the flame turns blue."

"U-um, interesting," I said, "very interesting."

We carried on walking deeper into the mine, along one of the tunnels. A conveyor belt ran throughout the length of the tunnel and running alongside was a small steel track on which small four-wheeled bogies ran. These bogies were like trolleys, only slightly bigger. The tackle lads used them for carrying timber, props, girders, bricks, blocks and other materials to the coalface. The tunnel was constructed in a similar way to the entrance drift, but was much smaller and also much wetter.

"By 'eck," I commented, "this is a flippin' wet tunnel, innit?"

"Naythen John Bill, let's get one thing straight from word go," rapped John Bill, "we don't call 'em tunnels when they're running from the coalface, we call 'em 'gates'. Aye, and this one is the main gate and there's another running parallel to it a hundred yards on the lower side called the tail gate."

"Oh reighto, I'll remember that."

We eventually reached the coalface, which to my surprise was only about two feet six inches high. A scraper chain ran from the face, spilling coal on to the conveyor belt. This was a conveyor system, but instead of a rubber belt it was made up of steel link chains, which ran on top of, and underneath, specially designed straight steel pans. The belt attendant was there to stop the scraper chain in case the main conveyor belt stopped.

"Right, Young John Bill," my overseer continued, "there's something else you've gotta know. By law, until you're eighteen years old, you're not allowed within thirty yards of the coalface unless accompanied by someone of authority. I'm warning you now, cos if the fireman or the safety officer catches thi, you're forrit and could be sacked."

As it happened, there were two tackle lads throwing some props onto the face for the colliers.

"What about them, then?" I asked. "They're not eighteen."

"Aye you're reight there lad, but I'm telling you they're taking a risk and they could be down the road if they're caught. Anyroad, it's up to you what you do once you've finished your twenty days wi' me"

I pondered for a moment before asking, "U-um, it seems strange to me … how come they take the risk of being sacked, then?"

"A-ah, that's easy lad … you see, all the colliers encourage 'em to bring tackle right up to the face, cos it saves them a lot o'' hard work. Just look back along the gate and you'll see that the steel track ends about fifty yards short o' the face. That's a hell of a long way for colliers to hump the tackle."

"Yeah, fair do's, but it's also a long way for the tackle lads to hump it as well," I said, looking puzzled. 'If they're only allowed within thirty yards of the face, why don't they just leave it there?"

"You're catching on quick, Young John Bill. Well, what it is … for this service, the colliers give the lads some 'pey-brass' at th'end o' the week."

At this, my ears pricked up. "Pey-brass … what's pey-brass?"

"Well, on payday, after picking up their wage packets, them two young lads'll wait outside the cashier's office for the colliers to pick up theirs. This is the time of reckoning … each collier gives 'em half a dollar tip for their loyal services."

"Half a dollar!" I gasped, getting more interested by the minute. "And how many colliers are there on the face?"

"Let's see, on average there's about twelve … yeah, that's about reight, twelve."

My brain started to tick over. The thought of pey-brass gripped my imagination. In a flash I'd worked it out. 'Thirty shillings split two ways … fifteen shillings each – u-um, not bad … not bad at all." Now more than ever, I wanted to be a tackle lad.

During my twenty days' training, I did lots of different jobs with my overseer and once a week we had to attend a belt-end. I hated this aspect of the job, but it didn't seem as bad when there were two of us, because at least I had someone to talk to. Not many lads liked doing belt-end work, and the firemen were aware of this. Being fair-minded, they shared the task between the lads, so that each attended a belt-end on average about once a week.

On the second week after handing over our checks to the fireman, John Bill senior was told to go to the Bluebird.

"Oh no, not the 'Dreaded Bluebird'," he blurted out.

"Go on, get yourself up there and stop your moaning!" replied the fireman.

Some of the colliers laughed as they passed, making comments: "Don't forget to take your compass with you,

John Bill." "Keep a sharp eye on that young fellow – mind you don't lose him in them old workings." "Cor blimey, rather thee than me, John Bill!"

I wondered what was going on, especially when one bloke tapped me on the shoulder, saying, "Eh, God bless thi … you're such a young lad too, try not to take it too hard!"

"Come on, John Bill, what's the joke?" I asked, getting a little agitated.

"It's no joke, lad … we're goin' to the Dreaded Bluebird and believe you me it hasn't got that name for nothing. I've got to admit, young un … this is one time when I'm glad I've got a trainee with me."

"Oh come off it, you're trying to wind me up … you're having me on," I insisted.

"Have it your way lad, you'll see … you'll see."

After leaving the Landing we walked some distance along number 4 gate, then turned left and went through two air-lock doors. On the other side of these was another tunnel, but it was only two feet high.

"Reight lad," quipped my senior, "this type of tunnel is called a heading and this particular one is about 500 yards long and leads to a maze of similar ones. We'll have a minute here, cos we've a few headings to go through afore we reach the Bluebird and it's no fun walkin' under the low – it's back-breaking, cos you have to walk on all fours."

John Bill was right. It was too low to walk proper, even when you were crouched over. I kept catching my back on the roof and had to revert to scrambling on my knees. I wasn't too concerned about this, as I was quite fit, but what did concern me was the chilliness of the place. As we progressed deeper into the mine, the more eerie it got. After the first 500 yards, we came to a T-junction and another heading. This one had a very large scraper chain running throughout its length.

"Naythen, Young John Bill, if you crawled left for about a thousand yards you'd arrive at number 2 face. We're going right for the same distance until we come to th'end o' this here scraper. As you may have noticed, this scraper is much bigger than any o' t'other scrapers that you've seen already. This is the Bluebird."

I glanced left and the light from my lamp zoomed into the distance until it faded into total darkness. I then glanced right with the same effect. We had to climb over the scraper and crawl along the other side of it.

"I'll tell thi what, John Bill," I commented, "it's bloomin' draughty and cold round here, innit?"

"Aye, that's because this is a main airway for ventilating the coalface and the different gates, the wind's much stronger cos we're under the low. Anyway, let's go … we've got a bit of a trek ahead of us yet!"

Finally we arrived at our destination. Talk about eerie, this place was enough to put the shivers up the hardiest of men. The scraper emptied its contents onto a conveyor belt that went off in another direction through another tunnel, running into oblivion. Just a few yards on the other side of this belt were the openings to at least five other headings, which veered off in various directions. All the openings were blocked off with strong sack sheeting.

"If you're ever tending to this belt on your own, Young John Bill," said my carer, "don't ever go foraging in any o' them headings o'er yonder cos they lead into a labyrinth of old workings and you could easily get lost. Besides, there's not much ventilation beyond them sacking curtains and there could be gas hanging about."

"You must be joking!" I quivered. "Go foraging in there? It gives me the shivers just looking at 'em."

John Bill didn't make things easier, as he went on to tell me some scaremongering tales that had spread throughout the pit about ghostly figures wandering about the old workings. I wasn't one for believing in ghosts or evil spirits, but this was a frightening, awesome place even though there were two of us.

My thoughts were interrupted as the conveyor belt started. "Reight lad, push that button o'er there and get the Bluebird going," said John Bill senior. Within ten minutes, the large scraper was full of coal, feeding its contents onto the conveyor belt. During the procedure, lots of spillage accumulated and some started to backtrack onto the underside of the Bluebird. "Reight lad, get hold o' that shovel and make sure you stop them scuftings from cloggin' up the scraper chain."

"What's scuftings?" I asked.

"Oh, it's just another name for loose coal ... you'll soon get used to it being called that, especially on the face."

The day passed very slowly; minutes seemed like hours ... we never saw another soul until a young lad, who was taking over for the afternoon shift, relieved us.

"All reight lads," he greeted us, "you can go now, you lucky sods."

"Bloomin' 'eck," I thought, "I'd hate to be in his shoes." The very thought made me shiver. I couldn't wait to leave the place.

*   *   *

The twenty days soon passed ... now I was on my own. It soon became apparent that the nickname 'Young John Bill' was to stick. No matter where I went working in the mine, that was how I was known. It wasn't just the colliers, either. From the firemen to all the pit top workers ... even the safety officer, George Riley, referred to me in this way.

As I progressed, I got my chance to tackle drag, but I also spent many shifts attending belt-ends and hated it. However, I took it in my stride, knowing that it was only fair that I should take my turn along with the others. Then came the dreaded day when I was told to go on the Bluebird. A cold shiver went through me at the thought of having to crawl through all those isolated headings alone. I knew it was no good protesting, as someone had to do it and today was my turn. I reluctantly handed over my check then slunk off, despondently. I made my way through the two air-lock doors and crawled warily through the heading as far as the T-junction.

After climbing over the large scraper chain, I hesitated for a moment, paralysed with fear, not daring to go any further into the eerie darkness. I gradually built up some courage, but every few yards I kept peering over my shoulder, imagining that someone or something was there. I eventually arrived at my base and set the Bluebird in motion. For a while, I just sat there frozen to the spot, as my gaze was drawn to the maze of old workings, imagining all the ghastly figures that John Bill Senior had talked about.

My mind started wandering, and I began to imagine all different kinds of things. "What's that creaky noise? Who's there? What's that moving?" To make matters worse, the odd rat would occasionally scurry from under the conveyor belt across my path.

That awesome place wasn't just chilly in the frightening sense, but also temperature wise. I started shivering and my teeth began to chatter; I really was scared. Even the droning of the Bluebird's engine and the clanking of the thick chain seemed to make a weird sound.

"Oh, blow this for a tale," I muttered to myself, after pondering for what seemed an age, "I'll have to do something to take mi mind off them old workings." I grabbed hold of the shovel and started shovelling the scuftings for all I was worth. This helped a little, for I felt warmer, but the eerieness remained.

After what seemed an eternity, the conveyor belt stopped, so I switched off the Bluebird.

"Oh thank goodness, it must be bait time," I thought, "John Bill told me the belt would stop for half an hour then. Mind, it feels like I've done two shifts already." I'd just taken a bite out of a jam butty when I became aware of the stillness of the place ... it was so quiet, you could literally hear a pin drop.

"Oh flippin' 'eck," I mumbled, "it's more eerie now than when scraper were droning away!" Just then, I heard a creaking sound. I felt the hair rise on the back of my neck as a chill ran down my spine.

"Who's that ... who's there?" I shouted, trembling. My lamp shone into the pitch darkness, but I could see nothing untoward. "It must have bin a cob o' coal falling off the belt, or maybe a rat ... or maybe my imagination working overtime," I reassured myself.

I settled down to finish my bait, and was taking a slurp of coffee from my flask when I heard another creaking sound. This time, I knew for certain that it wasn't my imagination. All the same, when I peered along the heading, everything was motionless; I could see nothing. Not being able to weigh up what was happening, I became more un-nerved, as lots of bizarre thoughts ran through my head.

"I'm not usually nervous like this," I mumbled, "but this bloomin' place is enough to give anybody the creeps. I know bloody well now why nobody likes looking after this belt-end." My mumbling was interrupted as a minute piece of coal struck my helmet.

"All right, that's it!" I shouted, "Come on out whoever you are ... I know there's somebody there." Nobody answered, so I climbed over the belt to the other side and started to crawl down the heading. I'd gone about thirty yards when a glint of light reflected back at me from the glass of a miner's lamp. My heart skipped a beat as I spotted two bodies lying flat out on their bellies by the side of the belt. After getting over the initial shock, I shouted, "All reight, come on, you can get up now ... the game's up, I've seen thi!"

When they realised they'd been spotted, two lads turned their cap lamps on and burst out laughing. "Eh, that got you, dinnit, John Bill? You looked freightened to death!"

"Too true I was bloody freightened ... so would you have bin if it had happened to thi. Anyroad, how did you get here with no lights without making a noise?"

"Oh, that was easy ... we crept up on you whilst the belt was still running and we used the light from your own lamp to guide us here." They went on to tell me how it was a kind of ritual to do this to every trainee on their first stint on the Bluebird, and we all ended up having a good laugh about it. I wasn't bothered in the least – I was only too glad of the company as they joined me for bait-time. After they'd left, it still seemed a daunting place, but somehow it didn't appear quite so eerie any more.

This was my first solo experience on the Bluebird, but not my last. Other lads tried to play the same prank on me, but I was wise to their game. They'd sneak up on me in the same manner, making similar eerie, ghost-like sounds. On realising that someone was there, I turned the tables on them. I would settle myself down in a comfortable, safe position, then switch off my cap lamp. The roles were now reversed. Without lights they were in a much more precarious position than I was. Before long they had to switch on their lights and the laugh was now on them. I enjoyed these little pranks, because it relieved the boredom and also made me a lot of friends. When I was tackle running, I actually played the same prank on new unsuspecting trainees, with the same effect.

*　*　*

The mine worked on a three-shift system: days, afternoons – known as back-shift – and nights. The day shift was seven in the morning till two-thirty in the afternoon, the back-shift from quarter-past two in the afternoon till nine forty-five at night and the night shift from eleven at night till six-thirty in the morning. All three shifts had a half-hour break for bait-time.

By law, no one could work nights until they were sixteen years old. However, they could still work the afternoon shift. After working at the mine for two months, George Riley, the safety officer, approached me.

"Reight John Bill, as from next Monday I want thi to come in on the afternoons and from then on, you'll be alternating weekly from back-shift to days."

Each fireman had his own team of men and each team worked the three-shift system, alternating weekly from days to back-shift to nights. This meant that I would work with one particular team for two weeks and then change over to another, as they progressed onto nights and I progressed back onto days. Consequently, after leaving one team, it would be another four weeks before I met up with them again and so on.

Little did I know that I was to spend some very unhappy times during the next few months. Of the three teams, two of the firemen were very fair and I got my share of tackle running, but the third … he was different altogether. This particular fireman was referred to as G.T. and for some reason, from the word go, he took an instant dislike to me and made my life unbearable. On my first day under G.T., he told me to go on the Bluebird. I frowned and this was noted. The following day, he ordered me to attend the Bluebird again.

"But I went on there yesterday," I protested, "it's somebody else's turn today."

"Oh did you now?" he snarled. "Well, you can bloody well get your arse up there again today, you cheeky little swine!"

I protested again, but to no avail, "Hey that's not fair … you know that we all take turns!"

"Oh we all take turns do we?" he scoffed. "Well I'm the gaffa round here and I'll tell thi just one more time, you little rat … move your arse or I'll kick it all the way to the flamin' Bluebird!"

I wasn't happy about it, and felt like walking out of the pit, but I knew that wouldn't help my cause. I was left with little alternative but to make my way to the Bluebird full of foreboding. What made matters worse was that some of the other young lads started mocking me – they were highly delighted at not having to go on the dreaded scraper themselves. Every day that week and the following week on the back-shift, G.T. ordered me to attend the Bluebird. I was extremely unhappy, to say the least. G.T. seemed to derive a sadistic pleasure from sending me to the Bluebird.

However, some good did come of it. For starters, I became much more acquainted with the place; it didn't seem quite so eerie and I wasn't scared any more. I overcame my fear, realising that I had to do something about it in order to save my sanity.

"Blow this for a tale!" I mumbled to myself one day. "I've got to do somet to alter things around here or I'll go round the bend. U-um, for a start, if I'm gonna be coming here on a regular basis, I might as well have a bit a o' comfort. I need to build a den o' somet to ward off the cold draughts." I pondered for a little while longer, then came up with an idea. Looking towards the old workings, my brain started to tick over. "Yeah, that's it ... there's bound to be some materials in there that I can use." The thought of it made me feel very uneasy, but I wasn't to be put off. "Sod it! In for a penny ... in for a pound! Anything's better than having to put up with these conditions."

As I got nearer to the old workings, I could feel every hair on my body standing on end, but I was determined to carry out my plan. I wasn't stupid enough to venture into the disused workings – I remembered the warning that John Bill Worseley had given me not to go beyond the sack sheeting because there could be lingering gas in the old tunnels. All the same, as I shone my light beyond the old sheeting into the darkness, I could see that just a few yards inside there were a few mouldy wooden props and some rolls of sacking lying about. Quick as a flash, I nipped in, got what I wanted and was out again. I got a roll of sacking and four wooden props, which I set up in a square formation by the side of the Bluebird.

"This sacking is used for diverting the airflow around the pit," I told myself, "so it should be good enough to ward off the cold." Within a short time, I'd fixed the sacking around the props and formed a nice, cosy cubbyhole. There was plenty of sacking left over, which I used to make a comfortable seating arrangement.

"U-um, not bad," I thought, rather pleased with myself, "it's like a home from home."

Taking everything into account, things were better, although I was still unhappy with the situation. I did not realise it at the time but this was not the end of the matter … not by a long way!

For the whole of the two weeks, G.T. revelled in sending me to the Bluebird every day deriving pleasure from both my misery, and from making the other young lads laugh. The sense of power that he held over me seemed to boost his ego. Unsurprisingly, I began to despise him. The time passed slowly but gradually the Friday of the afternoon shift arrived.

I sat there reflecting on things. "Thank goodness, this is my last working day under G.T. – at least for another four weeks, anyroad." Sure enough, the following Monday morning I was working with another team. The fireman treated me like any other lad and I got my fair share of tackle running. Nevertheless, the next four weeks passed very quickly and before I knew it, it was Sunday evening. I couldn't bear the thought of working under G.T. the next morning. I was agitated, and mentioned it to Dad.

"Get him bloody well reported, our John. He's not allowed to treat you like that, it's victimisation."

"Aye, I know that Dad, but it's not as easy as that. I've got to try and sort it out another way. You never know, I might be going on about nothing, cos he might treat me different this time. Anyroad, if he does send me on the Bluebird, I'll act like I'm not bothered. I'll pretend to be happy about it."

"That's the idea, lad! Don't let the so-and-so grind you down!"

"Right, Dad, you're on. I'll not let him get to me."

No such luck … things didn't go to plan! I'd only just arrived at the pit and was getting changed in the shower room when I heard G.T.'s mocking voice from behind me.

"Aye, look who we've got here! How you going on, Young John Bill you little rat-bag. I hope you're lookin' forw'd to the Bluebird." His face lit up with sheer delight when a few lads started laughing.

I tried to contain my frustration, but realised it was useless trying to reason with this fellow. "Get lost!" I growled, "You're nowt but a bullyboy. I'm gonna report thi."

That didn't help … G.T. just laughed. "Report me … do what you want, you little git, but you're still going on the Bluebird!"

I did complain to the union chap, but was told there was nothing he could do about it. At that, I became very demoralised – it meant me having to put up with the ridicule and, of course, the Bluebird again. I felt like packing the job in, but thought better of it.

"Why should I for the likes of him?" I groaned. "I won't let the bastard grind me down!" Every day that week, I had to attend the dreaded scraper; and the thought of working under G.T. the following week on the back-shift spoiled my weekend. But then, on the Sunday, I had a brainwave.

"I know what I'll do tomorrow," I sniggered. "I'll go in on the morning shift instead of the back-shift … yeah, why not, nobody'll know difference." The more I thought about it, the more convinced I became that it was a good idea.

So I did it, and everything went smoothly … I even got to tackle-drag that shift. However, this was the easy part; the hard part was getting out of the pit undetected by G.T.

I knew that at two-fifteen in the afternoon, each fireman would be stood at the Landing organising his workforce. The shift passed quickly and by two o'clock I had to think of something.

"I've already picked up my round disc, so that's not a problem," I said to myself as I made my way to the Landing, "but getting by G.T. is a different matter. I'll try to blend in with t'other colliers leaving the pit."

When I reached the Landing, my luck was in. To my delight, there were about fifteen full mine-cars waiting to be connected to the loco. "Great," I mused, "I'll be able to sneak out behind them and make my way to th'exit tunnel." I warily made my way forward sneaking from mine-car to mine-car, inwardly congratulating myself on outwitting my foe.

Unfortunately, my little ruse did not come off. Unbeknown to me, G.T was onto my little scheme and was watching out for me like a hawk. Prior to entering the mine, G.T. had noticed that I wasn't there. On checking with the lamp-chap, he'd discovered that I was already in the pit. After weighing up the situation, he'd fathomed out exactly what had happened ... and he was absolutely fuming.

When I reached the last mine-car, I paused a little before making a dash over the last few yards to the safety of the dark tunnel. But alas, G.T. was waiting behind the mine-car and he grabbed me as soon as I made my move. He was a strong man, and literally lifted me off my feet and pinned me up against the rock-face. My helmet fell off and dangled by the wire of my cap lamp.

"You little bastard, John Bill!" he growled, curling up his lips, "so you thought you could gedda way with it, did you? I'm telling you now, you little git, you'd best come in on the back-shift tomorrow, or you're sacked! Aye, and don't just take my word forrit, you little rat, cos I've had a word with the manager about it and he backs me up!" I struggled and tried kicking out, but couldn't get out of his grasp – he was too powerful.

I couldn't move, and had to protest in the only way I could, by shouting, "Get your bloody filthy hands off me! You're the bastard, not me! And I'm tellin thi, if you ever get hold o' me again I'll bloody well kill you when I get bigger!"

G.T. laughed mockingly, and started shaking me. 'When you get bigger, you little swine? Just look at thi, you're nowt but a little wimp – there's nowt about thi!"

I felt intimidated by this thug, and tears welled up in my eyes. My body shook in trepidation, but still, I resolutely stood my ground.

"Yeah, you think you're a big man tackling a little un like me, don't you? Well, I think you're nowt but a bloody coward!" I looked defiantly into his eyes, adding, "And you're wrong. I will get bigger and I'll remember this day for the rest of my life … so you'd better watch out!"

G.T. clenched his fist and the venom showed in his eyes. 'I've a good mind to fist thi right now, you little git … you wouldn't be so bloody fly then, would you?"

"Yeah, why don't you, then? I wish you would!" I taunted, actually willing him to hit me. "At least you'd be off mi back – you'd be goin' down the road then, not me!"

At this point a passing collier interrupted us. "Whoa, hang on a minute G.T.! What do you think you're laking at … you're goin' a bit o'er top wi' Young John Bill, aren't you?"

G.T. had no option but to release me, but as he did so he sneered sarcastically, "Right, you can go now you little bastard, but you'd best remember to come in on the back-shift tomorrow ... you'll be needed on the Bluebird!"

My lips tightened, but I still couldn't resist saying defiantly, "Right, I'll be here. Now get your bloody dirty hands off me, and you'd better not touch me ever again!" I then fired off a contemptuous parting shot, so as to get his back up: "Anyroad, I noticed you never answered that bloke back ... mind, he was as big as you, wasn't he, you bloody coward!" And just to rub salt in his wounds, I added, "At least this is one day that I don't have to work under your stinking authority." I was still trying to incite him to hit me ... I didn't fancy it, but it seemed worth it at the time.

G.T. glared at me and then walked off, snarling obscenities under his breath. I started to walk out of the pit, singing a happy song loud enough for him to hear.

Reluctantly, I made my way to work next day. The scoffing started even before entering the pit.

I was just putting on my cap-lamp when G.T. approached me. "Aye, if it isn't Young John Bill! Have you brought plenty o' bait with you? Cos you're gonna need it on the Bluebird!" I felt my blood boiling, and to make matters worse, even some of my mates seemed to find it amusing.

I felt that I couldn't stand any more of this kind of treatment. But then I got to thinking. "Blow this for a tale," I reasoned to myself, "why should I let him think I'm bothered?" From then on, rather than show my disappointment, I actually expressed my delight when handing over my check.

"Oh great! Another cushy shift on the Bluebird ... I didn't feel in the mood for tackle-running today," I would say cheerfully, adding "it's money for old rope working down the pit, innit?"

I could fair see G.T.'s mind ticking over and sensed what he was thinking – "Does the little swine really like working on the Bluebird or what?"

I added food for thought by whistling merrily as I made my way to the Bluebird. Even the lads got to thinking that I actually enjoyed it, but I wouldn't let onto them – no way! Over the next few months, this was the way of things. But I have to admit, although I felt better about it in some respects, I still hated working on the Bluebird.

Time passed and one day I was tackle-running for another team – Jerry Dawson was the fireman in charge. I had worked very hard this particular shift, carrying tackle for the colliers and was sat down in the Landing having my bait when Jerry approached me.

"I'll tell thi what it is, Young John Bill. You're only little but, by 'eck, you're a bloody good tackle lad. I only wish you was on my team permanently."

I didn't need any prompting. "Oh I'd love that! And I'm sixteen tomorrow, so I'll be able to rotate on nights with you as well."

Jerry pondered for a moment, then replied, "Right lad, I'll see what I can do. I'll see the manager about it first thing tomorrow and fix things up."

I couldn't contain my excitement, and blurted out, "Oh fantastic – that's the best news I've had since coming to the pit!"

"Whoa, hang on a bit Young John Bill," Jerry cautioned me, "don't build your hopes up, it's not in the bag yet! One thing I do promise you, though – I'll try my best."

At that moment, I knew how Mum must have felt on her first day in London all those years ago, when Mr Baron had agreed to find her a job in a hotel.

True to his word, Jerry did speak to the manager and the request was granted. I was highly delighted; it was a great birthday present. What made things better still was that two lads in Jerry's team didn't like tackle-running and actually preferred belt-end work. From then on, I became a permanent tackle-runner and I loved every minute of it. I also derived lots of satisfaction from the fact that I would never again have to work under G.T.

Before the week ended, something else happened that added to my delight. Jerry asked me if I would like to work some overtime.

"John Bill, how would you like to start your first night shift on Sunday? You'll get paid double time."

"Sunday night," I replied, a bit puzzled, "but I thought that the pit was shut down then?"

"No, not exactly, John Bill. It's not a working shift but even so every face throughout the pit has to be inspected in case there's been a build up o' gas."

"Oh right, but excuse me for being a bit thick – where do I come in?"

"Ah well John Bill," replied Jerry, "you see … nobody, no matter who, is allowed to go into the pit on his own in case owt happens to him. All you have to do is to give me some backing and moral support, a kind of partner, if you like." I remembered what John Bill Worseley had told me.

"Do you mean that I'll be able to go onto all the coalfaces with you?" I asked, eagerly.

Jerry's reply left me in no doubt as to how he felt about this. "Aye, that's reight lad, but only because you're with me. You know the ruling on this, so let's get one thing straight from the word go. I think you're a good worker and that's why I've picked you for my team, but make no bones about it … if I ever catch you on the coalface without proper authorisation, I'll have thi in front o' the manager afore you can blink … understand?"

That's the way Jerry was – strict but fair – and that's the way I liked it. I enjoyed the shift, as we toured every face in the mine, including those in the lower mountain seam. The lower mountain faces went much deeper into the pit and we had to walk down a steep one-in-four incline to reach them. It was quite a daunting experience because the lower bed faces were only eighteen inches high.

Next morning, after the shift finished, I was having a shower and felt absolutely great. The reason was twofold: one, I'd just completed a double-pay shift, and two, I was eagerly awaiting the arrival of the morning shift workers … G.T.'s team. I purposely waited in the shower until I saw G.T. coming, then I started briskly drying myself, exaggerating my movements so as to be noticed. It worked a treat. It was great to see the look of astonishment on G.T.'s face when he spotted me.

"Hey, what are you playing at, you little rat!" he rapped. "Have you swapped shifts again?"

I just stood there, grinning defiantly. "And wouldn't you like to know?" I replied, with a wry smile.

"I'm warning you, you fly little swine, if you have … you're for the sack!"

I grinned all the more. "Oh haven't you heard? I'm on Jerry Dawson's team now," adding so as to rub salt in the wounds, "yeah, and permanently at that!"

"You lying little rat! I'll have you for this!"

"Please yourself!" I retorted, not being able to suppress the giggles. "Eh, I'm surprised you haven't heard about it … has nobody told you?" I felt absolutely great. G.T.'s bottom lip tightened, and his face became a bright red mask as it screwed up. At that moment, Jerry happened to be passing.

"Hey Jerry," growled G.T., "is it true you've taken this little wimp onto your team?"

Jerry, who'd noted the mocking tone in G.T.'s voice and the angry look on his face, answered quite coolly. "Yeah, that's right G.T., he's the best little tackle-runner in the pit. I'm surprised you didn't snap him up afore I did."

The look on G.T.'s face said it all ... my victory was complete. All the grief that he'd given me was now in the past and at that moment, everything seemed worthwhile. Ironically, shortly afterwards, G.T. left Thorney-Bank Pit to go working in a coal mine in South Africa. As for me, I never again went on the Bluebird.

9

LEISURE TIME

During my free time, I loved nothing better than going to Sandygate Youth Club, which stood at the junction of Trafalgar Street and Sandygate. And what a club it was, an ideal place for teenagers to congregate in the evenings and Sunday afternoons, having many facilities – including table-tennis, snooker and dancing – and even held a special physical training night, which included weightlifting. Three lads from Trafalgar took a great interest in weightlifting and carried off a few trophies in the Lancashire championships. Two of them, Terry Carter and John Topping, lived on Bedford Street, and the other one, Billy O'Connell, lived in the local barber's shop, near the corner of Sandygate. All three were highly competitive and did exceptionally well in their chosen sport.

Some of the lads took up boxing under the expert eye of Derek Clarke, an ex-boxer. Derek Gallagher, a well-built lad, was really keen on this sport and fared very well.

"Blooming 'eck!" I remember thinking as I watched him sparring fiercely in the ring, "I wouldn't fancy doing three rounds wi' Derek."

I will never forget the one and only time I ventured into the ring. My opponent was called Les Holroyd and he was about the same age as me.

"How do you fancy sparring three rounds with me?" he asked one day.

Les was the same height as me, but not quite as stocky.

"Yeah, why not," I replied, feeling cocksure that I could easily beat him. That was my undoing. Whether Les had done a bit of boxing before, I don't know ... what I do know is that he taught me a lesson that I remember to this day. He was a left-hander, better known in boxing circles as a southpaw, and therefore led with his right hand. I couldn't get through his defence at all and every time I tried to land a punch, his right fist jabbed forward, catching me time and time again on the nose. Those three three-minute rounds were the longest minutes of my life. I was absolutely outclassed, and never ventured into a boxing ring again.

The youth club also had a splendid football team. Martin Grogan, a regular team player, was renowned for his footballing skills and was a prolific goal-scorer for the club. Being a great player, Martin was an automatic team choice. I enjoyed playing football too, but with names like Derek Duerden, Billy Kershaw, Frank Neville, Roy Swift and other talented players, I was never good enough to gain a regular team place, and usually participated as a reserve. One game in particular, which I watched from the sidelines, is very memorable, for obvious reasons: Sandygate Youth Club played the Boys' Brigade and won 53–0, a record that stands to this day. Roy Swift created another record, which earned him a place in the *Guinness*

Book of Records ... he actually scored twenty-seven goals. The amusing thing was, Jack Preston, the opposing goalkeeper, finished up getting an award for his performance. Jack received his unenviable prize from Sam Bartram, Charlton Athletic's goalkeeper, during a televised edition of *Sports Round-Up*. All the members of Sandygate Youth Club were glued to their television sets that night, as the famous goalkeeper presented Jack with a leather football.

As Sam Bartram handed over the football, he asked, jokingly, "Well lad, what do you think about letting in fifty-three goals?"

"Well it could have been a lot more," Jack replied cheekily, "cos I made a few good saves!"

"Aye, I suppose it could, lad," laughed Sam, "I suppose it could."

It was in the youth club that I learned how to bop. Les Harrison and Brenda Taylor merrily bopped the night away, and good they were too. They complemented each other well on the dance floor – and in other ways as well ... it wasn't long before a courtship began.

Alan Billington, the club leader, came up with many ideas for generating lots of healthy competition between the club members, creating a good atmosphere. I was quite a good table tennis player, but never good enough to get into the first team. The 'A' team consisted of George Wilton, Brian Bunting, Jazz Wilkinson and Ralph Foster; all four were masters at the game, winning every trophy in sight. Still, I was content to be picked for the 'B' team alongside Granville Town, Derek Ratcliffe and Alan Carter. I had just turned sixteen and the other three were of a similar age.

Derek and I became very friendly and spent many happy hours competing against each other at the club and also at

Ken Stanley's Table Tennis Hall. One Sunday night we had a longer game than usual, because, being well-matched, neither of us could gain the upper hand.

I'll never forget our parting words as I walked along Trafalgar and Derek made his way towards Lord Street.

"Eh, I'll tell you what John," said Derek excitedly, "that were a bloomin' good session o' table tennis, weren't it?"

"It was that, Derek. I can't wait till next Sunday to give you another good whopping."

"Whaddaya talking about," he replied, "aren't you coming down the club tomorrow night?"

"I can't, Derek, I'm on the flamin' back-shift this week," I complained, "so I won't be getting home till nearly eleven o'clock every night."

"Oh bloomin' 'eck John, just when we were getting into our stride. Still, never mind … I'll see you next Sunday. But there'll be nowt for you cos you'll be a bit stale not being able to practise for a week."

"Yeah, sure Derek, just you wait and see," I joked. "Anyroad, I'll see you later … so long."

"Don't forget what I said, Johnny," shouted Derek, after walking about twenty yards, "there'll be nowt for thi next Sunday … ha, ha, ha!"

I laughed and waved in acknowledgement. However, I will remember that conversation for the rest of my life. The next day when I got home after completing my shift, Dad was in the house.

"All reight Dad, have you had a good day?" I asked, cheerfully.

"I have, our John," he answered, solemnly, "but there's one young lad, who lives on Lord Street, who hasn't. Poor lad's been killed at th'end of Trafalgar on the corner of Manchester Road."

"He-ey Dad, what happened?" I asked.

"Well, from what I can gather, he was delivering some meat on a butcher's bike and was run over by a coal wagon!"

"A young lad, a butcher's bike ... lives on Lord Street," I thought ... then the horrible truth started to dawn on me! "Oh no Dad ... they didn't call him Derek Ratcliffe, did they?"

"Aye our John, they did ... why, do you know him?"

I didn't have to answer; it was obvious by the expression on my face ... I couldn't believe what I'd just heard.

Dad noticed the shocked look and tried to comfort me. "E-eh, I'm sorry our John, I didn't realise he was a friend of yours."

"Yeah Dad, he's the lad I kept talking about every night last week when I came home from the youth club." Dad was very sympathetic and tried his best to comfort me but, all the same, I still felt really upset.

Young Derek was buried from his own home a few days later. It was the first time in my life that I had been badly affected by a death. Sadly, it was not to be the last.

* * *

I never played snooker much at Sandygate Youth Club, but I did like the occasional jive. The rock 'n' roll era had arrived in Burnley, and local interest reached fever pitch as films such as *Love Me Tender*, *Loving You*, *Jailhouse Rock* and *King Creole*, all starring Elvis Presley, were shown at the local cinemas. One occasion that all the local teenagers of the time were to remember occurred when the film *Rock Around The Clock*, starring Bill Haley and the Comets, was shown at the Empire Theatre. When Bill Haley started to sing 'Rock Around The Clock' on screen, lots of teenagers in the audience got up and started to bop in the aisles, while the rest of their peers started clapping and chanting. Up to that point it was all innocent fun, but then some unruly lads went wild and started ripping out seats and throwing missiles through the air; inevitably, fighting ensued. Luckily, nobody was badly hurt but, all the same, an enormous amount of damage was caused to the theatre. This particular event was the main topic of conversation in teenage circles and during the next few weeks, the same pattern repeated itself. Things settled down, and life eventually returned to some kind of normality. However, rock 'n' roll was here to stay; bopping had taken on a new meaning.

Going to the pictures was a popular pastime, and it was commonplace to see long queues at the cinemas every Saturday and Sunday evening. An up-and-coming film actress named Marilyn Monroe was making a name for herself at the time, in films such as *Niagara* and *The Seven Year Itch*. She'd only recently come to stardom and was every young lad's dream – mine included. I had a large photograph of Marilyn pinned up in my bedroom – a famous image from *The Seven Year Itch*, in which she is standing over an outside air vent, with the skirt of her dress billowing up around her waist, showing her undergarments. She became the ideal woman for me and millions of other teenage lads like me.

*   *   *

It was a great time to be young. We had several good dance halls to frequent in the local area. The 'Arcadians' was run by Sam Clegg, an ex-dancer who, with his wife, had won various competitions. Upon retiring from the dancing scene he hired a room underneath the Roxy Picture House and opened it as a rock 'n' roll venue for teenagers and this lively place soon became very popular with us young ones, who referred to it as 'goin' down th'arcs'. Sam was a trusting man and, if any teenager didn't have the admission price he would waive the cost till a later date … nobody ever let him down.

The last record of the night was titled 'Sam's Song'.

> Here's a happy tune
> I love to croon,
> They call it Sam's Song.

From the Arcadians we progressed to the 'Big Band Sound'.

The Empress Ballroom and the Nelson Imperial were the 'in places'; both staged live bands, featuring famous stars such as Cleo Laine and Johnny Dankworth, Eric Delaney's Band, Ray Ellington, Alma Cogan and many more. Every Saturday night, young folk flocked to these popular venues from far and wide, creating a wonderful atmosphere.

I worked at the pit and for me, like other teenagers, the weekend was the highlight of the week – especially Saturday night. I'd meet up with my friends, Ronnie Hopkinson, David Whittaker, Pete Holroyd, Pete Fletcher, Billy Pounder and Barry Birks. All spruced up in our Teddy Boy suits and our Tony Curtis hairstyles with a D.A. at the back, we'd strut down Albion Street like bantam cocks. Our first port of call was the Nelson Hotel. where there was always an air of friendly rivalry. After playing darts, we'd make our way to the dance hall. Once inside, the atmosphere was absolutely electrifying. Occasionally, tensions rose among some of the lads and a fight would ensue. But the local bouncer – Tommy Kenny, an ex-boxer – would quickly sort things out.

The air pulsated with energy from hundreds of young folk; it was the ideal time for chatting up the girls and asking them for a date, especially on the dance floor. I wasn't too bad at rock 'n' roll dancing, but when it came to the waltz, quickstep or slow foxtrot, I was hopeless, and as I was shy, the opportunity to chat up a girl eluded me. Still, one time during a waltz, I did finally pluck up the courage to ask a girl if she'd like to go to the pictures with me on Sunday night. The girl's name was Mary McCulloch, and very nice she was too. I arranged to meet her under the clock in the Town Centre. We went into the best seats upstairs at the Odeon and afterwards I walked her home to her house on Annie Street near Burnley Football Club. I liked Mary a lot, but as I wasn't a good conversationalist, we spoke very little – and sadly, that was the end of what might have been a romantic friendship ... I didn't even get a kiss.

* * *

The fifties were great years, especially for teenagers and I relished every moment.

However, I had a bad experience with the local milkman that dampened my ego, making me feel humiliated and even ashamed. For reasons of my own I'll call him Harry Black.

He delivered milk to most households on Albion Street and his mode of transport was a horse and cart. He used to tether the horse to the lamppost outside our house and many a time I fed it a carrot.

Harry was in his early thirties and renowned for his fine physique and reputation of serving in the Royal Marines, a commando outfit. He was in peak condition and as strong as an ox.

The incident happened one Saturday night after enjoying myself dancing in the Empress Ballroom to the sound of Ted Heath and his band. All my mates had clicked, leaving me a bit despondent as I made my way home.

"Not to worry," I thought, "better luck next time. Anyroad, I'm starving … I'll just take myself off to the chippy for some nosh."

The chippy was next to the Coach And Horses Pub about two-hundred yards from the dancehall. As I stood in the queue I noticed Harry in front of me. "All reight young fella," he said cheerfully, "you're a Trafalgar Waller aren't you?"

"Yeah I am," I responded, "I live on Albion Street … it's on your milk round."

"I thought I knew your face. Anyroad, you look as if you've enjoyed yourself … have you been dancing?"

"Yeah I have," I gloated, "I've been down th'Empress with some o' my mates … it's absolutely great down there."

"Your mates," he queried, "how come they're not with you?"

"'Cos the lucky sods have all got fixed up … I'm the only one who's missed out. Never mind eh … I'll just have to settle for a fish and chip supper."

"You could do a lot worse lad," he chuckled, "at least you'll not get into any trouble, eh?"

"Aye, you could be right there," I said, stuffing a chip into my mouth, "but a chance would have been a fine thing. Anyroad, I'll be seeing you … so long."

"It's a long way to Albion Street," he said as I attempted to pass him, "I'll give you a lift if you want … my car's parked on t'other side of the road."

"Yeah, fair enough Harry," I replied, not thinking anything of it, "that'll be great."

I felt comfortable with the situation until we'd crossed the road and I couldn't see any sign of a car. He started to walk towards a large expanse of derelict ground at the back of the Odeon Cinema where large steel factory boilers were stored. As a child I'd played amongst these gigantic boilers and knew that the canal ran just beyond them. The spare ground had no lighting and the Odeon cast a dark shadow over the area making it pitch black.

As he walked into the eerie darkness I got strong vibes telling me he was up to no good but I couldn't put my finger on why I felt this way.

"There's no way I'm going behind them boilers with him," I thought, "I don't even think he's got a car ... maybe he just wants to try it on with me."

"Are you coming then?" he said interrupting my thoughts. "My car's over yonder near to the canal."

"U-umph, no way," I mumbled, "on your bike!"

"What's that?" he shouted.

"Oh nowt, Harry," I lied, "I've decided to leg it home ... it's a nice night and I need some fresh air."

I took my leave, walking sprightly back past the dancehall towards the town centre.

I'd just reached Manchester Road when Harry pulled up alongside me in his car.

"Well lad," he said, leaning over and unwinding the passenger window, "d'you want a lift or what ... th'offer's still on?"

I felt shamefaced for mistrusting him ... he really did have a car after all. My confidence restored I accepted the lift and got into the passenger seat. I felt relaxed as he laughed and joked, driving up Manchester Road; but I started to feel uneasy again when he speeded up, driving past Trafalgar.

"Whoa Harry!" I shouted. "You've passed my turning ... can you drop me off at Piccadilly Road instead?"

Paying me no heed he put his foot down on the gas and sped for the outskirts of town.

"What are you doing?" I spluttered in panic. "Let me out ... you're taking me miles out of my way."

"Eh, don't worry about it lad," he said smarmily as he put his hand on my leg, caressing the inside of my thigh, "I'm taking you to a great nightclub in Rawtenstall where we can have a ball."

I was now frightened and my fear intensified, as my initial feelings were confirmed. The thought of being driven into the open countryside by this man terrified me, but I kept my wits about me ... I knew I had to think of something quick. We were fast approaching the summit traffic lights and I prayed they would be on red. I knew that the bleak moors of Crown Point lay beyond and had visions of this monster having his wicked way with me. To my utter dismay they were on green and he sped through them.

"Come on John, think of some't afore it's too late," I prayed. I was young, strong and fit but I knew I was no match for this powerful man.

By God's grace or intervention it came to me that I had to play him at his own game. Luckily there was a tiny slip road that turned back on itself just before the Bull and Butcher Pub.

"Harry," I said nudging him and giving him the eye, "if you really want a good time I know a fantastic place in Padiham. Just turn down this snickit onto Rossendale Road and I'll take you there."

To my relief he took me at my word.

"Great!" he said turning the corner on two wheels. "Now you're talking."

"Thank goodness for that," I thought sighing with relief, "at least it's given me a little leeway."

I knew I had to keep calm but inwardly prayed that the traffic lights at Rosegrove would be on red. No such luck ... they were on green and he sped through the interjection at breakneck speed as he had done the previous one. Now I really began to panic as my chances of escaping were running out, knowing full well that once we reached Padiham he would call my bluff.

As he accelerated towards the Padiham Road T junction I geared myself up mentally to risk life and limb by jumping out of the car rather than let this evil pervert get his filthy paws on me. I was still a virgin and terrified of being abused by this depraved monster ... the very thought repulsed me. My thoughts raced wildly as I pictured myself lying dead in some moorland ditch. I placed my hand on the door handle in preparation for a quick exit, but then Lady Luck smiled on me. A large wagon was speeding down Padiham Road and forced Harry to slow down.

I didn't need any coaxing ... in a flash I nipped out of the car and ran like a bat out of hell; Roger Bannister couldn't have caught me. I made for the nearest field, bolted over a wall and crouched in a corner like a frightened rat. I shook uncontrollably and couldn't for the life in me move ... I was rooted to the spot, cold and bedraggled but I remained there until dawn. I didn't dare lift my head for fear of seeing his beady eyes bearing down on me. Before I took off I scanned the area in every direction ... my adrenaline was pumping and I was ready to bolt at the first sign of danger. As I made my way home I felt jittery and kept looking over my shoulder.

Even though I came out of my ordeal unscathed bodily it affected me inasmuch as I felt ashamed and never mentioned it to a living soul for many years. I was the innocent victim and shouldn't have felt this way ... but I did. Like a lot of victims of this kind of atrocity I felt I was to blame ... had I encouraged him in any way by giving out the wrong signals? But clearly I hadn't ... I was just a normal young lad enjoying a good night out. In my anguish I thought about women who had been the victims of sexual abuse and how terribly helpless they must feel.

"There but for the grace of God go I," I thought.

I kept the secret to myself for fear of being ridiculed by my work colleagues and friends. The stigma of guilt, shame and humiliation stayed with me into my adult life ... and even then I shuddered at what might have happened.

I never set eyes on Harry again ... he'd most likely absconded, thinking I would report him to the police. Looking back I should have exposed him but I was too ashamed and lacking in confidence.

Ironically, I later saw some graffiti on the wall of a public toilet, which read:

'HARRY BLACK THE BUMBOY!'

"U-um," I thought, "he must have been trying it on elsewhere ... I'm not the only one who knows about him."

* * *

I was a good swimmer but my mate, Peter Holroyd, who lived on Albion Street just above the railway bridge, definitely had the edge on me, both in speed and stamina. We were very competitive and every Saturday morning went to the Central Swimming Baths. The two of us could easily swim a length underwater, but Pete would always turn and swim that extra couple of yards more than me.

"I'm gonna swim two lengths o' this flamin' pool underwater if it kills me," said Pete one day.

"Yeah me too," I replied, 'but I don't think it'll be for a while yet … I can just about manage a length an' half."

"I'll tell you what John … you dive in first and see how far you can get and then I'll try to beat it." This set the course of events at the swimming pool during the following weeks, and we both gradually improved.

The length of the pool was divided into five segments by four dark lines running across the breadth. Each one of us in turn would swim as far as he could, but if I swam to the third line, Pete would reach the fourth when it was his turn, and so on. Neither of us smoked, so we were both in peak condition and it wasn't long before Pete broke the two-length barrier. A healthy competitive spirit built up between us and I was determined to beat him eventually. Then one day I too broke the two-length barrier; my lungs seemed near to bursting but I knew that if I was to beat Pete's record I had to carry on. Somehow I managed to turn and actually made it to the second line. Not to be outdone, Pete dived in and not only passed my mark but also carried on to the third line. That was it … I realised I could never beat Pete at this game. Afterwards, it became routine for us both to swim two lengths underwater.

*　*　*

I had a good set of mates and we all knew how to enjoy life without doing anything stupid. But like most teenagers we sometimes went a little bit over the top. We certainly enjoyed our weekends in Burnley and Nelson, however we also had something else – something fantastic – at our disposal: the 'Four o'clock Special'. This was a special train, so called because it was laid on specially every Saturday evening and would leave Central Station at four o'clock, heading for Blackpool. We couldn't afford to go every week but made a pact to go at least once a month. Every week I'd scrimp and save, putting some of my spending money to one side, but it was worth every penny – when we got to Blackpool we always had a ball.

One Saturday afternoon after a game of football, Ronnie asked me, "Whattaya doing tonight John, are you going down th'Empress?"

"Am I 'eck as like, Ronnie, I'm going to Blackpool on the four o'clock special with David, Pete, Barry Birks and Billy Pounder ... are you not coming?"

"Oh aye, I forgot. It doesn't seem two minutes since the last time we went ... time flies, don't it?"

"Well it's four weeks since. I should know, I've bin skint for the last month."

"Bloomin' 'eck, I'd best get mi skates on and get home to get ready."

"You'll be all right Ronnie, there's bags o' time ... it's only three o'clock and we don't have to catch the train till five-past four at Barrack's Station.

Ronnie was ready with time to spare and meeting up with our other mates on the platform, all dressed up in our glad rags, we boarded the train that was almost full with other excited teenagers, all raring to go. A load more boarded at Accrington and by the time we reached Blackburn the train was bursting at the seams.

"Great ... I can see the Tower," bellowed Ronnie, as the train got nearer to Blackpool, "we're gonna have some fun in there tonight."

The excitement built up as we pulled into the station; many lads opened the carriage doors and jumped off the train before it came to a stop, eagerly making their way along the platform.

"I'm starving," said Ronnie, "I could eat a scabby donkey."

"Aye, so could I," put in Billy. "Are we going to that little chippy near to Central pier?"

"Yeah why not," I said, "we allus get good grub in there."

After a plate of fish, chips and mushy peas, we all made our way to the Western Bar on the Pleasure Beach.

"It's a great atmosphere in here," David said, "I love it."

"It is, innit," said Ronnie, taking a swig of beer, "it's as good as being in Uncle Tom's Cabin."

"Where are we going after," I asked, "to the Tower or the Winter Gardens?"

"Well, I think the Winter Gardens is great," said Pete, "but most of 'em on the train said they were going to the Tower, cos Eric Delaney's playing there."

"Aye, I heard the same thing," said Billy, "they were all saying it should be bouncing in there tonight."

"I'll go along with that," David chipped in, "how about a show of hands?" The vote was unanimous in favour of the Tower.

"Right," said Billy, "now can we get down to some serious supping?"

We had a few pints of beer, then cheerfully made our way along the 'Golden Mile', where hordes of youngsters were happily meandering back and forth between the Tower and the Pleasure Beach. This was a great opportunity to chat up the girls.

"Come on, girls," one or other of us would quip, "get yourselves along to the Tower Ballroom – it's gonna be raving in there tonight. You never know … this may be your lucky night!" Another of our favourite chat-up lines was, "You look gorgeous luv … is there any chance o' borrowing your body for a bop later on?"

When we reached the ballroom, it was packed to capacity; you couldn't move. The dance floor was full of boys and girls, standing shoulder to shoulder. We met up with Bobby Cheetham, Martin Grogan and many others from Burnley, but there were lots from other towns as far afield as Southport and Liverpool, and everyone was there to enjoy themselves.

"Bloomin' 'eck Billy," I said, "you were right when you said it'd be bouncing in here tonight. It's heaving! I can feel the floor going up and down."

The night passed very quickly and the bewitching hour to leave arrived only too soon. We had to leave before eleven o'clock as the last train for Burnley left at eleven-fifteen. Addresses were exchanged between boys and girls and letters would follow. All in all, the atmosphere was wonderful … innocent and naive, maybe, but wonderful all the same.

If a lad didn't make it out on the dance floor he wasn't too bothered … there was always a good chance on the way back home on the train – the 'Passion Wagon'. It was a single-compartment train and once it left the station, the fun began. Lads removed light bulbs from their sockets and threw them out of the window and the 'necking' session began. If a lad hadn't 'clicked', as it was quaintly put, he'd think nothing of climbing out of the window and making his way to the next carriage by edging along a narrow ledge that ran along the length of the train, clinging onto anything to hand. This happened frequently, but in all the times I did the trip I never heard of anyone getting hurt or killed.

"By 'eck," said Ronnie as we walked along Trafalgar after disembarking from the train, "that was a bloomin' good night, weren't it?"

"It was that," agreed David, "you can't beat the four o'clock special, canya?"

"You're right there Dave," I chipped in, "it were well worth all the scrimping and saving – there's nowt like it. I'm looking forward to the next time, if it's only to meet up with them Liverpudlians again … they're reight characters, aren't they?"

"Aye, you're not kidding," Ronnie said as he turned onto Derby Street, "they were really funny. Anyroad lads, I'll see you tomorrow down the club … adios!"

Dave, Pete and I chatted a little under the gas-lamp outside our house, before turning in at about one o'clock in the morning. "What a good day," said Dave. "See you."

* * *

Sunday was a quiet day. Usually, after breakfast, Dad, Jimmy, and I would go round to Peter Barrett's house on the next street for a game of cards. We'd meet up with six other blokes and then get settled down for a long session of three-card brag.

The Barretts were even poorer than the Cowells and their home was forever untidy. Mrs Barrett never threw newspapers away – she used them as a tablecloth and even as make-do curtains. Still, the atmosphere was good and, besides, Mrs Barrett baked the most delicious scones and buns. She'd mix all the ingredients in a large aluminium bowl prior to putting them into the oven and it wasn't long before tantalising smells filled the nostrils, whetting everybody's appetites.

Dad was always very particular and would never eat or drink anything in anybody else's house. Nevertheless, all the others heartily scoffed the buns washing them down with a brew. I too was faddy but all the same, I couldn't resist Mrs Barrett's delicious buns. This went on for months – it became a proper Sunday ritual – but then, one morning, it came to an abrupt end.

It was about quarter to twelve in the morning and Mrs Barrett tapped Peter on the shoulder. "Nip upstairs, our Peter, the jerry hasn't bin emptied yet." Minutes later, to everybody's horror, Peter came downstairs precariously carrying an aluminium bowl – the same bowl used for baking – with all its contents swishing about!

"Will someone open the back door for me," said Peter, unconcerned, "so I can empty this down the lav!"

We all sat there in disbelief, with our mouths open.

The only person to see the funny side was Dad. "Serves thi bloody well right," he murmured to me, revelling in it.

However, thanks to our Mary, Dad didn't get the last laugh. He used to love Mary's baking and looked forward to her special dishes. And that was his downfall.

One day, Mary was in Mrs Barrett's and the kindly lady asked, "How would you like some potato pie, Mary? It's only just come out of the oven." The delicious aroma filled the air, but Mary politely declined, as she'd heard of the aluminium bowl episode.

"No thank you Mrs Barrett, I've just had my tea," Mary excused herself. But, as an afterthought, she added, "I wouldn't mind taking some home for mi supper tonight, though."

"Yeah, righto love, I'll just get you somet to put it in."

Mary couldn't wait to get home to prepare it for Dad along with some vegetables. Sure enough, he came home at the expected time.

"I've made something different tonight Dad, a potato pie with a crust on top," Mary said, slyly, "I hope you like it." He didn't just like it ... he loved it!

"By 'eck our Mary, that were good, did you learn to make it in the cookery class?" Dad asked, after cleaning his plate. Mary composed herself before dropping the bombshell.

"Well no, Dad, in fact, I have a little confession to make; I didn't make it at all ... Mrs Barrett did!"

"Oh, I thought it tasted different. Anyroad, who's Mrs Barrett ... is she one of your cookery teachers?"

"No Dad ... Mrs Barrett, where you go playing cards every Sunday."

"*You what!*" Dad gasped, the awful truth dawning on him. "You mean to say it were med in that bloody aluminium dish of hers?" he grimaced, retching. "A-ar-rgh ... I feel like I'm gonna be sick!"

When Jimmy and I got home, Mary told us what had happened and we both burst out laughing. Dad was not amused!

"Well Dad," quipped Jimmy, "it serves you right for laughing at us ... you've got to admit it's funny."

Mary rubbed salt in the wound, chuckling as she said, "And Dad, you can't deny you enjoyed it ... it must have been the secret ingredients that Mrs Barrett used!"

*   *   *

I was seventeen when I had my first experience as a decorator. One Saturday morning Mum felt rather disgruntled, as the front of the house was looking very shabby and she couldn't affod a tradesman to do the job. I'd always fancied having a go at painting and decorating, so I raised the subject with her.

"I'll do it for you if you want, Mam. I would love to try my hand at painting the front of the house."

"How can you do that, our John," she asked, "we don't have any ladders."

"Oh it'll be all reight, Mam, I'll paint the upstairs window by standing on the window sill. Our Barry said he'll hold the paint tin for me."

"No, you can't do that, you could fall off and hurt yourself or even be killed."

"Don't worry Mam, I'll be all reight, honest!"

Mum was a little reluctant, but after I'd pestered her for a while, she relented. Thirty minutes later I was back from the paint shop with four tins of paint, some putty, a bottle of turpentine, some sandpaper and two paintbrushes.

"Why have you bought four tins?" asked Barry.

"Well, I'm painting th'house black and white, so I need two tins of undercoat and two o' gloss."

"Oh aye, I never thought o' that."

"Right," I thought, "I've never done any painting afore, so I'll start on the downstairs first, for a bit o' practice."

After rubbing the window frames down and re-puttying where necessary, I started to apply the undercoat. The grey undercoat blended well with the white, and I was quite impressed.

"U-um," I said to Barry, "not bad, eh … what do you think?"

"Yeah, I've got to admit it looks a lot brighter already."

"It does, don't it?" I agreed, feeling pleased with myself.

"I wouldn't feel too chuffed yet our John," said Barry, "that's the easy part … you've still got to do th'upstairs window."

"Aye, I know that, don't remind me, our kid. Anyroad, I've figured a way o' doing it and I'm gonna put th'undercoat on this afternoon and the gloss tomorrow."

"I'll believe it when I see it," quipped Barry.

"Come on then, let's get cracking," I said as I made my way upstairs.

"Righto! I'm coming, I'm coming!"

"Well here goes," I said as I lifted up the lower frame of the sliding sash window until it almost touched the head lintel, and then lowered the top frame a couple of inches. "I'm gonna climb out onto the window sill now and get started."

"Why have you lowered the top window and left the lower one a bit short of the lintel," asked Barry. "Wouldn't it have been better if both of 'em were right up to the top to give thi more room to get through?"

"No Barry, I want them open a bit at the top so that I can hold onto somet."

I climbed through the window and hung on precariously with one hand whilst I did the preparation work with the other. I then climbed back into the room.

"That weren't too bad our kid," Barry said, as we chatted over a brew that Mum had just made.

"That's all reight for you to say ... you had the easy job on the inside. Even so, you were a good help, our Barry."

"Yeah I know that, you couldn't have managed it without my advice could you?" Barry joked.

"No, I suppose not our Barry. Anyroad," I continued, as I clambered back out of the window, "now comes the crunch – I need your help to hold the paint tin for me ... here goes ..."

It worked a treat. I painted the woodwork first, followed by the head lintel and then the stone jambs.

"Great!" said Barry. "All you need to do now is paint the window sill."

"Yeah, that should be easy," I said, as I climbed back into the room, "cos I can do that from th'inside o' the bedroom."

"It looks like your little plan to paint th'upstairs window without a ladder's gonna work all right our John. You've only to put the gloss on tomorrow and that shouldn't take too long, cos you wont have to do any more rubbing down."

"Aye, you're right there our kid, it'll be easy peasy, eh! Anyroad, we'll start soon in the morning and seeing that I've now got the hang of it I'll do th'upstairs window first."

"Hey that's a good un our John … got the *hang* of it. Do you get it … *hanging* on? Ha, ha, ha!"

"Ha, ha … very funny!" I quipped back.

Next morning, after going to church, I got started.

"Are you gonna paint th'upstairs first, our John?" asked Barry "It should be a piece o' cake after yesterday."

"That's easy for you to say our kid … you're not the one hanging on for dear life."

Once again I climbed out on to the window sill and everything went well. By three o'clock, I'd applied the finishing touch to the downstairs window and proudly stood back in the cobbled street to admire my handiwork. Jack Bickle, who was passing at the time, stopped to look as well.

"Bloomin' 'eck Johnny!" cracked Jack. "It looks like a Massey's House."

"A Massey's House?" I repeated. "What are you talking about?"

"Well that's the colour scheme of Massey's Brewery, innit," he laughed, "all Massey's pubs are painted black and white."

"I'll have a pint o' bitter," joked Jack Smithson, as he passed the house, "ha, ha, ha!"

"You can laugh all you want, but I think it looks all reight," I said, a little annoyed. "Anyroad, it looks a lot better now than it did afore and a sight better than some o' t'other houses around here."

"Aye it does," said another voice from behind me, "in fact, I thinks you've made a good job of it, lad." Turning round, I came face to face with a small, slim fellow in his late forties.

"Thank you!" I said, a little bewildered. "Do I know you?"

"No lad, I'm not from round here, I live o'er in Nelson. My name's Sam Sykes and I'm a self-employed decorator and I've just been pricing a job up in one o' them big houses o'er the bridge."

"Oh yeah," I replied, a little nonplussed as to why he was telling me this. He soon enlightened me.

"I've got a lot o' work on, lad, and I could do with a good helper ... are you interested?"

"I'd like to," I said, "but I can't. I already have a job workin' down the pit."

"Oh I'm not talking about full-time, I just need someone to help me now and again. Happen you could work for me at weekends or evenings?"

"Yeah, fair enough," I said. "In fact, I'm on the back-shift this week, so I'll be able to help you in the mornings."

"Right lad, if you bring yourself to number 20 at nine o'clock in the morning, I'll find you somet to do."

"Great!" I muttered to myself. "It'll be a bit extra spending money and I'll be able to pick up a few tips on decorating at the same time."

I worked with Sam for about six months. He was a good tradesman and he taught me quite a few tricks of the trade.

Consequently, I did quite a lot of experimenting on Mum's house. The first time I attempted wallpapering was on the staircase, and it turned out really funny. I was working with Sam one day and I asked him what he did with all the short ends of wallpaper when he'd finished a job.

"Well I throw 'em away, they're no good for owt else."

"Oh, can I have 'em then? They'll come in handy in our house."

"You can if you want, but I don't know what you'll be able to use 'em for."

"Waste not, want not!" I thought, "I'll paper the staircase with 'em." Before going home, I asked Sam if I could have a little bit of adhesive to stick them on with.

"Aye, take a packet o' Lapcell, lad. It'll come out of your wages, mind!" he said, jokingly.

I took every short roll that I could – red ones, blue ones and rolls of all colours, even some nursery wallpaper with cartoons on it.

"U-um, it doesn't matter," I thought, "at least they'll brighten the place up. It'll be better than looking at the bare plaster every time I come down the stairs, anyroad."

I did the job one weekend and was proud of it, though Mum wasn't quite so impressed.

"What the 'eck's going on? What sort of wallpapering is that?"

"It's a new style, Mum," I quipped, "it's what they call contemporary."

"Contemporary? I don't know about that," she replied, "all I can say is it's definitely multicoloured ... it looks like Billy Smart's Circus."

"Well, every time you come downstairs now, Mam," I joked, "It'll remind you of Joseph and his coat of many colours."

"It'll do that all right," she replied, holding back a smile.

This was the beginning of my decorating experiences. I remained interested in decoration, and always kept my hand in. In fact, with lots of help and advice from Sam, I became quite the expert.

Sam wasn't only a good tradesman; he was also very witty and comical. He had me intrigued one day with one of his stories and really caught me on the hop. Some kids had just broken a window and Sam was re-glazing it.

"I'll tell you what," he said, "I've glazed a lot o' windows in my time but I'll ne'er forget the time I glazed one for old Mrs Gorton."

"Oh aye," I said, "what happened then?"

"Well," he went on to say, "it were only a small pane o' glass, so it didn't take me long to bed it into the putty, fix it with some panel pins and then smooth the putty off with mi putty knife. After that, I went home for a bit o' dinner. I'd only bin in th'house ten minutes when the phone rang. It was Mrs Gorton and she said that I hadn't smoothed the putty off. I tried telling her I had, but she wouldn't have it. Anyroad, sure enough, when I got back on to her house, the outside putty was missing."

"So you had forgotten to do it, then?" I asked.

"Well I wasn't sure, so I just re-puttied it and went back home. I'd only just taken mi coat off when the phone rang again. I couldn't believe mi ears … guess who it was?"

"Mrs Gorton?" I asked, curiously.

"Aye it were, and she said that I still hadn't put any putty on th'outside o' the glass. I telt her that I'd just left her house ten minutes ago but she wouldn't have it. She said she were there now and insisted there were definitely no putty on th'outside of the frame. When I got back to her house I couldn't believe it … there were no putty in it again. But this time I knew something was going on."

"So what did you do?" I asked, intrigued.

"Well, I re-puttied it again, but this time I hid at th'end o' the block and waited. I could just about see the window from where I was standing and it was about ten minutes afore I saw it … I couldn't believe my eyes."

"Saw it … you saw what?" I asked, now more intrigued than ever.

"It were an animal, weren't it … a bloomin' animal!"

"An animal," I said, all fired up, "what sort of an animal?"

He looked serious for a moment, then burst out laughing before coming out with the punchline, "It were a putty cat, weren't it … a bloomin' putty cat … ha ha, ha, ha!"

I stood there for a few seconds with my mouth open, but then I saw the funny side and joined in the laughter. I liked the joke very much and later used it myself on many of my unsuspecting friends.

* * *

Being an early riser and an outdoor type, some Sunday mornings during the summer months – especially if it was a sunny day – I loved to set off on my bike. I regularly did a circular route to Bacup via Rawtenstall and Stacksteads. One Sunday, I pedalled all the way up Manchester Road, through the traffic lights at the summit, as far as the Waggoner's pub.

"Great," I muttered to myself, "downhill now all the way to Rawtenstall!" There were some flat bits after passing through Dunnockshaw and Crawshawbooth but it was quite easy going. On the downhill stretches I freewheeled, singing out loudly,

> *"Oh what a Beautiful morning,*
> *Oh what a beautiful day.*
> *I've got a wonderful feeling,*
> *Everything's going my way."*

The inspiration for the song stemmed from the fact that I'd recently been to the Odeon Cinema and seen Gordon Macrae in the musical *Oklahoma!.*

After a brief stop in Rawtenstall I headed for Bacup, cycling through Waterfoot, passing through a narrow gorge, which always intrigued me, then Stacksteads, finally arriving at 14 Mowgrain View – my grandparents' home in Bacup.

"Hiya Granma," I said, giving her a peck on her cheek.

"E-eh, look who's here, it's our Johnny fro' o'er Burnley … come here and gimme a kiss."

"All right Granma, how are you?"

"All the better for seeing thi lad … sit thisen down and I'll mek thi a nice cuppa tay and tha can have one o' mi buns."

"Great, Granma … what d'you think I've come all this way for?"

"Go on, you cheeky young monkey!"

I laughed a little, "I'm only kidding Gran … you know how much I like to see you. Mind, I do really love your buns, cos nobody in the world bakes 'em like you do … I think they're smashing."

"Never mind the bleedin' buns, lad," put in Grandad, "how about coming and havin' a word wi' me?"

"Right, Grandad, how are you feeling … a bit better than last weekend, I hope?"

"Never mind me, lad ... how about thi?"

"Ah well, I've got to check up on you, Grandad, cos mi mam were a bit worried last week when I told her you weren't so well."

"Oh aye? Well think on tha tells her I'm all reight when tha gets home today ... I don't want mi lass worrying none, she's got enough on her plate as it is."

"Righto Grandad, I promise. Anyroad, while I'm here, is there any chance of you telling me any more tales of when you were in the trenches during the First World War?"

"By Gum, our John, you're more inquisitive than a cat. Nobody else asks me any questions about the war like you do."

"Well that's cos you make it sound so interesting, and anyway, I'm proud of you, Grandad."

"Nay lad, there's nowt to be proud of, we were out there cos we had to be. Another thing – many a good lad died out yonder ... u-um, a sheer waste it was!" His face turned a little sad and his voice lowered as he added, "Aye, and many a mate o' mine died since cumin' home from that blasted war!" I loved to catch him in this kind of mood when he'd relate to me some of the horrors of the First World War.

"U-um, I know you don't always like talking about it, Grandad, and I know it makes you feel really sad, but that's one of the reasons why I'm proud of you ... you went through so much."

"Aye, all reight, our John, but that's enough for today ... I'm not feeling up to any more. Mind, you'd best not tell your mam that."

I just laughed and left it at that. I loved his stories, but I knew when to back off. I stayed a little while longer then bade them farewell.

"Ta-rah Gran, see you next weekend, please God ... same to you, Grandad."

"God bless you, our John ... give our love to everyone o'er in Burnley, said Granma. And think on ... tek care when tha's cycling back o'er them tops," she shouted, waving from the doorstep.

In spite of a steep two-mile uphill gradient passing through Weir as far as the Deerplay Pub, I always enjoyed the trek back. On reaching the Deerplay, I took a short respite admiring the beautiful countryside. I loved nothing more than to sit down on a grassy verge and take in all the scenery.

"Just look at the beauty all around, as far as the eye can see ... what a contrast to working down the pit all week." I took a long, deep breath breathing in God's good fresh air to the very depths of my lungs. "By 'eck but it's good to be alive," I mumbled, adding, "u-um and especially when I'm on my bike and I can freewheel it all the way back to Burnley."

Then, to my amusement, I saw a baby rabbit hopping by just a few yards in front of me and became intrigued and wanted to get a bit closer. So as not to frighten it, I crouched down onto my hands and knees and started to stealthily crawl nearer. Too late ... the little rabbit spotted me and scurried off over the moor. It was then that I spotted a piece of coloured paper crumpled up amongst the tall grass.

"Can that be what I think it is?" I thought, feeling a tinge of excitement. On unfolding the small scrap of paper, my suspicions were confirmed ... it was actually a pound note! I was highly delighted.

"Yeah, great, fantastic ... what a good do!" I whooped, "that's two weeks' spending money ... I'm loaded!"

I niftily sat astride my bike and set off as happy as a lark, singing the second chorus of my song as I freewheeled the long downhill journey home:

"There's a bright golden haze on the meadow
There's a bright golden haze on the meadow.
The corn is as high as an elephant's hide,
It looks like it's climbing clear up to the sky.
Oh what a beautiful morning,
Oh what a beautiful day.
I've got a wonderful feeling,
Everything's going my way,
O-oh what a beau-tiful da-ay!"

When I reached home, I had a sandwich and a swig of pop and then couldn't wait to set off again, but before doing so, I mentioned my good fortune to Mum.

"Anyroad Mam, here's ten bob here for you … it'll help you to get by till next week."

She was extremely grateful, making it obvious in the way she knew best: "E-eh, I'll tell You what it is, God … none of my kids have much, but whenever they have anything they like to share it with me."

I interrupted her little invocation. "Right, Mam, I'm going now … I'll see you later tonight."

"Are you off again so soon, our John," she asked, "you never stop in th'house for long, do you?"

"Not on a nice day like this, Mam. We don't get many … I've gotta take advantage while I can."

"Aye, I suppose you're right there. By the way … how was my dad this week?"

"Oh he was all right Mam, he seemed much better."

"Are you sure? You're not just saying that cos he told you to?"

"No Mam, honest!" It was a white lie, but what else could I say? "U-um," I thought as I pedalled off, "she's a right wise ole bird, mi mam is … she misses nowt."

By the end of the day, I'd covered a lot of the surrounding countryside and loved every minute. Before going into the house, I looked down Albion Street at the beautiful clear red sky. Even though we lived right in the very heart of the Weavers' Triangle, I was still taken aback in awe. I was mesmerised by the sight of Pendle Hill in all its glory, dominating the background. The lights from the looming factories contrasted with the sultry hills in the distance and were testimony to the insignificance of man in comparison to the majesty of nature. I gazed in wonderment at the glory of the sunset and pondered over the beauty of the night. The setting sun and the beautiful red sky were a sweet contrast to the clusters of chimneys and soot-stained buildings. It struck me that nature makes no distinction between rich or poor … it is there for all to enjoy.

"Even amongst all the large ugly factories," I said to myself, "the beauty of God's creation comes shining through."

*   *   *

I was always intrigued by the way the older women walked the streets dressed in clogs and shawls. Many were only in their early forties, but looked much older because of their attire. They made me laugh, as they clip-clopped along, especially when they came out with their comical expressions: "By gum, just hark at him"; "Naythen luv, just keep tha pecker up"; "I'm just tekkin misel off to petty", and many more.

One day, just as our Mary had got home from a date, our Barry came out with one of these funny sayings. He wasn't too keen on the lad who Mary had been out with and vented his feelings.

"U-ugh our kid, I didn't think you'd o' gone with him …
I don't like the cut of his jib."

"U-umph, who cares what you like," she replied,
indignantly, "I like him and that's all that counts."

"All reight, all reight, our Mary, keep your hair on … I
was only tellin' thi what I thought."

"Well, keep your opinions to yourself … I'll go out with
who I please. Anyroad, where did you dig that expression
from … 'the cut of his jib'?"

"Eh I don't know, it's just that I've heard loads o' people
saying it. Anyroad, do you know what it means?"

"Do I 'eck as like … I haven't got a clue."

At that moment I happened to be parking my bike in the
lobby.

"Our John's just come in," said Barry, "ask him '

I'd hardly set foot in the living room before she pounced
on me.

"Hey, our John … do you know where the expression
'the cut of his jib' comes from?"

I pondered for a moment, before replying, "I'm not sure,
but I've a sneaky feeling it comes fro' working down the pit."

"How's that, then?"

"Well, the miners on the coalface use a cutting
machine that has a large jib attached to it that undercuts
the coal."

"How do you mean, a large jib?" Mary asked, looking
rather puzzled. "What's a jib?"

Again, I thought a little before answering. "Well, the best
way I can describe it is it's like the long blade of a chain saw
except it's fifty times bigger. It works on the same principle
and has a load of sharp tungsten bits attached, which
undercuts the coal seam prior to it being fired by explosives.
So you see our kid … it's a cutting jib.

"U-um very good … aren't you a clever clogs?"

"Oh aye, a clever clogs am I? All reight then … where does the expression 'clever clogs' come from?"

"I don't know, but knowing you, you'll probably know, Mr know-it-all."

"Hey, don't go on at me our Mary. It were you who asked the question in the first place. Anyroad, go and mek a brew … at least you know how to make a good cup o' tea."

Seeing the funny side, Mary just grinned and went to put the kettle on. We got settled around the fire with our pots of tea and some broken biscuits and the conversation continued.

"Right, our John," said Mary, "now I've got one for you. D'you know where the word 'spinster' comes from?"

"I haven't a clue, our kid, but I've got a feeling I'm gonna find out."

"Too true you are … you're not the only one with a bit o' working knowledge!"

"D'you really know?" put in Barry.

"Yeah course I do … it's to do with working in the mill. Most of the spinners in the spinning department were young unmarried girls and over the years, any young girl who'd reached a certain age and was still single got tagged with the nickname spinster … so there."

"Very good, our Mary," I said to her, "it's a good un is that. Now who's the clever clogs!"

* * *

The following Saturday afternoon, as I cycled to Bacup as usual, I decided to go via a different route, directly over the moors. I was pedalling up Todmorden Road when I saw our Barry and Barbara coming out of the top gates of Towneley Park.

"Where are you going, our John?" asked Barry.

"I'm going o'er to my granma's and mi Aunt Katie's."

"Oh, can we come with you? I haven't seen mi gran and grandad for ages," said Barbara."

"And how the bloomin' 'eck can you do that?" I asked her.

"Well, you can tek us on the back of your bike … you've done it loads o' times with them kids on Trafalgar."

"Aye maybe I have, but don't forget they're a lot smaller than you. And another thing – there's two of you."

"Ar-gh it's not fair, I never get to go anywhere," moaned Barbara.

"Well, I'm sorry, there's not a reight lot I can do about it," I replied, getting ready to set off. I'd only gone a few yards when I stopped and shouted back to them. "Come here, I've got an idea if you're willing to try it out."

"Yeah, go on then … what is it?" they both asked, impatiently.

"Well, you start walking, our Barry, and I'll carry our Barbara on the back of mi bike."

"No way, I'm not walking it all the way to Bacup!" he replied.

"Hang on a minute, our kid, let me finish! I'll drop Barbara off about a mile up the road and whilst she's walking I'll come back for you. Then I'll carry you until we're a mile past Barbara and so on till we reach Bacup."

"U-um, I suppose so … we can give it a try," agreed Barry. "I'm willing if you are." So off I went, carrying Barbara on the back of my bike as far as the Towneley Arms pub. After a short respite, I gave my little sister some brief instructions.

"Reight, our Barbara, now you keep walking up Bacup Road until I pick you up again." As planned, I went back for Barry, picked him up, and started cycling furiously.

"My, our Barbara's done well," I commented, as we passed the Towneley Arms, "she's way up there in the distance."

As we passed Barbara, Barry made some kind of gesture encouraging her on, "Come on our kid, you're doing well." This time I pedalled arduously up the steep gradient until we reached the brickworks.

"By 'eck our Barry that were bloomin' hard work," I groaned. "I'm having a breather afore I go back for our Barbara."

"Righto, our John, I'll get going ... I should be way up the road before you catch me up." It was hard going, but we finally made it over the open moors, reaching the Deerplay Hotel.

"Right, this is where I usually take a breather every Sunday when I'm coming back from Bacup," I said, pointing to the spot where I'd seen the baby rabbit and found the pound note, "so we'll have a short break here before the downhill run." It was downhill all right ... two miles to the centre of Bacup and some of it quite steep.

"Are you two ready?" I grinned. "This is going be fun, cos this time it's gonna be three on a bike." I put our Barbara's coat over the crossbar and she sat on it. I then straddled myself behind her with one foot on the floor and the other on the pedal, ready for the off. "Just make sure you keep your feet on the lower bar so you don't touch the front wheel," I warned her.

"Bloomin' 'eck, this seat's hard!" moaned Barry, as he perched himself behind me and clung on to my back.

"Reighto you two," I laughed, "I'm ready when you are ... let's go!"

What a ride! We sped down the road with the wind blowing in our faces, thoroughly enjoying every minute.

"Yippee," shouted Barbara in sheer delight, "Bacup here we come!"

It was about five o'clock when we reached Grandmother's house. She was very surprised and a little taken aback to see the three of us.

"What the flippin' 'eck's going on," she quizzed, "what aya doing over here at this time?"

"I were coming over to see you on mi bike like I usually do, Granma, and they wanted to come as well," I replied.

"What, you mean to say our little Barbara's pedalled all the way o'er from Burnley on a bike?"

"Oh no, Gran, she's come on the back o' mine."

"Tha's never peddled all the way o'er them moors with her on the back o' thi, surely to goodness!"

"Aye I have Granma ... gospel truth!"

"Oh aye, and what about Barry, then?"

"Yeah, I've brought him as well."

"I don't believe thi," interrupted Grandad, "it's impossible to do that trip wi' three of thi on a bike."

"Oh no, Grandad, there were only three of us on the bike on the downhill stretch coming into Bacup." I went on to explain exactly what had happened.

"By 'eck, that's some feat, our John ... tha must be a fit lad."

"Aye, but don't forget Grandad, I'm used to it cos I'm always pedalling over here, aren't I?"

"Aye, that's reight lad, but there's a hell of a lot o' difference in doing that to what tha's just done."

"Now just hang on a minute," Granma interrupted. "It may well have been a mean feat, but what I want to know is, how long did it take you to get here?"

"About two hours Gran, but don't forget, I had to keep doubling back on myself."

"Two hours ... oh dear," she mumbled, with a frown on her face, "you can't set off back there tonight, cos it'll be dark in less than two hours." She thought about it a moment longer before saying, "Right that's it, I'll mek thi somet to eat then your grandad'll put all three of thi on the seven o'clock bus."

"I can't go on the bus with 'em Gran ... what about mi bike?" I said

"Never mind your bike, I don't like the thought of thi pedalling o'er them bleak moors at night."

"Don't worry about me, Gran, I'll be all right, honest! Anyroad, if I set off twenty minutes afore the bus, I'll be able to wait for 'em both at the bus station in Burnley."

"Aye I suppose so, but I'm tellin' thi now, our John, I don't like it ... I'll be on tenterhooks till I see thi again."

"I'll tell you what then, I'll come and see you again tomorrow morning to put your mind at rest ... how's that, Gran?"

"Go on then, tha could talk a bird out of a tree. Anyroad, afore tha sets off, tha can sit thasen down and have a bite to eat wi' t'others."

I heartily scoffed the lot before setting off back to Burnley. As promised, I waited at the bus station for Barry and Barbara to make sure they arrived safely, and next morning I made my way back to Bacup.

"E-eh, I'm reight glad to see thi our John," Granma greeted me warmly. "I've bin fretting about thi e'er since tha left last night."

"I'm sorry, Granma, I didn't mean to worry you, it won't happen again."

"Oh don't tek any notice o' me," she sighed. "I were a bit cranky yesterday, cos I weren't feeling so well."

"Why Gran, what's up?" I asked, concerned.

"Well, I've got a swollen leg and it's bin giving mi some jip lately."

"Oh I'm sorry to hear that, I'll tell mi mam when I get home." I did tell Mum and, after that, she went over to Bacup at every available opportunity.

As it turned out, my grandmother had phlebitis in her leg and was started on a course of medication. However, despite this, she gradually became very run down and contracted pneumonia, her condition deteriorated rapidly and sadly, she died within two weeks. I was sixteen at the time and completely devastated ... it seemed unreal that Granma would never again be there to greet me. Her memory will remain with me forever.

It came as a terrible blow to everybody in our family, especially Mum, but the person most affected was Matthew, my grandad. My grandmother, Mary, was his whole world; he'd loved her from the moment he'd first set eyes on her, and there was no consoling him. I still went over to see him on a regular basis, but things were never the same. Never again did Grandad ever talk about his time spent in the trenches or anything else for that matter. All he wanted to do from then on was join his beloved Mary.

*   *   *

I bought my first motorbike for five pounds and it looked like it had just come out of a museum. It was antiquated, with solid forks at the front and rusty springs at the back – a real boneshaker. Hand gears were fixed to the right side of the frame, near to the petrol tank.

The first time I took to the road I got a quick lesson in what not to do, as I drove along Trafalgar attempting to change gear without pulling in the clutch. As a result, I went flying over the handlebars and finished up sprawled in the middle of the road. I hurt myself a little, but I was more concerned about the state of my bike. It didn't look damaged, but I couldn't get it to start.

Not to be beaten, I decided to have a word with Malcolm Davis, our next-door neighbour, who was a dab hand at mechanics.

"You must have damaged the carburettor, John," he said, "you'll have to strip it down and give it a reight good cleaning."

"Clean the carburettor … is that an easy job?" I asked.

Malcolm knelt down and pointed to the engine. "Aye, all you have to do is loosen those bolts and that fuel pipe. When you've done that, give everything a good cleaning and then swill the carburettor out with petrol afore you put it back on the bike." I carried out his instructions to the letter and, to my delight, the engine kicked up first time.

"Great, I'm back in business!" I thought, highly delighted. However, my pleasure was short-lived. I'd only gone about two hundred yards when it started spluttering and backfiring and came to a full stop. Once again I went back to see Malcolm.

"U-um," he said stroking his chin, "it seems to me that the timing's off."

"Crikey … how do I fix that, then?"

"Well, I'm afraid it's a bit more tricky this time. I'll tell you what … I'll do it for you and you can watch me for chance it happens again." Malcolm then re-set the points whilst I watched him like a hawk. After he'd finished, I tried kicking it up and once again it started straight away.

"Oh well, here goes," I said with fingers crossed, "let's see what happens this time." I did a full circular straight up Albion Street, left at Scott Park Road, down Manchester

Road and back along Trafalgar. "It's great Mal," I gushed, as I stopped outside his backyard, "it's running like a dream. Thanks a lot!"

Two weeks previously, our Jimmy had bought a 125 BSA Bantam and he was bursting to try it out on a long run. That weekend, Jimmy, Malcolm, Arthur Ratcliffe, Kenny Clayton, and I all set off in convoy for Blackpool. Not to be outdone, a neighbour, Mr Daley, caught us up on his motorbike and asked if he could join us. The six bikes headed off in convoy, with Malcolm up front, motoring along effortlessly on his well-maintained bike. Arthur had just acquired a two-stroke Francis Barnett and he was really chuffed as he put-putted along. The other three bikes ran smoothly, and I chugged along after them with loads of black smoke belching from the exhaust. The others kept making fun of me but I didn't mind. The little bike got me to Blackpool and back and I thoroughly enjoyed it.

During the following months the bike was forever breaking down with one fault or another; but with perseverance and a bit of advice from Malcolm, I became quite adept at repairing it. One day, though, my mechanical knowledge let me down and caused a bit of a stir. I was about to go on a run with Kenny Clayton and Arthur Ratcliffe, but once again the bike wouldn't start.

"Let's take it into the cellar, John, and strip it down," suggested Arthur. "It'll be easier than working out here on the cobbles."

"Aye reighto Arthur, but you'll have to give me a lift so we can do it quicker."

After a bit of a struggle, we had it set up on its stand on the cellar floor ready for working on. Within two hours we'd stripped it down, cleaned the parts and reassembled it.

"That should o' done the trick," said Arthur. "Get it cracked up, John."

"Reight, fair enough ... here goes." I stood at the side of the bike, holding the handlebars with my foot on the kick-start pedal. "Are you ready lads ... the moment of truth!"

I took a deep breath and then thrust my foot down as hard as I could. The bike started all right ... it backfired, making one almighty bang, blowing out thick black smoke and some flames. It took me by surprise, spinning round in circles on its stand, whipping the handlebars from my grasp. Within seconds the cellar was full of thick dense smoke and sparks kept belching from the exhaust.

"Bloomin' 'eck, it's gonna blow up," shouted Kenny, "we're gonna be killed!"

"Let's get outta here whilst we can still see where we're goin'!" bellowed Arthur.

Arthur was the furthest from the door, but he moved so fast that he was outside on the backstreet whilst Kenny and I were still thinking about it. I was the last to leave, as I was concerned about my bike, but I too sensed the danger and decided to follow the others.

"Oh, blow this for a tale, Kenny might be right," I thought, "the bloomin' petrol tank might blow up!"

The bike spluttered for a few more minutes and then ... silence. On re-entering the cellar we couldn't see the motorbike; in fact, we couldn't see anything.

"Blimey, look at all this smoke ... I can hardly see mi hands in front o' me," said Kenny.

"Aye, and it's all going up the cellar steps into the living room," added Arthur.

"A-ah flippin' 'eck, mi mam'll go mad," I panicked, 'I'd better nip up and open all the windows." When I got up to the living room, my worst fears were realised ... the room was full of smoke and it was making its way up to the bedrooms. After opening the front and back door, and every window in the house, I shouted to Kenny and Arthur.

"Quick, get yourselves up here reight away and help me to clean up this mess afore mi mam gets home ... she'll go up the wall if she finds it like this." All three of us got stuck in shaking the pegged rugs and wiping down every stick of furniture. We worked hard and did a decent job, but we couldn't get rid of the smell of smoke. When Mum got home it was evident that something had happened.

"What's been going on here then ... what's been burning?"

"We've had a bit of a soot fall Mam and the chimney set afire," I told her, hoping to stave off the inevitable telling-off. It didn't work.

"Oh yes, and why can I smell petrol then?"

"Well Mam, I ...."

"Never mind well Mam, I want the truth ... have you been starting that bike o' yours up in the cellar?" I knew it was useless lying ... Mam was too canny for that.

"Yeah, I'm sorry Mam, it won't happen again ... I promise you."

"Too true it won't, cos you can get that bike out of the cellar right now ... and keep it out!"

"Oh don't say that Mam, I can't keep it on the backstreet ... it'll go rusty."

"You should have thought of that before you set it off inside the cellar. Anyway, have you no more sense? You could have set the flamin' house on fire."

"Hey, that's a good un, Mam ... you just cracked a joke!" I said, trying to play down the situation.

"What are you talking about ... I cracked a joke?" she asked, a little puzzled.

"Set the *flaming* house ... on *fire*! Get it?"

As she thought about it, a little smile came to her face, "Ha ha, very funny ... but don't think you're getting around me that easy."

Despite her words though, I knew she was weakening. "Oh come on Mam ... I promise thi it won't happen again."

"Use the Queen's English will you, for crying out loud," she corrected me. "I promise *you*, not I promise *thi*!"

"All right Mam, I promise you ... I promise *you*."

She smiled again and relented. "Right, I'll let it go this time, but it had better not happen again ... this is your last warning. Another thing, you'd best get yourself down the cellar right now and clean up the mess. I want the floor shining like a new pin." I happily settled for that – I knew I'd got off lightly.

Thereafter I spent many happy hours on that bike, covering much of the Lancashire countryside. But the thing I enjoyed most was riding up Albion Street, especially when there were loads of neighbours sat on their doorsteps; I felt like Sir Lancelot charging forward on his trusty steed!

Motorbiking was the love of my life during the next two years. The little bike finally gave up the ghost but by then I had saved £60. I'd seen a Triumph 500 speed-twin advertised in the *Burnley Express* for £55. Malcolm Davis went with me for a bit of moral support and expertise and after some negotiation I purchased the bike for £50.

"Great," I thought highly delighted with the deal, "that leaves me enough money to tax and insure it." That bike was the best machine I ever had, a good starter, good on petrol and it never once let me down.

Shortly after procuring the Triumph I put in for my driving test and on the day I was all keyed up but quietly confident. I met up with the driving assessor, a rather surly gentleman, at the Ministry of Transport Office on Nicholas Street.

"Right," he said, "when you set off from here I want you to drive along Grimshaw Street, turn right into Manchester Road then right again at the traffic lights. Drive through the town centre and turn right into Park Lane and right again into Grimshaw Street. Just keep driving around this circuit until I wave you down. During the drive I will test you for an emergency stop. I'm going to intermingle amongst the crowd but when I step to the kerb waving this newspaper, I want you to stop as soon as you can in a safe manner. Do you understand all these instructions?"

"Yes I do," I replied, edgily.

"Right then, off you go."

After the test I felt good, thinking I had driven steadily and done a good emergency stop. All I had to do now was answer questions on the Highway Code, which I did proficiently. I was shocked when the man informed me that I'd failed ... in fact, I was absolutely gutted. The official wouldn't go into any details; he just handed me a slip of paper with the reasons for my failure written on it. The main reason was not glancing behind over my shoulder when signalling to turn right. I felt dejected, but that made me more determined than ever to pass the test. Six weeks later I was there again, but this time I got a different assessor.

"Thank goodness for that," I thought, "this one doesn't look as grumpy as the other chap." All the same, I knew I couldn't take things for granted.

He gave me the same instructions as the other official and, setting off on the same route, I was determined this time to glance over my shoulder ... if anything, I tended to exaggerate the movement. Once again I thought I'd driven well, but this time I wasn't so confident. Then came the Highway Code questions.

"Give me five instances when you can overtake on the inside of a person"; "What is the difference between a road sign with a triangle above it and one with a circle above?" One question was a little more tricky: "If it had been snowing and all the signs were covered in snow ... how could you tell it was a 'Halt at the Major Road' sign?"

I smiled to myself. "Oh, it's shaped like a letter 'T' and the word 'HALT' stands out boldly in the top section of the sign."

"U-um," he muttered, "but what if you can't see the letters because of the snow?"

"Well, like I said, the sign has a definite 'T' shape, which distinguishes it from any other sign on the road.

"Anything else?" he asked.

I faltered a little before I realised what he was getting at. "Oh yeah, it has a circle above it indicating that it's a sign that must be obeyed, unlike a triangle that gives a warning."

The official pondered for what seemed an age before saying, "Right Mr Cowell, I'm pleased to inform you that you have passed!"

Those words were like music to my ears ... I could have kissed the bloke! The first thing I did was to remove the 'L' plates and then I drove up Manchester Road full of the joys of spring, raring to give one of my brothers a ride on the pillion.

A few days later, on Saturday afternoon, a funny thing happened. Our Jimmy and I had just been to Bury on our motorbikes and on the return journey were riding through Crawshawbooth. Dad and his friend Billy Cook had been out on the binge in the Black Dog and they were both tottering at the bus stop as Jimmy and I drove through the village.

Our Jimmy saw Dad and pointed his finger towards the bus stop.

"Bloomin' 'eck!" I thought as we slowed down, "That's mi dad and Billy Cook and they look as if they've had a reight skinful."

"Come on, let's ask 'em if they want a lift back," shouted Jimmy.

"Good idea, our kid," I agreed.

"Hiya Dad … do you want a lift home?" I said, pulling up near to the kerb.

"No way, our John, you must be joking, I'm not geddin on back o' that thing with you … I'm not that drunk!"

"Oh come on, Dad, I'm a good driver … anyroad, you've just missed a bus, so you'll have to wait ages for the next one."

At that, Billy Cook intervened. "Aye he's reight, Barney … you get on the back of him and I'll get on the back o' Jimmy's bike."

"U-um, I suppose you're reight, Billy." Dad inched forward and climbed aboard, muttering, "I only hope I don't regret it later."

"All reight Dad … are you sitting comfortable?" I asked, as he perched himself on the pillion. I set off in low gear as I negotiated the steep hill out of the village, keeping up a nice steady pace until we'd passed through Dunnockshaw. But then … Jimmy came tearing past me with Billy hanging on for dear life! That was it; I put my foot down in hot pursuit, overtaking him in the open countryside prior to reaching the Waggoner's Inn.

"Whoa, slow down, our John … you'll get us bloody killed!" bawled Dad, clinging on even tighter than Billy.

"Righto Dad, that's it, I just wanted to show you what it could do. Not to worry, though … I'll take it steady down Manchester Road." Dad and Billy may have been well canned before they got on the bikes, but they were both stone-cold sober when they got off. Dad was fuming and he gave me a right rollicking.

"You bloody swine, you're nowt else, that's the last time you get me on the back of your flamin' bike!"

"Oh come on, Dad, it were a bit o' fun, weren't it?" put in Jimmy.

"And you can wrap up as well," growled Dad, "He probably wouldn't have gone so fast but for you trying to show off!"

"Oh come on, Barney," said Billy Cook, "there's no harm done … at least they got us home in one piece."

"Aye, I suppose you're reight, Billy," Dad replied, "but there's one thing for sure … I'll never ride pillion with any of 'em again." He never did, either!

* * *

I enjoyed the occasional drink with my mates, but I'll never forget the time that I had my first beer … it proved to be a very memorable occasion. It was a Saturday night and I was all spruced up in my Teddy Boy suit to go dancing down the Arcadian's with my mates Billy Pounder, Ronnie Hopkinson, David Whittaker, Pete Fletcher, Barry Birks and Pete Holroyd. It was David's eighteenth birthday and he wanted to celebrate it in a pub. Billy was already eighteen, but the rest of us were under age.

"How about going for a couple o' pints down town afore going to th'Arc's?" David suggested.

"I'm gam if t'others are," said Barry.

"How about you, John?" asked David.

"Yeah why not ... it should be a bit o' fun," I answered, not wanting to appear a killjoy by revealing that I hadn't drunk alcohol before.

"I know a good pub down the Croft," said Billy, enthusiastically.

"Oh aye, which one?" put in David.

"The Miller's Arms," said Billy, "it's a good pint and you never get any coppers calling in there."

"Reight, that'll do me," enthused David, "come on, lads!"

What a good do it turned out to be ... I really enjoyed myself, playing darts in the taproom and with every drink my confidence increased.

"Here," said David handing me a pint, "get this down you ... it'll do thi good!" By the time we left the pub I'd drunk three pints of Massey's bitter and I felt on top of the world. For the first time in my life I didn't feel shy in the presence of girls. On reaching the Arcadian's I was brim-full of confidence and I chatted openly to the opposite sex, hardly missing a dance and my personality was second to none.

"No wonder mi dad enjoys going for a drink," I thought, "this is great ... I've never felt like this in my life afore." Alas, I overdid it. As the atmosphere built up, becoming warmer and warmer, I began to feel sick and ended up vomiting in the toilets.

"Oh 'eck David," I muttered, "I'm sorry about this, spoiling your birthday an' all."

"Don't worry about it, John," he reassured me, "get it up ... you'll feel better for it!" When I left the Arcadian's I walked around for ages trying to sober up before going home.

"I daren't go home like this, David," I groaned, "if mi mam sees me in this state she'll go up the wall." Luckily she was in bed when I arrived home. But I didn't get away with it altogether ... I had a real ding-dong stinker of a headache the next day!

From then on, we frequented the pubs every Saturday night prior to making our way to the dance hall. We would go the Nelson and the Healey Wood but our favourite venue was the Corporation, close to the Market Square where they sold Scotch bitter, a strong beer and dark in colour, like a Guinness.

One incident that stands out in my mind was the time I went into the Big Window with David Whittaker, Pete Fletcher and Billy Pounder. It was my round and I'd just ordered four pints at the bar when I heard a voice behind me.

"You'd better make that five, lad!"

To my horror, when I turned round, my dad was stood there with a stern look on his face.

"Oh 'eck," I thought, "how am I gonna get outta this? I stood speechless for a few seconds before stuttering nervously, "Well I ... I were just gonna ...."

"Never mind you were just gonna," he joked, a grin spreading across his face, "whaddaya think you're doing in here?"

"Well I ... I ...."

He cut me short again. "I know all about it, our John, I haven't just come in on the banana boat. I'm not thick, so don't try and pull the wool o'er mi eyes."

"It weren't his fault, Mr Cowell," interrupted Pete, "we talked him into it."

"Oh it weren't his fault, were it not ... has he not got a mind of his own, then? Anyroad, while we're on the subject, Peter Fletcher, you're even younger than he is ... how would your dad take to seeing thi in here?"

"Well I ... I'm not sure," stammered Pete, thinking he'd put his foot in it.

"You're not sure, are you not? Well I'll tell thi what he'd do ... he'd kick your britches' arse reight up to Trafalgar!" There was a stony silence for about three seconds, and then Dad started laughing. "Ha ha ha!" he roared, thrusting his glass forward, "Just look at your gloomy faces, the four of you. Anyroad, I'll let it go this time, so long as each one of you buys me a drink." Then. on a more serious note, he turned to me. "Your mam'd better not find out about this, our John, she'd go mad. And while we're at it ... it'd best be the last time I catch thi in a pub until you're eighteen, or you're forrit mi lad!"

* * *

Sunday night was the culmination of the weekend. My mates and I would go to the Empire, Roxy, Odeon, or the Palace etc., and the film usually ended about nine-thirty. Crowds of youngsters would then walk 'The Drag' which stretched about half a mile along St James's Street from the bottom of Manchester Road to the Cross Keys Hotel at the bottom of Sandygate. When we reached one end we'd walk right back to where we'd started from, all the time exchanging glances and greetings with girls, it was very similar to walking the Golden Mile in Blackpool. This was our last chance of the weekend to chat up girls and so we'd promenade up and down several times until everyone gradually dispersed. We'd then make our way home and chat for a short while at the bottom of Albion Street before reluctantly parting.

"Bloomin' 'eck!" David would comment. "Don't time fly when you're enjoying yourself?"

"Ah well, that's another weekend o'er with ... back to flamin' work in the morning," Pete would say.

"Yeah, back to the bloomin' grindstone," I'd reply. "Still ... there's always next weekend to look forward to."

Tackle-Running

I really enjoyed the pit life and was very happy now that I was tackle running for Jerry Dawson. Tackle lads always worked in pairs and my mate was called Pete. Like me, Pete was just sixteen years old. We got on well, working hard together, and made a good team, feeling that we had found our niche. Materials were carried into the pit in the mine-cars and it was our job to empty them and stack everything neatly in the Landing prior to transportation to the coalface. Together with another team of tackle runners, Pete and I had to regularly empty five mine-cars containing bricks, wooden props, steel girders, corrugated tin sheets, large wooden blocks and steel rings, which were roof supports shaped like giant horseshoes. There were many more things including steel telescopic props, each weighing about a hundredweight ... these were called Dowties. This aspect of the job took about three hours and was usually done on a Saturday morning. However, depending on demand, a mine-car could arrive at any given time containing 2,000 bricks and had to be manhandled there and then. The four of us would form a chain, throwing two bricks at a time from one lad to another, which we stacked in a heap. This was no easy task, as they were Accrington Nori bricks, which were notorious for being hard and heavy. In fact, they were the hardest bricks in the world … thus the name 'Nori', which spelt backwards is Iron.

During the course of a day, Pete and I would make two trips to the coalface … one before bait-time and one after. An average load consisted of steel rings, Dowties, bricks and large wooden blocks. The bogies were well constructed but even so, the wheels would buckle under the tremendous weight. The inward journey was uphill for about seven hundred yards, which meant a lot of hard shoving, huffing and puffing. To get the bogey rolling, we had to get well down behind it, place our feet against a wooden sleeper and grab hold of the steel tracks. Placing our heads against the back of the bogey we pushed with every ounce of strength we had, using every muscle in our bodies. Once we'd built up a momentum we didn't dare stop until we got to the top of the incline for fear of not being able to get the bogey going again. As we strained with all our might, sweat dripped off the end of our noses. At the top of the incline we'd have a breather before resuming the downhill run. This was quite steep in parts and so we locked the bogey's wheels with a sprag in order to stop it running out of control as we held it back with a long rope. On our first day some colliers were waiting for us at the end of the track. Pete and I had already discussed the matter of 'pey-brass' and decided that I would be the spokesman. Right away one of the colliers broached the subject of carrying the tackle as far as the coalface.

I remembered the advice that John Bill Worseley had given me, and took this as my cue to bring up the matter of pey-brass.

"U-um, I don't know about that," I said winking at Pete, "we're not allowed to go any further than th'end o' this track ... you know that."

"Oh come off it, John Bill, you know only too well that t'other tackle-draggers do it," moaned one of the colliers.

"Aye, maybe they do, but that's up to them, isn't it? I don't want the sack."

"How about if we give you some pey-brass at th'end of the week ... say a shilling from each of us?" the collier said, with a smirk on his face.

"You must be joking!" I retorted, "The going rate is half a dollar each ... not a shilling."

"Aye, but you're only little lads and, anyroad, you've only just started."

"What difference does that make? It'll be bloomin' hard work humping all the tackle to the face," I pointed out, "surely, if we get the job done that's all that matters to you?" The colliers soon found out that, despite my size, I wouldn't be put upon.

"Aye, reighto John Bill, but you'll have to work a week in hand, same as you did for your wage."

"No way!" I responded immediately, "We work for you this week ... you pay us this Friday!"

"Bloody hell! I can see nobody's gonna pull the wool over your eyes, lad," interjected another collier.

"And why should they?" I answered back. "A fair day's pay for a fair day's work, that's what I say."

Just then the main belt stopped and a load of colliers came off the face and sat down in the main gate.

"Come on John, it looks like it's bait-time," said Pete, "let's go and squat down with 'em." As we all sat together, the colliers who had negotiated with me, told the others what had been said.

"You cheeky young buggers," blurted out a few in unison, "you're only apprentices ... you've got to prove yourself first!"

"Whoa, hang on a minute fellas!" put in Tommy Lowe, a union representative. "Let's give the lads a chance to see if they come up to scratch. If they don't ... they don't get paid. On t'other hand, if they prove worthy ... they deserve half a dollar."

Some agreed, though not all.

"No, I don't go along with it ... they're too inexperienced," moaned one collier as he took a bite out of his jam butty ... "I think it's too much!"

"Aye you would, you tight swine Archie ... everybody knows you could split ha'penny in half," quipped Tommy.

"Never mind about that," he snorted, "if I'm gonna have to give half a dollar, I want mi money's worth!"

"Yeah we know that ... that's what we all want," stressed Tommy. "I'll tell thi what ... let's have a show of hands." Much to Pete's and my pleasure, the vote was almost unanimous in our favour. The only dissenter was Archie. He mumbled a little but went along with the decision. Afterwards, Pete and I thanked Tommy Lowe for speaking up on our behalf.

"Hey, don't thank me yet, lads. Don't think I'm a soft touch. Just like Archie said ... you'll have to earn every penny o' that half a dollar."

This was the way of things throughout the mine. Men would argue readily amongst themselves, but always in an open and fair way. There was no back-biting at all ... once an agreement had been reached, that was the end of it. Overall, there was a definite affinity amongst the men ... a comradeship second to none.

I loved this aspect of the pit and from then on, Pete and I regularly ate our bait sat amongst the experienced pitmen listening to their friendly squabbles.

"Great," said Pete as the colliers returned to the face, "come on John, let's get cracking, we've got to haul the bogey back to the Landing afore we can do another trip."

"Reight Pete, I hope you're feeling fit, cos it's hard graft shoving it back up that long gradient."

"Hang on, I've got an idea," said Pete, "why don't we jump onto the conveyor belt and pull it with the rope?"

"Aye, we can try it, but don't forget ... we're forrit if Jerry catches us."

"It'll be reight ... we'll see his spotlight-coming from a mile off."

"U-um, I suppose so ... come on then." It worked a treat. We had to grip the rope tightly when the bogey came to the steep parts but, on the whole, it was easier than shoving it.

Pete and I proved worthy of every pennyworth of pey-brass we got and soon earned the respect of all the face-workers. Mind you, we didn't just hump all the materials to the coalface, we actually ventured onto the face and helped the miners.

"Can we help you to shovel some o' the coal?" we'd ask.

"Aye, course you can, but we don't call it shovelling on the face," said one of the colliers, "it's called 'filling'."

Pete and I were aware, as were the men, that we could be dismissed instantly for this, but it still seemed worth the risk. Everyone, including the belt-end attendant, kept a constant vigil for the approach of a fireman or any other official, who could be seen coming a mile off, as they had special spot lamps, which were very distinct from the ordinary miner's lamp. Jerry enforced the ruling about untrained youths venturing onto the coalface and was very strict about it; but all the same, although he knew what went on, he turned a blind eye because he knew how much timber lads depended on their pey-brass. However, woe-betide any lad who actually got caught in the act. Pete and I knew this and never once became complacent about it.

At the first sign of anyone flashing their lamps and shouting, "Spotlight! Spotlight!" Pete and I would scurry down the face and make our way back to the Landing via the tail gate. This didn't create the problem of having to explain our whereabouts, as we frequently ran tackle on the bottom gate as well.

During the process of filling the coal the colliers put up steel roof supports every few feet and propped them up with Dowties or wooden props. Large wooden chocks were also used and these had an extra special function of reinforcing the other supports. The chocks were formed from large wooden blocks built into a square formation. This was done by laying down two blocks parallel to each other about eighteen inches apart, and then two more on top but diagonal to them. Before a third layer was applied, a half-brick was placed at each corner. More blocks were applied on top of these until the chock was roof high.

After the filling was completed the perilous job of 'striking' followed, which entailed the removal of all the back supports from the coalface. This unsupported area behind the miners from where the coal had been extracted then became known as the 'Gob'. The ideal situation was for the roof to collapse in once the props were removed. However, this sometimes took days to happen and created a dangerous situation as the hanging roof would put colossal pressure onto the coalface supports. A daunting place to be working!

One day, whilst striking, I was helping a very friendly collier called Jimmy Howarth.

"What's the idea of the chocks, Jim?" I asked him.

"Ah well," he stressed, "they're really important. Just shine your light into the Gob, John Bill, and you can see the roof hanging." I shone my light into the empty space of the Gob and could see way back. The floor looked spacious, just like a ballroom until the sagging roof restricted my view.

"It's not good when the roof's hanging like that, John Bill," said Jimmy, "in fact it's downright dangerous. This is the reason why we need to build chocks. When the roof hangs like it's doing right now, all the weight is being pushed o'er onto the face. Without the chocks in place the weight would skirt out the props like knocking o'er a set o' dominoes."

"Bloomin' 'eck Jim … does it not scare you, then?" I asked, feeling a bit edgy.

"Too bloody right it scares me! Sh-ssh, can you hear that creaking noise," he whispered, "that means that the Gob's shoving right now … it could go at any time…."

Suddenly, the Gob roof caved in! There was a deafening roar as thousands of tons of solid sandstone rock crashed to the ground, billowing up loads of dust. Jim rolled about laughing as I nearly jumped out of my skin.

"See what I mean, lad … don't say I didn't warn thi!"

Still shaking from shock I asked, "Is it safe now, Jim? Flippin' 'eck, that were scary."

"Aye, John Bill," Jim roared, unable to contain his laughter, "a bloody lot safer than what it was afore. Right lad, now you've got o'er the initial shock, how would you like to learn a bit about striking?" I liked this bloke and right away said I'd have a go.

"Reight, watch me first and then I'll let thi have a go at striking out one o' these chocks." I watched with interest as Jim wielded a seven-pound hammer and began to strike one of the bricks in the chock. "This is the reason why we have to use bricks, lad … otherwise we'd never get the chocks out once the weight had settled on 'em." After painstakingly knocking out all four bricks, the wooden blocks came tumbling down. Jim then built another chock nearer to the coalface, before striking out the next one. He'd only knocked down a few chocks when part of the Gob roof came crashing down.

"That's better," said Jim, "that's what should happen all the time, then there's not as much weight being thrown o'er onto the face."

Whilst some men were striking, others were moving the heavy scraper pans into the empty space in preparation for the next batch of coal. Once the striking was completed and the scraper pans were moved into position, the jib of a special coal-cutting machine was used to undercut the new seam of coal. Holes were drilled six feet into the coal throughout the length of the face in readiness for the shotfirer, who would fill the holes with explosives and then, using special detonators, 'fire' them. After being fired, the coal was again ready to be filled. Overall, I found face-work very interesting, albeit dangerous. My experience of the hazardous life of a miner increased daily working alongside these courageous, hardworking men.

* * *

As the months passed, Pete and I gained the respect of our seniors. The colliers held us in high esteem and willingly gave us our pey-brass. This was great for us two lads, as it fairly boosted our wage packet. However, something happened that Pete and I didn't like ... not one little bit!

It was bait-time and one of our mates, Les, who liked attending the belt-end at the top of the face, complained to the colliers that he should get pey-brass as well.

After discussing it, one of the colliers said, "Yeah, it's only reight, young Les is only on a little wage like t'other lads. I'll tell thi what ... why don't we give all the pey-brass to him this Friday?"

Pete didn't usually say much but on this occasion he did. "Hey hang on a minute! He doesn't do any humping like me and John Bill and anyroad, he's attending to belt-end outta choice, cos he doesn't like hard work."

"Take no notice of 'em Pete," I interrupted, "they're having us on ... don't take the bait!"

"Never mind don't take the bait, John Bill," said Archie, "we're not kidding ... just wait and see!"

Throughout the week, we both carried out our usual routine, humping, filling, striking, etc. But every bait-time, the topic of conversation amongst the colliers was the same. Pete showed his obvious annoyance and even I began to feel irritated.

"You know somet, John Bill," complained Pete, "I'll be as sick as a parrot if they give our pey-brass to Les ... I'd be in a reight mess without it, cos I've come to rely on it."

"Don't worry about it, Pete, there's no way they'd do that. Anyroad, can you honestly see Archie handing o'er half a dollar to Les?" Despite trying to reassure Pete, I was beginning to feel uneasy myself.

Finally, payday arrived. At the end of the shift, Pete and I raced through the showers and, after collecting our wages, we stood outside the pay-office waiting for the colliers to hand over the pey-brass. Sure enough, as hard-faced as anything, there was Les.

Pete sniggered at him. "I don't know what you're standing there for ... you haven't got a cat in hell's chance o' getting any pey-brass."

Les just sniggered back, "Well, we'll just have to wait and see, won't we?"

"Right," I said, "we'll stand in our normal places and see what happens." It wasn't long before the colliers started filtering through. Tommy Lowe was the first one to pick up his wage packet and on opening it he approached the three of us.

"All reight John Bill, how's it goin' then?"

"All right Tommy, and you?" I replied thinking, "Aye, I knew they were only kiddin' us." Be that as it may, Tommy did the very thing I least expected ... he actually gave half a crown to Les!

"Hey what are you playin' at Tommy ... that's our pey-brass!" I protested.

"Listen here, John Bill ... we've been telling you all week what we were gonna do, but you obviously didn't take any notice." Pete and I were fuming!

"I don't believe this, Tommy, especially from you!" I snapped.

"Don't blame me, John Bill," he replied shrugging his shoulders, "this is nowt personal, it was a unanimous decision ... you know how things work round here."

"That's all right in some circumstances, Tommy, but in this one you're wrong," I growled. "That's mine and Pete's money you're messing about with."

"Hey, don't get cocky, John Bill … I'll give flaming pey-brass to who I please. Anyroad, why don't all three of you share it between yourselves?"

"Because he hasn't done any of the humping," rapped Pete. "Me and John Bill have done all the grafting while he's been sat on his arse all week doing nowt!"

In the meantime the other colliers approached, and all of them did the same as Tommy Lowe. All of them, that is, except Jimmy Howarth.

Jimmy protested to the other miners – but to no avail: "Come on fellas, I think you're taking things too far. These two young lads have worked their socks off for us this week." Turning to Pete and me he said, "I'm sorry about this lads, but there's not a reight lot I can do about it. All I can say is, here's my half a dollar."

"Thanks Jimmy, thanks a lot, it's not your fault. Anyroad, don't worry about it … we'll get our pey-brass all right," I told him.

"Well you won't bloody get any off me," quipped Les, "if you think I'm splitting it with thi, you've got another thing coming!" Just then, Archie, the last miner to collect his pay packet, approached.

He gloated as he gave his half a crown to Les. "What did I tell you, John Bill … serves thi bloody well right for not taking any notice."

Pete was frantic, and started yelling, "You bloody swine, you're nowt else … after all we've done for you!" Archie simply laughed and walked off.

"Just look at this, John Bill," Pete moaned, "bloody one and thre'pence a piece, I feel like throwing misel in the Cut."

"Not to worry, Pete! I feel as bad about it as you do but we'll sort it … you'll see," I told him. Completely powerless for the moment, we both made our way to the bus stop full of gloom.

The weekend passed and the Monday afternoon shift commenced at two-fifteen in the afternoon. Pete and I had discussed the matter between ourselves and decided to take action – or, better still ... no action! We went about our tackle-dragging in a proper manner, but that's all; we stuck implicitly to the rules. We carried all the tackle to the end of the rails, and there it stayed!

"We'll just hang around here for a while, Pete," I said, "it won't be long before they're wanting some tackle on the face."

"I hope you're reight, John Bill. I couldn't do with missing out on the pey-brass again."

"No, neither could I ... anyroad, I have a gut feeling about it."

Sure enough, it wasn't long before two colliers came traipsing off the face, asking for some help. "Come on lads ... give us a lift, we're behind schedule!"

"You cheeky, hardfaced swines you're nowt else!" rapped Pete. "After what you did on Friday, there's no chance!"

"Oh come on, it were only a joke ... it won't happen again."

"Too bloody true it won't!" we shot back. "If you want a lift, get Les to give you one."

"Please yourself," said one of them as he made his way back to the face, "but there'll be no more pey-brass for any o' you any more."

"Oh blimey, that's done it!" exclaimed Pete. "We've messed it up for good now, haven't we?"

"I don't know so much, Pete, they both looked knackered carrying them Dowties. Don't forget, they may be used to working on the face, but they're not used to carrying the tackle as well. Anyroad Pete, I just know we've got to stick to our guns ... I'm convinced that we're doing the right thing."

"I only hope you're reight, John Bill ... I really do."

The day passed and the same thing happened on Tuesday. Once again we both waited patiently at the end of the track. It wasn't long before a couple of colliers came to pick up some bricks. One of these happened to be Archie.

"All right, Archie, how's it going then?" asked Pete.

"Never mind how's it goin', you little ratbags, you know bloody well how it's going!"

Just then the main belt stopped and everybody got settled down for bait. Pete and I joined them.

I sat down at the side of Jimmy Howarth, who gave me a hearty greeting – "All right, John Bill, nice to see you ... keep up the good work, lad, I'm proud o' thi."

"What bloody good work!" rapped Archie. "I ain't seen any bloody good work around here!"

"Hang on a minute, Archie!" said Tommy Lowe. "I know what Jimmy means, and he's right ... we treated these here lads shabby and you know it."

"Whattaya talking about, Tommy?"

"Come off it, Archie! You know only too well what I'm talking about ... we've bin out of order. You were only saying yourself t'other week that they were the best two tackle lads in the pit."

One of the other colliers intervened. 'I'll go along wi' that Tommy ... I've got to admit it's been bloody hard graft without 'em."

"Aye it has," said another, "and don't forget it's only Tuesday."

Pete and I were listening intently and lapping up every minute as the debate began to heat up a little.

Pete sniggered and whispered in my ear, "We've got 'em by the short and curlies, John."

"I think you're reight there, Pete, they're wavering."

Jimmy Howarth nudged me from the other side. "Well done, John Bill … keep it up, don't let 'em off the hook."

"Don't worry about that, Jim," I said, munching a jam butty, "there's no chance o' that."

After more discussion, Tommy Lowe acted as spokesman for the colliers. "All reight lads, you've made your point … start bringin' tackle onto the face and we'll give you your pey-brass at th'end o' the week."

"Oh yeah, and what about our pey-brass from last week?" I replied.

"You must be joking!" splurted Archie, nearly choking on his coffee. "I'm just giving thi half a dollar … you'll have to get rest of it from t'other lad."

I stood my ground. "No, you get it from him Archie … you gave it to him!"

"You bloody cheeky little git … I'll drum your ribs if I get hold o' thi!"

"Now hang on Archie, the lad's right!" a few colliers chimed in, "it's our own doing, so we'll have to pay 'em."

Archie grumbled a little before replying, "Yeah go on then, I suppose you're reight … I just don't like thoughts o' coughing up five bob."

Turning to me and Pete, Tommy Lowe said, "Reight lads, I know you've been listening to everything that's gone on … well, you've won and we'll all give you double pey-brass on Friday. So now, how about getting stuck in after bait and humping this bleeding tackle to the face?"

"At your service Tommy, with pleasure," we answered together.

As the men made their way back to the face, Jimmy Howarth tapped us both on the shoulder. "Congratulations lads, I'm proud of you … that were better than going to the pictures."

"Yeah and thanks to you, Jim," I replied, "I don't think we could o' done it without your help."

"Oh yes you could lad, don't underestimate yourself … I don't."

That was it. Both Pete and I were elated. "We've done it … we've done it!" bleated Pete, excitedly.

"Not quite," I said. "Let's wait to see what happens on Friday."

On the back-shift, the wage was paid out before work commenced. Pete and I made sure we were at the pay office in plenty of time to catch everyone. One by one each collier handed over five shillings. Then came Archie's turn. He slipped half a crown into Pete's hand and started to walk off.

"Come on, Archie, another half a dollar … you'll have to cough up like the rest of 'em," shouted Pete.

A grin came to Archie's face. "Oh well, you can't blame me for trying, can you?" He then handed over another half a crown, which he already had clasped in his other hand.

Finally, Jimmy Howarth came and he too handed over five shillings.

"That's too much Jimmy … you paid us half a dollar last week," I told him.

"Take it lad, it's been worth every penny seeing you at work … it were like watching a pantomime."

I turned to Pete. "Great, we've done it! We can really celebrate in th'Hapton Inn tonight after the shift's finished." Thirty shillings pey-brass each … we both felt like millionaires.

Pete and I carried on with the good work, remaining partners and friends for nearly two years.

* * *

Tackle-running for the colliers suited me down to the ground. I loved every minute of it. It must have been good for me too, because in those two years I grew and grew. By the time I was eighteen, I'd grown to my maximum height of five feet seven inches and I was fit and strong with it ... nobody called me 'Little' John Bill anymore.

Eighteen years old and the time had come for me to do my coalface training. This consisted of twenty days' 'coaling', twenty days' 'ripping' and twenty days' 'striking'. I did my coaling on number 4 face and my overseer was none other than Archie.

"Right, John Bill, you're under my wing now for the next twenty days, so think on you don't step outta line ... you might well o' grown a bit, but I'm still capable o' drumming your ribs!" Having worked with Archie before, I knew only too well that his bark was worse than his bite. We worked well together and before I knew it, I'd acquired my coaling papers, which meant I could now officially work on the face filling the coal ... on collier's rate!

After completing my coaling training I worked odd days on the face earning £4 a day, but this wasn't as regular as I would have liked. Most of the time I was 'day'tling' on normal pay, working on belt-ends, tackle running or other things.

I did my twenty days ripping training on the back-shift. When the coal had been extracted and the coalface advanced, the job of the rippers was to blast away the stone above the coal to give height to form a roadway and lengthen the tunnel. It was an experience I won't forget in a hurry. I worked alongside four experienced men, whose team leader was Lawrence Smith, nicknamed Loll, a big fellow with a bald head, who liked to get the job done. At the time, the pit was experimenting with a new shift system whereas, on completing his particular task, each collier could leave the pit for home, receiving a bonus into the bargain.

Loll liked to finish early and he made this quite clear to me on my first day: "Reight lad, let's get one thing streight from the start … I'm not keen on taking on a trainee, so don't expect to be pampered, you'll have to get stuck in like the rest of us."

"Righto Loll, I go along with that. I don't expect any favours … you just tell me what to do and I'll do it."

"Well first thing … the shot-firer's gonna fire the ripping. so you'd best grab a bit o' bait now. cos you won't have time to eat owt after that."

I had barely taken a bite when there was a loud blast. Hardly had the dust settled, before Loll issued his orders: "That's it, John Bill, if you haven't finished your bait yet, you can leave it for the rats."

As the smoke cleared, I could see a mountain of shale that had been dropped by the tremendous explosion … it was nigh impossible to get out of the gate onto the face.

"Come on, don't just stand there gawking at it … get hold o' that shovel and start clearing a way through!" rapped Loll.

"Righto," I replied, "I'm going … I'm going."

It took about ten minutes to form a small opening before Loll started issuing orders again.

"Reight lad, that should be big enough for you to crawl through onto the face … now get your arse through there and start shovelling from t'other side so we can all get through."

"Bloomin' 'eck Loll, that hole's not big enough for a rat to crawl through … never mind me!"

"I don't want any back chat, just get yourself under there … now!"

Being very nimble, I dragged myself through the gap on my belly and started shovelling. Finally, the hole was big enough to allow the men through and once again Loll started giving the orders.

"Reight, John Bill, we're gonna form a line and start 'backening' the shale from one man to t'other. You'll be the last in line, so you'll have to build a 'pack' as we throw it to thi."

I was well-versed in pack-building – I'd helped the colliers on number four face to build plenty. I also knew the importance of the packs, as conveyed to me by my collier friend, Jimmy Howarth. Jimmy had taught me how to use the larger pieces of shale to build two dry walls and then to throw all the loose shale in-between them to form the pack.

"U-um, I'd better make a good job o' this," I thought, knowing that the packs played an all-important part in controlling the weight of the roof.

I was eager to make a good impression, but my diligence soon wore off when I realised what a wet hole I was working in. Water poured in from the layers above and, to make matters worse, being blocked by the loose shale, it dammed up on the floor. We were all wearing oilskin waterproofs, but these didn't help much, as the water trickled off our helmets and down our necks. It didn't take long before the water, where I was kneeling, was six inches deep and above my kneepads. I was like a drowned rat but I couldn't complain, as the other four men had to cope with the same conditions. Mind you, the thought did enter my head that they were on a lot more money than I was.

"Come on you little swine, John Bill, keep going," growled Loll, "the sooner we get the job done the sooner we get home!"

This certainly spurred me on. 'Yeah, reighto Loll, I want to get finished and outta the pit as much as you do," I shouted back.

"Aye, well get your flamin' back into it and stop mucking about!"

"Come on, John lad," I mumbled to myself, as the hot showers on the pit top beckoned, "get stuck in so we can get out o' this rat-hole!" It got me to thinking how my grandad survived four long years on the Western Front. "Bloomin' 'eck, Grandad, I know now how you musta felt cooped up in them wet trenches twenty-four hours a day ... I'm wiltin' and I've only done three hours." I worked furiously shovelling the shale, gradually forming a channel, which allowed some of the water to flow from the coalface to the gate.

Every now and again, Loll would throw big flat stones, which kept landing in the water smack in front of me, drenching me even more.

"He-ey, you're doing that on purpose," I moaned, "you've just splattered me full in the face with a load o' slush ... watch it!"

Loll roared with laughter. "Whattaya talkin' about, you little runt, we haven't got time to mess about ... just get on with it." It happened a few times, but I was never sure whether he did it on purpose or in the course of trying to get the job done.

"Oh never mind, it doesn't matter," I reassured myself, "I'm soaked to the skin as it is already ... what difference does a bit more water make?"

On the first day, we finished the task in less than three hours, and I actually caught the twenty-to-six bus at the Hapton Inn.

On the bus home I was quite pleased, reflecting on the day, "By 'eck, I'm gonna be in th'house afore our Mary gets home from the weaving shed ... won't she be surprised!" Taking everything into account, I didn't mind working in the wet conditions if it meant finishing so early.

The twenty days' ripping training passed quickly and I then went on to complete my final twenty days working amongst my former colleagues on number 4 face.

I was now a qualified collier, but didn't get regular face work and had to spend many days day'tling on low pay.

A few weeks before my twentieth birthday, I was on the early shift. Prior to going into the pit most colliers went across to the canteen for a brew or to buy some chewing tobacco and as the firemen were allowed to the front of the queue. On this particular morning, I was stood in the queue and who should walk in ... no other than G.T. And he was no longer a fireman, but an ordinary collier like me.

"By 'eck, look who's back from the gold mines in South Africa," one of the colliers remarked.

"All right, G.T., how's it goin'," said another, "I never expected to see thi back here again?"

I turned round and on seeing him my mind flashed back to the Bluebird days and the way that he had made my life a misery.

"Not to worry," I thought, "that's in the past way behind me." I would have let it go at that, but then G.T. did something that got my back up. He actually walked right to the front of the queue, as bold as brass, as if he was still a fireman.

"Hey what d'you think you're doin G.T.?" I yelled. "There's a queue here … now get to the flamin' back of it!"

"And who the bloody hell are you, then?" he quipped. Suddenly a look of recognition came to his eyes, 'By 'eck, is it little John Bill?"

"That's right, but not quite so little anymore, and I'm tellin' you agen … get to the back o' this bloody queue!"

"Oh aye … and who's gonna mek me if I don't?"

I knew I could be asking for trouble, but I was determined not to let G.T. get away with it … besides, by now my adrenaline was flowing.

"I'll bloody well put you there," I growled, "I'm not that little lad any more that you pinned up against the wall behind the mine-cars!"

G.T. weighed me up for a while glaring at me and I could tell by his eyes that he was annoyed. "Aye, you might o' grown a bit," he growled, "but I can see you're still a fly git!"

"It takes one to know one," I sneered, exaggerating a wry smile. I was full of foreboding and shaking a little, but I didn't let G.T. know that. However, my fear was unfounded and soon laid to rest. G.T. glared at me again for what seemed an age before grunting, "Arg-gh, you're not bloody worth it … I didn't flamin' want owt anyroad!" At that, he stormed out of the canteen, looking rather dejected – it wasn't quite the kind of reception he'd expected. Despite a feeling of self-satisfaction, I still sighed with relief.

But I couldn't help muttering to myself, "Great … every dog has its day!" And I'd just had mine!

NATIONAL SERVICE

It was shortly after the G.T. incident that I decided to leave the pit. I'd become a little unsettled of late, as there had been talk of the mine closing down. One thing swayed me: Dad asked me to go into partnership with him in the scrap-iron trade.

Also, the way I saw it, the cotton industry was on the decline, as by the late Fifties, it was reeling from the effects of cheap imports from abroad. 'King Cotton' was soon to be a thing of the past. The unfair competition had taken its toll on the cotton mills and most of them were dying a slow death. One by one, many of the tall factory chimneys were demolished, symbolising the end of the 'Great Cotton Era'. Burnley's main industry had literally hung on a thread, and that thread was now wearing very thin.

I could foresee the closure of lots of other factories, which got me to thinking, "If that happens, there's going to be lots of scrap iron for the taking. Yeah, I think this is a good time to go into business with Dad." So I did and we made a formidable team. He taught me the tricks of the trade, introducing me to factory owners with whom he negotiated fat contracts for their scrap iron.

We worked well together. I sensed that I was influencing him by my willingness to work hard, as he didn't seem to spend as much time in the pubs as he used to, and concentrated more on the business. This made me feel good because the business was taking off and I felt that I had won Dad's respect. Yes, things were really looking good.

However, I'd only been working with Dad a few weeks when he lost Peggy, our beloved horse, in a stupid game of cards in the pub. So, in order to carry on working, and with the help of a loan from my elder brother Jimmy, he acquired a motor wagon – as he quaintly called it, and despite missing Peggy, we now got through much more work in a day. He still did most of the wheeling and dealing directly with the factory owners, but now always took me into the office with him.

"Don't say a word, our John, leave it all to me," he'd say. "Just look, listen and learn … you'll soon get the hang o' things."

One day, whilst in the Salford pub, Dad made a good deal with the manager of Barden Mill.

"Isn't that the mill where our Mary works?" I asked as we made our way to the factory.

"It is that, our John. Why do you ask?"

"Well, I were thinking … our Mary'll go mad if she knows we're collecting scrap iron from where she works."

"Hey, John lad, there's no sentiment in business. You'll learn that quick enough."

"Aye, I suppose you're reight, Dad. It were just a thought."

"There's no supposing about it, our John, you can get them sort o' thoughts outta your head right now. You'll be no good in business if you don't."

We arrived at the factory just after half-past twelve, on a nice sunny day. As I started to load the wagon there were a few weavers sat around outside enjoying their dinner break. I'd just climbed on the back of the wagon to move some of the scrap iron when I saw our Mary coming out of one of the shed doors. As she approached us, I made the mistake of letting Dad know.

"E-eh, all reight our Mary," he shouted cheerfully as she came into view, "it's your dad."

When she saw us, a look of sheer horror came to her face. For a moment she was dumbstruck.

"Oh 'eck," I thought, realising what was wrong, "she feels humiliated in front of her friends." If looks could kill, I'd have dropped on the spot. Mary's face reddened, she tightened her mouth and hissed through gritted teeth. Without saying a word, she turned around and walked straight back into the factory.

"What the flippin' 'eck's up with her?" asked Dad. "Who the flamin' 'eck does she think she is, anyroad … Lady Muck?"

When we got home that night, Mary was in a right mood.

"What d'you think you're playing at, Dad? You've really shown me up!"

"Whaddaya talkin about, Lady, who d'you think you are, anyroad? I've got to mek a living, just like anybody else!"

"I know you have," she screeched, "but coming to the bloomin' shed where I work is a bit much, innit?"

"And what am I supposed to do, then … let a flamin' good deal slip through mi fingers?"

"I don't know, but at least you could've ...."

"Never mind what I could've done. It's obvious you're ashamed o' me. I'll tell you this for nowt, our Mary – I'll not stop coming to that mill or any other for you or anybody else. And there's one thing for sure ... I won't ever acknowledge you any more when I'm about mi business."

If Dad was expecting an apology from Mary, he didn't get one ... she just tutted arrogantly and strutted out of the house. In a way, I could see her point ... but I could also see Dad's.

* * *

I still often went over to Bacup on my motorbike to see my relatives. But the main reason was that Grandad was grieving badly for Granma and his health was deteriorating rapidly. However, I also visited Aunt Katie's house and often took Michael, one of my young cousins, for a spin on the pillion. I was nineteen and he was nine years younger than me, but despite the age gap, a strong bond formed between us. I frequently took him over to Burnley and he loved every minute of it, as the many cobbled streets and high factory chimneys intrigued him.

"Bloomin' 'eck Johnny," he'd comment, "I thought we had a lot o' big chimneys o'er in Bacup but there's millions o'er here, in't there?" Michael also enjoyed it because there was more going on in Burnley than Bacup. He especially liked it when I took him home to Albion Street.

"Are you gonna tek me to see mi Auntie Winnie and mi Uncle Jack?" he'd ask.

"Aye, all reight, but I know why you want to go there," I joked, "you get med a fuss of by mi brothers and sisters ... that's reight, innit?"

"Yeah, course it is," he'd answer with a cheeky grin, "wouldn't you if you were me?"

"U-um, I suppose so," I replied with a smile.

He also liked my mother because she spoilt him and often took him down town for little treats.

I occasionally took one of my other younger cousins for a ride on the back of my motorbike, but more often than not, it would be Michael – we just seemed to jell together.

About three and a half years after Grandma's death, the sad news came from Bacup that Grandad had died whilst sat in his armchair. Aunt Katie contacted my mother saying she had found their dad whilst visiting him. It was yet another sad time for my family, especially Mum. I was in the house with her a few days after the funeral and she reflected sadly on her younger days.

"E-eh, mi poor mam and dad, they tried their best but they didn't stand a chance. I know Dad could get a bit grumpy at times but he were never a well man … what with having to work out in all weathers and the war an' all. U-um, and they never got any hand-outs from the government like they do nowadays; mind you, Dad was too proud to accept anything anyroad." She paused for a moment wiping a tear from her cheek before mumbling to herself, "I'll tell you what, Dad … you were a stubborn old so-an-so but I'm still going to miss you."

"E-eh Mam, I'm gonna miss mi grandad as well," I consoled her, "but at least he's not suffering or fretting anymore for Granma, is he?"

"No, you're right there, our John. There's one thing for sure … he certainly wanted to join her."

"He did that," I agreed, as I pondered on the way he'd cut himself off from everyone since my grandmother had died.

Things were never the same now that Granma and Grandad had died, but I continued to visit Bacup frequently and often went straight after work to take Michael for a ride on my motorbike around the Rossendale Valley.

* * *

Ironically, three months after my twentieth birthday and only four months after going into business with Dad, I received my 'call-up' papers conscripting me to serve two years' National Service with Her Majesty's Forces. Two of my mates, Billy Pounder and David Whittaker, had recently been called up to serve in the Catering Corps and another two, Pete Holroyd and Barry Birks had signed on for nine years in the Royal Marines. Pete Fletcher and Bobby Cheetham had also received their call-up papers, but both had opted to sign on as regulars in the Service Corps and were serving in the Far East.

After reading my papers from the War Office, I made my feelings clear. "Bloomin' 'eck Dad," I commented, "just my luck … just when we were geddin started."

"Never mind, lad, it's not th'end o' the world," he replied, consoling me. "Two years isn't all that long, it'll soon pass."

"Aye, I know that, but it would have to happen now just when we've got a few good contracts on the go."

"Don't worry about it, our John," said Dad, patting me on the back. "I'll keep everything shipshape while you're away."

"I hope so, Dad … I hope so." I wasn't happy with the situation, but there wasn't a lot I could do about it.

I had to go to Preston for a medical and and a recruitment briefing. After the initial formalities, I was informed that I had been placed into the Royal Army Medical Corps, working as an auxiliary nurse in the army hospitals. I protested strongly to the officials, asking if I could be placed into the Service or Ordnance Core. I knew if I enlisted into any of these I would at least obtain a driving licence, which would be useful when I was demobbed.

A rather strict regimental officer told me, "If you want to go into the regiment of your choice, my man, then sign on as a regular soldier ... if not, you go where we put you." I gave it a lot of thought, but I didn't fancy signing on for three years.

"No, what if I don't like it," I pondered. "Two years doesn't seem a long while, but three ... I don't know."

After the initiation ceremony, I was given a travel warrant and ordered to report to Queen Elizabeth Barracks, in Crookham, Hampshire on July 16th 1959 by four o'clock in the afternoon. I received my army number – 23633183 – and was officially placed into the Royal Army Medical Corps.

"Bloomin' 'eck Dad!" I moaned when I got home. "They've gone and put me in the Medics, working in flippin' army hospitals ... I don't fancy being a nurse, it's a woman's job. I tried to persuade 'em to put me into the Service Corps, but they wouldn't wear it."

"Never mind, lad, it'll be easier than workin' down the pit. Anyroad, when d'you have to go?"

"Next bloomin' Thursday. Oh, that reminds me, Dad ... will you do me a favour?"

"Aye course I will, our John ... what is it?"

"Could you sell my motorbike for me ... I don't like parting with it, it's the best bike I've ever had; but what else can I do?"

"Righto ... how much d'you want forrit?"

"If you get me twenty quid I'll be happy," I lamented. 'Somebody's gonna get a bargain … I give fifty quid forrit eighteen months ago and it's ne'er let me down once."

As it happened, Dad sold it to a mate of mine, Pete Abbott, for £20. Pete told me later that he ran the motorbike for two years and it was also the best bike he'd ever had.

*　　*　　*

As I stood waiting on Barrack's Station for the London train, I had one great thumping hangover – Dad had arranged a farewell party the night before in the Nelson Hotel and a few mates turned up, and along with my brothers and sisters, they gave me a really good send-off, plying me with loads of drink.

"Here you are, John, get this down you," said Jimmy, handing me a whisky, "it'll do you good."

"Right lad, down the hatch," said Dad, "here's to the future." By the end of the night I'd had a right cocktail of drinks – and did I suffer for it! As soon as I got outside into the fresh air, my face turned various colours, from green to grey.

"U-ugh, I want to be sick," I said, making my way back inside to the pub's toilet.

Our Barry was there to console me, "You'll be all right, our John … get it up, you'll feel better!" It reminded me of the night when I'd taken my first drink – except this time I felt worse … much worse!

Hence, the grotty feeling next morning as Dad and my two brothers saw me off on the train.

During my journey I reflected on the time Mum had made the same journey to the capital, nearly thirty years before. On reaching London I had to make my way via the underground to another station where I made my connection to Aldershot. Finally, that evening, I arrived at Queen Elizabeth Barracks, to commence my training as a nursing orderly. Once again I protested about being placed into the Medical Corps, but the officials gave me the same answer that I'd been given back in Preston.

"Right, that's it," I mumbled, resigning myself to my plight, "if I'm not going to sign on as a regular I may as well accept my lot!"

My home for the next four months was in a typical army barrack room, which I shared with about twenty other blokes in the same predicament as me. When I entered the billet all the mattresses were turned back off the bedsprings and the bedding was folded neatly at the bottom of the bed into a box formation. A soldier wearing two stripes on his sleeve, who introduced himself as Corporal Jenkins, greeted us.

"Right soldiers," he addressed us, "I'm the corporal in charge of this billet and you'll be under my charge for the duration of your training. This billet must be kept tidy at all times, and every morning the beds must be made up exactly as they are right now."

On Friday morning, we were officially kitted out with boots and full regalia. The weekend was a kind of settling-in period, allowing each one of us to get used to our new environment and each other. But on Monday, the serious business of rigorous training began ... this was to last for sixteen weeks. It consisted of square bashing on a large parade ground, in conjunction with some arduous studying in the classroom. The classroom layout was ingenious, leaving nothing to the imagination. It was like a hospital with models displaying different sections of the human body. There were many other modern teaching aids, including dummy patients and skeletons in the room. By the end of the sixteen weeks' training, my comrades and I were well versed in the functions and anatomy of the human body. Having undergone a strict course in first aid, we were also competent enough to cope with an emergency situation in case of any accident or illness occurring.

Every evening in the billet room, we had to spend at least two hours 'bulling' our boots, until they gleamed like a new pin. The same applied to our belts, cap badges and the brass buttons on our uniforms; everything had to sparkle and woe betide anyone if they didn't. Next morning on parade, the sergeant major stomped around with a stick under his arm, bellowing at the top of his voice. Anyone not passing the stringent inspection was put on a charge and ended up doing extra fatigue duties.

New intakes came into the camp every two weeks and were known as 'squaddies' or 'sprogs'. The Army numbered each intake according to the week and year in which it had been enlisted ... therefore, our intake was 59–14. As one intake commenced training, another one, having finished their stint, awaited transfer to a main camp somewhere in England. So, every fortnight, a booze-up took place to celebrate the occasion.

I met up with lads from many different walks of life. These included Jimmy Mitchinson from Wigan, Colin Hagan from Gateshead and Brian Holdsworth from Leeds. Brian was to become a lifelong friend of mine.

The gross pay was twenty-five shillings a week and after one shilling stoppages we were paid out to the nearest five shillings, which meant that most of the lads finished up with just twenty shillings in their hand. The rest of the money went into 'credits', a kind of saving fund. I was concerned about Mum not being able to manage whilst I was in the army, so I went to see my C.O.

"Right lad, we can allow your mother an army pension of forty-five shillings a week," he advised me, "but only if you're willing to contribute seven shillings out of your own allowance."

"Bloomin' 'eck," I thought, 'I'll only be left with seventeen shillings, and after they've taken out the credits … that'll only leave fifteen bob."

"Well lad, come on, what do you think?" barked the C.O. "We haven't got all day to mess about!"

"Oh sod it! What the 'eck," I thought, "we're all in the same boat … another few bob isn't gonna make all that much difference." So that was it, I was left with a paltry fifteen shillings with which to buy toothpaste, razor blades, soap and the like. Even so, I still managed to retain ten shillings … enough to buy eight pints of beer. I could have got onto Mum and she would have sent me the seven shillings, but I didn't bother.

"Anyroad," I told myself, "if I can manage on this pittance for two years, it'll put me in good stead when I'm back in Civvy Street. Another thing: I'm not into this boozing lark, so it'll give me ample opportunity to do some serious training and get myself fit."

So I trained hard during the week, but on payday, I joined the lads for a drink and had a right rave-up. It was on one of these rave-ups that I had my first army fight … I only had two fights during my army days and fortunately won them both.

The summer of 1959 was a scorcher and I took advantage of the pleasant evenings. Being determined to build myself up into peak condition, I spent most of my spare time on the playing fields or the army assault course.

But few of the lads were in the same frame of mind as me – they preferred drinking beer every night in the NAAFI Club. Some of them tried to persuade me to go out on boozing sprees with them during the week, but I wouldn't be tempted.

"I'm sorry, lads, but once a week is enough for me," I answered. "Besides, I haven't got enough money to go out drinking every night."

"What a bloody lame excuse!" quipped Jimmy Logan, a Londoner. "You've got twenty-five bob a week the same as the rest of us."

"No I haven't," I replied, "I'm only left with fifteen bob after stoppages."

"You're a bloody liar!" he barked. "You just want to ponce about pretending to be a soldier."

I didn't rise to the bait, but curtailed my natural instinct to fire back at him as I had done many times before to my peers at St Thomas's Junior School. I didn't go into detail as to why I only received fifteen shillings. Instead, I simply replied: "Please yourself, believe what you like … you do what you want to do and I'll do what I want to do."

That was it as far as I was concerned; I didn't think anymore about it till a few weeks later. The intake in the next billet to ours had just completed their sixteen weeks' training and the entire group went out on the town to celebrate the occasion in the NAAFI Club. All the lads from our billet decided to join them and I went along too, with my mates Colin Hagan and Brian Holdsworth. There was always a good-spirited rivalry amongst the different billets; however, on this occasion lots of beer was consumed and as the evening progressed, tempers became frayed as insults were exchanged. The situation got out of hand, and before long, two lads started fighting. The fight didn't last long, as the Regimental Police became involved and they marched the two lads off to the guardroom. There was a lot of tension in the air, but on the whole things seemed to settle down; however, that was not the end of the matter ... not by a long way.

When I arrived back at the billet, I decided to have a wash before going to bed. Directly on entering the barrack room there were four large red fire buckets filled with sand and four others filled with water, and next to these were two fire extinguishers. The billet was typical of any barrack room, having a corridor down the middle with beds on either side. My bed was the first one on the right.

I'd just dried myself when Jimmy Logan arrived back from the NAAFI Club with some of his mates. And he was in a right cantankerous mood.

"U-ugh, look who it is," he sniggered, "the keep-fit boy! Where were you, then, when the fight started ... you didn't hang about too long, did you?"

"What are you talking about?" I replied. "It was all done and dusted when I left."

"Done and dusted mi arse!" he snarled, "I noticed you didn't get involved ... you bloody coward!"

"No, you're right I didn't, I couldn't see the point," I said, adding sarcastically, "Mind you, I noticed that you stepped way back into the shadows when the fight started."

This obviously infuriated him, because without warning he caught me completely off guard as he took an almighty swing, catching me full in the eye with his clenched fist. I saw stars but the funny thing was, I didn't feel any pain ... I was fuming. Instinctively, I dived at him with fists flying.

All I could think was, "Right Logan, you bastard, it's either you or me!"

Immediately, a few of the lads got in-between and kept us apart, trying to calm us down.

"Come on lads," said one of them, "we don't want any fighting amongst ourselves, we've all got to stick together."

"Stick together!" I growled. "I'll kill the bastard ... just let me at him!"

"Ha, ha, ha!" mocked Logan, "let the bloody weasel go ... I'll murder the fly git!"

Despite trying to calm the situation, the lads could see it was useless.

"Right," said Jimmy Mitchinson, acting as a spokesman. "We'll all go outside onto the parade ground and form a circle and let these two settle their differences there."

"That'll do me," I snarled, determined to give Logan the same as he'd given me, "I'll show him which one of us is the weasel!"

"Great ... bloody great!" Logan shot back. "I've been looking forward to this moment for bloody ages."

We made our way to the parade ground in two groups so as to keep Jimmy and me apart. After forming a circle, they let us go. Jimmy Logan threw himself into the fight full of venom, baying for blood, but he was no match for me and I knew it. I was in tip-top condition, nimble and fleet footed. Besides, he had given me a reason to fight and my dander was now up ... I had never felt so strong. We both fought like tigers, using all the strength we had, but gradually I overcame him. In the past, under similar circumstances, I would have let up on him, but on this occasion I was determined to give him the same black eye that he had given me. After raining a few blows into his face I was happy with the outcome and that was the end of the fight.

Although I'd won, I sank to my hands and knees in an exhausted state. I was absolutely shattered. Before returning to the billet, Jimmy Logan offered me his open hand and we both shook on it.

"I hold my hand up, John," he said, wiping blood from his face, "I was wrong about you. That was a good, fair fight ... I didn't know you had it in you." He laughed before adding, "Perhaps we can be friends now?"

"You're on, Jimmy," I said, "that suits me fine."

"Great! Mind you, you might not think so in the morning ... it looks like you're gonna have a real shiner."

I just grinned and cracked back at him, "Snap ... I'm not gonna be the only one by the looks o' things – you don't look so clever yourself."

"No, I don't feel so clever at that ... how about having a can of beer back in the billet?"

"I'll go along with that," I replied, warmly.

By the time we got back to the barrack room, some of the lads had already cracked open a few cans of ale. Both Jimmy and I had one can each and then retired to bed ... we certainly didn't need any rocking to get to sleep that night.

But this was not the end of it. In fact, our troubles were just beginning.

I woke up next morning with the most horrendous headache and could hardly lift my head off the pillow, as with every little movement I felt the blood throbbing in my temples. I finally managed to sit up straight, but on putting one foot on the floor, I felt a pool of gritty water.

"What the flamin' 'eck!" I thought. "What's happened here?" On looking around, I struggled to focus my eyes on the scene that confronted me ... it was unbelievable. The barrack room was in a state of complete disarray. There were pools of water everywhere intermingled with sand, and floating on top of the slush was white foam from the fire extinguishers. The eight empty fire buckets were strewn around in different parts of the billet, as were the fire extinguishers. Most of the lads were still in bed but odd ones were beginning to stir.

"What's happened here, then?" I asked, puzzled as to what had gone on.

"You're joking," quipped Colin Hagan, "you mean to say you didn't hear anything last night?"

"No Colin," I replied innocently, "not a thing ... honest!"

"Bloomin' 'eck John," laughed Jimmy Mitchinson, "you must be a good sleeper to sleep through all the commotion that went on in here last night – especially with thi sleeping in the first bed ... there were enough noise to wake the dead."

"What commotion? I don't know what you're talking about, I haven't got a clue ... honest!"

"What commotion?" laughed Colin and Jimmy simultaneously. "That's a good un. All bloody hell let loose in here last night, it were complete mayhem." Just then, to make things even funnier, Jimmy Logan moaned from the other side of the barrack room.

"O-oh my head, I've got the headache of all headaches ... tell somebody to stop the room going round and let me get off." Then, just as I had done, he put one foot on the floor. "Who-oa! What the bloody hell's happened here ... there's a load of water under my bed!"

"What, you an' all, Jimmy," chuckled another lad, "you mean to say you heard nothing either?"

"What do you mean ... heard owt about what?" At that, all the lads started laughing.

"How anyone could've slept through that racket is beyond me," said Jimmy Mitchinson, "it were like Bedlam in here."

"All reight, it were like Bedlam," I put in. "Now is anyone gonna enlighten us as to what happened?"

"Well," said Colin Hagan, "do you remember the fight between the two lads in the NAAFI last night?"

"Do I remember it?" piped up Jimmy Logan, "That's what got me and John fighting in the first place."

"Right," carried on Colin. "Well, when you two were asleep, some of our lads went and raided the barrack room lower down and broke a few windows."

"Crikey!" Jimmy said, "I'll bet that got their backs up."

"You're not kidding, they were really fired up and the lot of 'em came charging up here like raging bulls."

"What ... do you mean to say you were all battling in this billet?"

"No, but it were like a battlefield on the corridor, cos most of our lads went to meet 'em head on," said Colin excitedly, getting psyched up now by talking about it.

"Well how come our billet's in this state?" asked Jimmy Logan.

"A-ah well," put in Johnny Church from two beds away, "some of 'em got through our barricade and they threw water and sand from the fire buckets all o'er the place."

"Cor blimey, I wish I'd bin awake ... I'd have got really stuck in. Anyway, what's all that white stuff floating on top o' the water?"

"Oh that's somet else" replied Johnny, "they triggered off the fire extinguishers as well."

"Ah, no wonder there's load's o' foam on mi bed," I said.

"Aye, and ours too," said a few of the others in unison.

"How did it finish up, then?" I asked, becoming more intrigued.

"You might know," said Brian Holdsworth, "the Regimental Police arrived and carted a few o' the lads off to the guardhouse."

"I'm absolutely amazed," I said, "I can't believe all this happened and I slept through it all."

"No, neither can I," laughed Jimmy Logan. "If it had happened to anybody else, I wouldn't have believed 'em."

We all started laughing about it. But our merriment came to an abrupt halt.

"Quick," shouted one of the lads, "the C.S.M.'s coming!" The warning was a bit pointless really, as there was no time to tidy things up before the company sergeant major was upon us … and he was livid. He was a man to be feared at the best of times but, at this moment, he looked absolutely nightmarish as he stomped into the barrack room splashing through the gritty water, bellowing at the top of his voice, followed by two tall regimental policemen.

"Ar-rghh," he roared as he yielded a wooden baton under his arm, "by your beds, the lot of you!"

Everyone scrambled to their positions at the foot of their beds and stood to attention, awaiting further abuse. Nobody dared to utter a word.

"Right, you scruffy lot, I want the name of the culprits who did this or so help me I'll put the whole flamin' lot of you on a charge!" Everyone stood by his bed … no one said a thing.

To his displeasure and obvious disgust, the sergeant major had to venture further into the room, getting his shiny boots wet. The first person he confronted was me.

"A-ahh, well at least I've got one of you," he barked as he glared at my bruised face and black eye. "Right, what have you got to say for yourself soldier?"

"Nothing, sir," I quivered as I felt his awesome presence draining my spirit.

"What do you mean '*nothing*?" he screamed. "You either come up with something now or you're going to the guardhouse with them other cronies! Now I'll ask you one more time ... what have you got to say for yourself?"

"Nothing sir ... I still have nothing to say."

"Right," he said, turning to one of the regimental police, "put this soldier under arrest!" The sergeant major then carried on around the billet until he arrived at Jimmy Logan's bed.

"A-ah, what have we got here then ... another slimy creature?" he growled, trying to intimidate Jimmy.

But there was no chance of that. Jimmy kind of smirked at the sergeant major and gave him the same answers that I had given. Consequently, both Jimmy and I finished up in the guardroom awaiting a charge of inciting a riot. We both had to go in front of our commanding officer the next morning and got sentenced to seven days inside the guardroom without privileges. But some good came of it, because after our release all the lads in the billet room rallied around and treated us like celebrities.

"Hey, this is great," laughed Jimmy, "I'm bloomin' glad we didn't blab to the sergeant major ... it's were well worth doing a week in the cooler, weren't it?"

"Aye, I suppose you're right Jimmy. Then again, if we had o' blabbed ... our life wouldn't o' bin worth living." We both laughed readily at that.

Jimmy Logan and I became firm friends from thereon in.

*   *   *

My second fight was similar, in the sense that another lad was forever trying to goad me into a fight, but other aspects of it were very different. This particular lad was called

Bernard Barem and he'd just been promoted to the rank of lance corporal. Lance corporals were always hard to get on with, because they were constantly striving to impress their superiors in order to get a second stripe. His attitude was commonly known amongst the soldiers as 'taping'. The name Barem always stuck out in my mind because the lads used to take the mickey out of him.

"Barem!" one of them would say. "It really suits him that name does ... I know I can't bloody well bear 'im!"

I wasn't over fond of Barem myself, but I didn't want to get into any conflict and tried to play things down.

Just like the kids of my junior school days, Barem resorted to barbed comments and insulting remarks.

"Ar-rgh you bloody yellow belly, are they all like that from your neck o' the woods?" he would say. I never rose to the bait or took any notice of his scurrilous remarks. Still, I had learnt from my previous experience to be on my guard.

But, one day, despite being wrong, Barem took me completely by surprise. I'd just come out of the washroom and was drying my face when he came up from behind and, without provocation, fisted me savagely in my back. The pain was excruciating, and as I fell to the floor like a stone unable to get up ... I could hardly breathe.

"You little wimp!" he mocked as he stood over me. "That'll teach you to mind your manners!" All I could do was look up into his jeering face; I couldn't even speak, as every breath was agony. My pain caused an involuntary moan. I knew I was badly hurt and needed medical attention, but he thought I was just too frightened to get up and the jeering continued. As luck would have it, a couple of my mates entered the room and noticed the pale, drawn look on my face. After administering first aid and assessing the situation, they called for an ambulance which took me to the army hospital. When Barem realised how hurt I was, he started to panic; but he wasn't bothered about me – he was only concerned for his own skin. He knew that if I reported what had really happened he would be charged and automatically lose his stripe. But I didn't want that.

"No," I thought, "I'll sort this my way. I've got to live with Barem. But there's one thing for sure, he's not going to get away with it scot-free."

When the doctors questioned me about the incident I told them I had slipped on the stone steps. As it turned out I had a pneumothorax due to broken ribs piercing and collapsing one of my lungs. The surgeon had to insert a tube into my chest to re-inflate the lung but luckily I wasn't in hospital too long and was discharged a few days later, my chest strapped up with wide Elastoplast. After a couple of weeks I had to report on parade every morning, but I was put on light duties.

Barem was all right initially, but it wasn't long before he started again with his snide comments. I knew in my heart that I had to put a stop to it but I wasn't fit enough to tackle him yet – the slightest exertion still creased me up. Time passed and every day my condition improved but even after four weeks I was nowhere near peak fitness.

One Saturday afternoon I was in the barrack room with a few of my mates and all the bed mattresses were turned back, displaying the bare steel framework underneath.

Things were fine until Barem entered the room and tried issuing orders. None of the lads took notice and this infuriated him.

"Get lost, Barem!" a few shouted. "Are you after another tape or what?"

"Go and play toy soldiers somewhere else," Brian Holdsworth quipped. Barem never answered Brian. Mind you, Brian weighed over sixteen stones and he was fit with it.

I couldn't help smirking, though, and Barem noticed.

"Tek that smile of your face, Cowell, or I'll wipe it off the same as I did last time."

I wasn't fit enough to have a go at him, but I shot straight back at him: "Get lost Barem, I don't want any truck with you. At least not yet, anyroad."

"What do you mean 'not yet', you little git … you'll have truck with me now and like it!"

"Oh no, he's coming for me again," I thought all tensed up, "he'll murder me!" I braced myself, as I could tell by the venomous look on his face that he was going to attack me. As he came for me I plainly remember praying to God for protection: "Oh please God give me the strength to ward him off … I don't know what I'll do if You don't."

It all happened so quickly. Barem came at me like a raging bull with pure hatred in his eyes. I somehow managed to side-step him and he fell onto one of the beds, sprawling on his back across the steel frame. As he tried to get up I instinctively dived on top of him. I couldn't throw any punches but I grabbed hold of the underside of the angle iron with both hands and pulled with all the strength I could muster. He couldn't move, as the corner of the angle iron was firmly pinned into the arch of his back. He tried pulling my hair but I simply pressed down all the more with my head and body. I kept up the pressure for what seemed an age, not daring to let go for fear of reprisal; the longer I hung on to the angle irons, the more laboured my breathing became. As my strength began to ebb I became agitated, but I didn't dare let up. Barem growled furiously at first, but then the growls turned to grunts, and finally to moans. I dared to lift my head, but with caution, as I wasn't too sure whether or not this was another of his sly tricks. Only when I looked at his face did I realise he was not kidding – it was deadly white and he was actually passing out. Justice or not, call it what you like … he actually finished up with a couple of broken ribs, just like me. He wasn't as badly hurt as I had been, but nevertheless, he was finished as far as this fight was concerned. It took about ten minutes before he was in a fit enough state to take himself off to the medical room. But before he did, I confronted him.

"Right Barem," I growled, "I've just beaten you with two broken ribs, so now I know you're no match for me. Anyroad, I'm warning thi … keep outta my bloody way in future or I'll rip your bloody throat out! Oh, and another thing whilst we're at it: when you get to the medical room you can tell 'em exactly what happened. I've got nowt to hide like you had, you slimy swine!"

That was it, I'd said my piece and finally laid the ghost to rest. I was very happy with the outcome. I didn't get joy from actually winning the fight so much as knowing that the taunting was finished. Barem and I never did become bosom buddies, but he never bothered me again after that.

* * *

As my ribs improved, I was determined to use everything at my disposal to get back to prime condition. This included using the camp's gymnasium and other facilities. I also decided to take up jogging and every evening I did a seven-mile run. I kept this up for two months, but to my dismay I began to suffer terribly from severe stiffness, especially in the mornings.

"I must be doing something wrong," I thought to myself, "surely I should be feeling a lot fitter by now?"

Then, one day, I approached one of the physical training instructors, a long-serving regular soldier called Tommy who was about forty years old and enjoyed the full respect of all his peers. I knew that he went jogging on a regular basis and I asked if I could join him.

"Aye you can if you want lad," he answered in a broad Lancashire accent, "but I won't hang about waiting for thi if you lag behind."

"Yeah that's fair enough," I replied, "I go along with that … I just want to get myself into prime condition the same as you."

"I'm glad to hear it, lad, there's too many young uns nowadays that just want to booze and laze about all the time. It won't be easy, mind … you'll have to work hard at it. Anyroad, we'll set off now, but think on what I said."

"Reighto, I'll keep as close on your heels as I can," I said, determined to make an impression.

He didn't run very fast, but kept up a steady pace non-stop for about six miles.

"We'll just have five minutes rest here and then we'll mek our way back to camp," he said, taking in deep breaths of air as he soaked up the last of the evening sun.

Surprisingly, I didn't have any trouble keeping up with him; in fact, I found myself slowing down to his pace. Nonetheless, despite doing everything he did, having a shower and a rub down after the run, I still suffered from terrible stiffness. After a month of jogging with this fit older man, I felt a bit dejected. And so one evening, after having a shower, I broached the subject with him once again.

"Excuse me, Tommy, but could I ask you something, please?"

"Aye course you can, lad … fire away."

"What it is, I were just wondering … how long have you been running like you do?"

"Well, it's bin quite a while now since I first started; in fact I'd be about the same age as you are now. U-um that's reight, I'd be about twenty, cos it were just after I joined up."

"That's interesting," I thought, "that's a bit of encouragement for me to carry on."

"Come on, lad," he said, intuiting my thoughts, "what d'you want to know?"

"Well, I was wondering whether you suffered from stiffness when you first started running? And if so … how long did it take before you reached the point when you overcame it?"

"Ha, ha, ha!" he bellowed, from the pit of his stomach. "That's a good un if ever I heard one."

"What's so funny?" I thought, a little flustered by his reaction.

"E-eh lad," he responded, seeing the bemused look on my face, "d'you really think you'll e'er get o'er being stiff if you carry on running every day?"

"I don't understand," I said, "I don't know what you mean."

"You don't know what I mean?" he said laughing again. "Bloomin' 'eck lad, d'you not know you've gotta have pain for gain?"

"Whaddaya talkin' about?" I asked, naively. "What d'you mean … pain for gain?"

"I mean what I say. If you want to keep yourself in good nick, you've gotta be prepared to put up with some pain."

"Yeah, I go along with that, but for how long? That's what I want to know."

"For as long as you keeps running," he said, "does that answer your question?"

"What … d'you mean to say you still suffer from stiffness?"

"Aye, that's reight lad, too flamin' true I do! I've bin running now for over twenty years and it's always the same … especially first thing in the morning."

"Over twenty years," I asked, rather surprised by his answer, "and it's still the same as when you started all them years ago?"

"Aye it is, but don't worry about it, it's somet you get used to. You've gotta programme your mind to it."

"Programme mi mind be blow'd," I thought, "sod that for a lark. If that's being fit, you can shove it!"

Once more Tommy noticed the look on my face. "You look a bit worried, lad. I haven't put thi off, have I?"

"Well actually," I replied feeling nonplussed, "in one word, yes."

"Don't fret about it, lad, you'll be all reight," he said, encouragingly, "you'll feel different about it in a couple o' months."

"No, I'm sorry Tommy I won't," I replied, my mind made up, "because I realise now this lark is not for me."

"Oh what a pity, and here's me thinking how well you were doing. It's a shame really, cos you really need to work at it to keep yourself in trim tha knows."

"Oh I know that Tommy and I intend to, but not by running."

"Oh aye, and what method are you gonna use then?"

"Well, I intend to go down to the gym every night or go swimming. Aye, and I'll tackle the army assault course a few times or do anything else that's interesting."

"I hope so lad, I hope so," Tommy put in, genuinely concerned. "I'll keep an eye on thi to watch your progress, cos I've taken an interest in thi and I wouldn't like to see you falter at this stage."

"Thanks, Tommy, I appreciate that and don't think I'm not grateful for everything you've taught me, cos I am."

"Tha's all reight lad ... just think on what I told thi and keep at it ... that'll be thanks enough for me."

For the rest of my time on the camp, Tommy and I kept in touch and despite the age gap we became good friends.

*　　*　　*

I did keep up various activities and definitely benefited from them. The beauty of it was that I no longer suffered from that crippling stiffness. Of all the exercises, I enjoyed swimming the best, and still frequently swam two lengths of the pool underwater as I had done back home in Burnley with my friend Pete Holroyd.

This put me in good stead when another physical instructor, a corporal whom we nicknamed Smithy, took a group of us out on an arduous keep-fit exercise. After an eight-mile route march at the double we finished off by fooling about in a large outdoor swimming pool. It was about half as long again as an ordinary pool. Unlike Tommy, this instructor was unfriendly and aggressive. He was also a show-off.

"Right, you toe rags!" he bellowed as we all stood around the pool in our swimming trunks. "I'm going to dive in now and swim underwater and I want to see who can get the nearest to me after I emerge."

"U-um, this should be interesting," I thought, "this is right up my street ... I can't see him being any better than Pete Holroyd."

I watched him dive in and he seemed to be going well, but I got a gut feeling that he wouldn't complete a full length.

"He's not doing too bad," I murmured, "but he's not deep enough in the water." I concluded this from the fact that I'd always found it easier to swim as close to the bottom of the pool as possible, almost scraping the bottom with my belly, as I found this way I experienced less resistance from the water.

To my surprise, lots of the lads started shouting eagerly as he reached the halfway mark.

"Blimey!" quipped one of them. "He's like a bloomin' fish ... he's never gonna come up for air."

"Yeah, but he'll never make it to t'other end," remarked another.

"He should do," I thought to myself, "after all the bragging he's done. U-um, it's nowhere near as far as two lengths of the Central Baths ... and it's a straight run, he doesn't have to turn around."

My gut feeling was correct. He'd only swam just over three-quarters of a length when he had to come up for a breather.

"Naythen you scruffy no-hopers," he bawled after a short respite, "I want you to dive in one at a time and try and match me."

He was a show-off but then again, so was I. I knew for certain that I could easily outclass him and that's what I intended to do. But first, I wanted to see how the other lads fared and so I purposely stood at the back of the queue. Some of the lads were non-swimmers and had to be helped out of the pool by the aid of a long bamboo pole immediately after diving in. Others emerged after only swimming a few yards. Two lads actually reached the halfway stage, but were still well short of their target.

"You feeble-hearted lot," bellowed Smithy from his position in the water, "this is what comes of smoking and boozing too much!" Then he noticed me still standing on the bank. "Right you ratbag," he yelled, "get yourself in and let's see what you can do!" This was to be my moment of glory and his downfall.

"Right you big-headed swine!" I smirked. "I'm gonna show you what a Trafalgar waller can do and bring you down a peg or two at the same time."

"Come on, you bloody sprog," he shrieked, "we haven't got all day to hang about!"

"Righto," I shouted back through cupped hands, "open your legs and I'll swim through 'em!"

This created a bit of a riot, as all the lads started laughing. Nevertheless, the laughing changed to cheers the nearer I got to the instructor and the cheers increased even more so when I actually passed through his legs and carried on to complete the length. I had enough in reserve to turn around and swim back through his legs the other way but I didn't bother ... I'd already achieved my goal. I knew that I'd done enough to ridicule the self-centred, arrogant bloke.

After that I never did hit it off with Smithy, unsurprisingly. Not to worry, though, the sixteen weeks training passed quickly and we all got a week's home leave prior to me being posted to Crownhill Barracks, in Plymouth.

EMBARKATION LEAVE

Time passed quickly and before I knew it, Christmas was upon us and to our delight we all got a few days' home leave. I arrived at Burnley Barracks Railway Station about seven o'clock in the evening and happily made my way along Trafalgar. Albion Street looked different somehow, not quite as busy as it had been in the past.

"It must be me," I thought, "most of my mates are serving in the forces. Yeah, that's what it is."

Nevertheless, something was different, as I discovered on reaching home. For the first time in my life the front door was locked.

"That's funny," I thought as I turned the door-handle, "I've never known this afore … I must be at the wrong house." I pondered a moment then noticed the gas lamp. "No, this is the right house all right … I should know, I've swung on that old gas lamp enough times." After shouting through the letterbox and rattling on the door, I heard a voice from above me.

"Hello there, is that Johnny?" As I looked up I saw Malcolm Davis from next door looking out of his bedroom window.

"Hiya Malcolm … it's me all reight. I've just got home on leave and I can't get into th'house."

"Bloomin' 'eck Johnny, has nobody told thi?" asked Malcolm.

"Told me what?"

"Well, your mam flit a couple o' days ago."

"Oh 'eck, she mustn't have had time to get in touch with me afore I left the barracks, maybe there's a letter in the post."

"I don't know about that, John. She never mentioned owt to us about you coming home."

"No, that's because she didn't know, Mal, I never told her cos I wanted to surprise her." I winced a little before adding, "It looks as though the shoe's on t'other foot now, don't it … I'm th'one who's surprised."

Maybe she's trying to tell thi something," Malcolm joked.

"Aye maybe, you could be right there Mal."

"Anyroad John, if you'd like to come in for a brew and a sandwich, I'll run you up there afterwards on the back of mi motorbike."

"Thanks a lot Mal, that sounds good to me."

Malcolm's wife, Ivy, was sat in the living room and she gave me a warm welcome.

"Oh look who it is, young Johnny Cowell, how are you? E-eh, but it's nice to see you."

"And it's nice to see you, Mrs Davis, I hope you're keeping well."

"By 'eck, the army life must be doing you good, Johnny, you're looking really well and you've filled out quite a bit as well."

"Thank you Mrs Davis ... you look really good as well."

"You can dispense with the Mrs Davis and call me Ivy now you're a grown man. Anyway, sit yourself down while I put the kettle on and make you a cup of tea and something to eat."

"Thank you very much, Mrs Davis."

"There you go again – 'Mrs Davis'."

"I'm sorry, it's just that …."

"Take no notice of me, Johnny," she cut in, "I'm teasing. I know only too well how your mother brought you up to respect others."

As it turned out, Mum had been offered the keys to a house in the Rosehill area and she couldn't get away from Albion Street fast enough. After a brief chat I thanked Malcolm and Ivy for their hospitality and then rode pillion to my new home at 76 Moorland Road on the Rosehill Estate, where I celebrated my home leave. To me the house didn't have the same feeling about it as Albion Street. I couldn't pinpoint why I felt like that about Mum's new home – I just did.

Our Barry and Barbara greeted me and they made a right fuss. It turned out that this meeting was to determine our Barry's future career.

"How are you liking in th'army, our John?" he asked eagerly. "Is it owt like you expected it to be?"

"Yeah, it's all right, our kid, I'm enjoying it, especially the comradeship."

"Are they teaching you to drive? You've allus fancied driving one o' them big wagons?"

"No they're not … the thing is they've put me in the Medical Corps and I've bin working in th'army hospitals." This got Barry really interested.

"You what!" he responded, "You mean like a nurse?"

"U-um kind of but they don't call us nurses … we're called nursing orderlies."

"So what do you have to do, then?"

"Oh we do everything from emptying bed pans to feeding the patients who can't feed themselves."

"So it is like being a nurse, then?"

"Oh yeah … we even give medicines and injections."

"Bloomin' 'eck! That's somet I've always wanted to do."

"I didn't know that, our kid – you've never mentioned it afore."

"Yeah, I know I haven't but it's true – honest! I've thought about going into nursing for ages, but I didn't say owt to anybody, cos I were frightened o' getting the mickey took outta me."

"Hey never mind about that … if it's somet you want to do our Barry, go forrit!"

"Are you sure our John? Would you if you were me?"

"I'm dead sure, our Barry, if that's the way you feel, do it! Anyroad, you're a lot different from me. With your nature you're cut out forrit."

Barry's expression changed as the excitement built up inside him. "That's it, our John, I'm gonna do it! You've convinced me, I'm definitely gonna do it."

"Good for you, our kid, good for you, go for it – follow your dream!"

Sure enough … the very next day he went to Burnley General Hospital and applied for nursing training, for a career that was to span forty years. Little did I know then that twenty years later I too would be pursuing the same career.

* * *

I was determined to enjoy my home leave, but as usual I went a bit over the top and did something very stupid. During the holiday I made friends with Alan Hargreaves, a lad who was three years younger than me and lived a few doors away on Moorland Road. On Sunday night we went down town and frequented a few of the local pubs, and by the end of the night we'd both drunk a few pints and felt quite fresh.

"Bloomin' 'eck John," drawled Alan, "I don't fancy that long trek back up Manchester Road ... how about catching the last bus?"

"Aye, all reight Alan, but it'll have to be a Ribble, cos the local buses stopped running at half-past ten."

"Well, what difference does it mek which bus we catch," Alan replied, "so long as it gets us up to Moorland Road ... that's all I'm bothered about."

"That's just it," I replied, "the Ribble bus doesn't drop off at the Rose and Crown ... the first stop is the Bull and Butcher, which means we'll have a long trek back."

"Oh aye, I forgot about that," moaned Alan, but then added as an afterthought, "anyroad, we can hop off at the Summit traffic lights afore it carries on towards Rawtenstall."

"Oh yeah, and what if the lights are on green?"

"Well even if they are, the flamin' bus hasta slow down so we'll still be able to jump off it, won't we."

"Right then, you're on Alan – let's go!"

So off we trotted and caught the bus from the bus station. As it sped up Manchester Road and approached the Rose and Crown, Alan and I alighted from our seats and perched ourselves precariously on the open-ended platform at the back of the bus. As it turned a slight left-hand bend the traffic lights, which were about a quarter of a mile up the road, came into view and they had just turned to amber.

"Great!" I said to Alan. "The red light's just coming on, so the bus'll have to slow down." What I didn't anticipate was that these traffic lights changed very quickly. The bus slowed down as it approached the junction, but then as it got within about two hundred yards, the lights changed to green. Inevitably, the bus driver put his foot down and the bus speeded up. I'd already committed myself to jump as I hung onto the steel handrail, and jump I did. As I landed, I tried running as fast as I could to retain my balance, but I couldn't run fast enough. Consequently, I went crashing to the ground banging my forehead on the flagged pavement.

"Oh no John, you idiot!" I groaned as I saw the blood dripping from my head onto the stone flags, "When will you ever learn?" After wiping my brow I looked up and to my horror I saw young Alan spread-eagled face downward about fifty yards further up the road. I realised that the bus must have been going even faster when he jumped and I feared for Alan's life. "Oh please God," I mumbled, "please don't let him be dead!" As I approached Alan, he was motionless, but I could hear him moaning.

"Thank Goodness for that!" I sighed. "At least he's alive … thank you God!" After weighing up the situation and putting my first-aid knowledge to good use, I could see that, in spite of a badly swollen face and a few cuts and bruises, he was going to be all right.

"O-oh, where am I," he groaned, "what happened?"

"You might well ask, Alan," I said, feeling happier now. "We both jumped off the bloomin' bus like idiots."

"Oh aye, I remember now, it were ... o-o-oh, mi bloomin' head, it feels likes it's bin run o'er with a steam roller."

"Come on, Alan, I'd best get thi up to th'casualty department."

"No way," he grunted, "I'll be all reight ... just get me home, I wanna go to bed."

We got home all right, but we both got a good rollicking from our mothers.

Alan and I slept well that night but we suffered for it the next day. I had a black eye and a few bruises, but he looked terrible – just like a boxer after being battered over fifteen gruelling rounds. Both his eyes were almost closed and his nose was swollen and squashy.

"Bloomin' 'eck!" I thought, feeling guilty. "I feel bad enough ... what must poor Alan feel like?"

From that day on nobody believed we'd jumped off a bus, especially Alan's brothers.

"Geddaway withee!" they'd say. "You've bin fighting! Who are you trying to kid?"

"Well, please yourself what you want to believe. That's the honest truth," I insisted.

"Tek no notice of 'em John," put in Alan, "we know what happened and that's what counts."

Luckily we recovered without any adverse effects. I felt very remorseful about the incident, albeit a little wiser. I went back to camp shortly after that, but Alan and I remained good friends thereafter. I put the incident down to experience and vowed never to do it again.

*   *   *

After six months' service we all got a pay increase of ten shillings. Twenty-five shillings still wasn't a lot of money to get by on, but it was a lot better than fifteen shillings.

Things seemed to be going well. But, as so often happens, a very dark shadow then came along, one that changed my whole life … my father died. He'd recently collapsed with abdominal pains and been rushed into Burnley General Hospital, to undergo emergency surgery for a burst appendix. I was immediately granted compassionate leave and went straight to the hospital to see him. During that critical time I spent many hours around his bed in Intensive Care along with my brothers and sisters. A blockage of the bowels had occurred and serious complications had set in. Still, after a week on Intensive Care, his condition improved and he was transferred to the main ward.

"Thank God for that," I prayed, as I made my way back to Plymouth the following day. But my delight was only short-lived. I had only been back at the camp two days when I received the most distressing telephone call from my sister Maureen informing me that Dad had died. I was summoned to the commandant's office at nine o'clock on February 27th, where our Maureen told me the terrible news over the telephone. Before she muttered one word I knew the worst – it's hard to say how, I just knew.

"Our John," she muttered, her voice trembling, "I've got something to tell …."

"Oh no, our Maureen," I stopped her in mid-sentence, "it's not Dad, is it? … Please don't say it's Dad!"

" I … I'm sorry, our kid," she mumbled in a shaky voice, trying to hold back the tears, "Dad died during the early hours of this morning."

I didn't answer – I couldn't. My whole body felt numb; it just didn't seem real.

"John … John, are you there?" Maureen asked, tearfully. "Please answer me!"

"U-um, I'm still here, our Maureen, I'm still here," I answered, after a few seconds. "I just can't take it in … please say it's not true!" But even as I was saying the words, I knew it was true.

Maureen was over three hundred miles away, but I could still feel her sorrow over the telephone, just as she could feel mine.

"I'm sorry, our John, that I had to be the bearer of bad news," she apologised, "but you had to be told and Mum thought it would be best coming from me."

"Yeah, I know that our kid," I said, as a tear rolled down my cheek, "thanks a lot." Then, as an afterthought, I asked, "How's Mam and t'others taking it, anyroad?"

"We're all feeling the same," she replied sadly, "we all need each other at a time like this."

"Righto our Maureen, give mi mam my blessing and tell her I'll be home as quick as I can."

When I put the phone down it was obvious to everyone in the office that something was wrong. I couldn't speak at first. I was devastated and felt numb all over. One of the lads sat me down whilst another offered me a cup of coffee and some biscuits.

The commanding officer was very good, again granting immediate compassionate leave and, within two hours, I was on the train, arriving home about ten o'clock that evening.

The next few days were very sad. My brothers and sisters and I held a constant vigil in the front room by Dad's coffin prior to the funeral service, which took place on March 3rd at Christ the King Catholic Church. He was buried in Burnley Cemetery and afterwards a reception was held at the Co-op tea-rooms on Hammerton Street.

Within two days of the burial I had to return to Crownhill Barracks to continue my army service.

In the months following Dad's death I was devastated, and didn't feel like doing anything ... everything seemed so unreal. Nevertheless, life had to go on. The army had been very lenient when Dad was ill, but now I had to toe the line and carry out my duties like any other soldier. In a way, the disciplined life was good for me and brought me back to reality. Also I had the support of my newfound friends. Six weeks after returning to camp, I celebrated my twenty-first birthday, but I was sad because, although I received lots of cards from home I didn't get the one I wanted ... the one from my dad. However, I did receive a nice card from my Aunt Lily and she'd enclosed three pounds.

"E-eh, that's nice," I thought, "and very generous of her ... I'll have to write and thank her. Yeah, Dad would like that. U-um, and he'd also like me to get on with my life; he wouldn't want me to be down in the dumps like I have been."

That night I went to the NAAFI Club in Plymouth, where I celebrated the occasion with some friends, after which I settled back down to army routine and gradually started to enjoy life again.

*   *   *

During my time at Crownhill Barracks I met another lad from Burnley, Ernie Christie, who'd just completed a strenuous course with the Para-medics – and had loved it. I was having a shave in the washroom one morning when I heard a voice behind me.

"All reight, Johnny, I've ne'er seen thee here afore. Whattaya doing here?"

"All reight, Ernie," I replied on turning. "I could ask thi t'same question."

"Me? I've bin stationed here for the last ten months."

"Aye?" I replied, rather surprised. "Then how come we've ne'er bumped into each other afore?"

"A-ah well, I've bin on a paratrooper's course for the last three months up in Aldershot and now they've sent me back here."

"What, d'you mean tha's bin parachuting outta planes?"

"Yeah, course I've bin parachuting fro' planes ... what the flamin' 'eck d'you think paratroopers do?"

"Bloomin' 'eck," I responded, enviously, "that's somet I've allus wanted to do!"

"So have I," said Ernie proudly, "and that's why I did it."

"So you'll have a red beret now and you'll be able to wear the wings on your uniform?"

"That's reight," Ernie said, going to his locker from where he proudly produced his red beret. "Aye and th'best thing is I get an extra two pounds a week on top o' mi pay. Mind thi, it were a bloomin' hard course ... you had to be as fit as a fiddle to get through it."

It was no idle boast. Ernie really was a fit lad. He didn't drink or smoke and during our conversation he told me he went for a long cross-country run every night over Dartmoor. I didn't offer to join him, but as I regularly went for a brisk walk over the moor myself I arranged to meet up with him. On warm summer evenings we would swim in one of the many streams throughout the grassland and loved trying to ride the wild ponies that lived on the moor. They appeared quite tame and would allow us to get close but when we attempted to ride them they kicked and jumped furiously, like bucking broncos in a Wild West rodeo show. Ernie and I became good mates during that summer, better than we'd ever been back in our home town.

Some of the army routine involved long route marches over Dartmoor and especially around Princetown, the place of the notorious Dartmoor Prison. It intrigued me to see a few prisoners working out in the open air around the town and I couldn't take in the fact that some of these men were serving lifelong prison sentences.

We patrolled a vast area of Devon exercising our manoeuvering skills, setting up camp for days or weeks on end and it was during one of these routine drills that Ernie met his future wife. The exercise took place in Taunton, a little town eighty miles east of Plymouth, where we were stationed for three weeks. It was Thursday night and a dance was being held in the church hall, and that's where he met the young girl ... he was smitten from the word go. I never saw much of Ernie after that, because he hitchhiked the eighty miles to Taunton at every opportunity to see his newfound love.

*   *   *

On reflection, the main reason why I wanted to go into the Service Corps was so I could learn to drive.

But after serving only a few weeks, I got to thinking, "I'm glad now that I got placed in the Medics, cos I really enjoy working as a nursing orderly in the field hospitals. Yeah, I might even apply to work as a nurse at Burnley General Hospital when I get demobbed. But it'd be an added bonus if I got my driving licence as well ... I wonder how I can do that?"

I racked my brains trying to think of something, but to no avail. Then, one Saturday afternoon whilst walking along Union Street in Plymouth, I passed a British School Of Motoring centre. There was an advertisement in the window that read:

A COURSE OF LESSONS WITH US GUARANTEES A 90% PASS RATE. COME IN AND ASK FOR A QUOTE.

"Why not?" I thought, "I may as well find out how much it'll cost me … I've got nowt to lose."

"Six shillings a lesson," said the receptionist, "and we recommend that you take at least two lessons a week for a period of six weeks."

"U-um, that's twelve bob a week," I pondered, "that'll only leave me with thirteen bob." I knew I'd struggle, but I felt a tinge of excitement building up in my stomach. "Oh blow it! I've bin skint afore … a few more weeks isn't gonna mek that much difference."

I started my lessons with enthusiasm but things didn't go too well and after eight lessons the school informed me that I would need to take at least another ten to come up to scratch. And then there was the added cost of a few pounds for the driving test. I became rather despondent as negative thoughts clouded my mind.

"Oh 'eck, what if I don't pass the test the first time? That'll mean more expense … I just can't do it!" I was feeling rather dejected but then I came up with an idea that paid dividends. I went to see my C.O. Colonel Peck, and asked for an advance on my future pay.

"And what's so important that you need this money now?" he asked me.

I explained the reason, emphasising that my driving licence would come in handy during my army career driving the ambulances and stretcher Rovers – or any other vehicle for that matter. To my surprise, he was intrigued and came up with something to my advantage.

"Private Cowell, I've got to say that I'm highly impressed with your enterprising scheme, I only wish I had more men under my command who thought like you. Yes indeed, anyone who would spend so much out of his meagre pay deserves some encouragement."

"Encouragement!" I thought. "This sounds interesting."

To my delight he then handed me a chit of paper, saying, "As from this moment, you don't have to spend another penny out of your own pocket … take this form to the Service Corps Depot." He looked at me with a pleasant smile on his face and asked, "Do you know what this is?"

"No sir?"

"Well, it's an authorisation slip, requesting the officer in charge of vehicles to arrange a full course of driving lessons and a driving test for you. I think it's a good idea what you've come up with and from now on, I'm going to arrange for every man in my regiment to undergo driving instructions." He muttered to himself as he stroked his chin. "Yes indeed, it should prove very useful to them and the corps during their spell in the army … especially driving the stretcher Rovers." Turning his attention back to me he said, "Right, Private Cowell, seeing as you came up with the idea I think it only fair that you should be the first to do it along with another lad. So, starting from Monday morning you will be excused normal duties … how does that sound to you?"

"Very good, sir," I stammered, obviously delighted, "thank you very much, sir!"

"Just one more thing before you go: have you anyone in mind who'd you'd like to join you?"

"Yes sir I have," I replied, hardly able to believe my luck. "Private Brian Holdsworth; he's in the same billet as me."

"Yes, I'm quite aware of where he's stationed, thank you. I'll make arrangements for him to be excused duties as well."

I couldn't wait to get back to tell my mate Brian. He was as excited as I was and went eagerly with me to the Service Depot.

"Right," muttered the officer in charge, after reading the slip of paper, "report to me the pair of you on Monday morning directly after inspection parade, and I'll get one of the corporals to take you out in a Land Rover."

That was it. Brian and I couldn't believe it!

"Great!" laughed Brian expressing his obvious delight, "no more fatigue duties for a few weeks and a chance o' geddin our driving licences in the bargain ... absolutely great!"

For the next three weeks, Brian and I thoroughly enjoyed ourselves, driving around Plymouth and the surrounding countryside. Our instructor, Corporal Gallagher, gave us our first driving lesson on an old disused aerodrome prior to taking to the roads of Dartmoor, driving through Princetown and other neighbouring villages. But we did most of our driving in Plymouth, passing through the docks, Plymouth Hoe, Union Street, and by the NAAFI club and the Drake Cinema.

Things were going great ... and then something happened in West Africa that almost put an end to our good fortune. There had recently been an uprising in the Belgian Congo, West Africa, and now the British Cameroons was fighting for independence. A state of emergency was called throughout the camp and all leave and special privileges were cancelled forthwith.

"Oh no, what lousy timing!" moaned Brian. "We'd o' bin going in for our test in two weeks … now this has blown it."

"I don't know so much, Brian," I mused. "How about us going to see the Service Corps' officer and asking him if he'll test us today?"

"Oh sure, and how do we get excused duties after th'inspection parade?"

"We'll just tell the sergeant major that everything's bin arranged."

"What, just like that? He'll have our guts for garters if he checks it out. We'll be thrown in't cooler quicker than we can blink."

"Oh come on, Brian, we've got loads to gain from it. I'm gam if you are."

"Aye, I suppose you're reight, it'd be a shame to give up at this stage."

So we did it, playing one officer off against the other. First we'd to get past our own sergeant major.

"What?" he screamed, his handlebar moustache twitching as the air gushed out of his mouth. "I haven't been told anything about it!"

"Yes sir, it's right," I said, lying as I stared him in the eyes, "the officer in charge of transport said we had to get there as quickly as possible." Luckily he just growled once more, then let us go. When we reached the vehicle depot, the officer in charge was just as puzzled.

"I'm afraid I don't know anything about it … have you got an authorisation slip?"

Feeling flustered, I had to think fast. "Well no, sir, but the sergeant major sent us down here to see if you could test us this morning. He said it would be handy to have at least two drivers amongst the Medics."

To our relief, he didn't question it further. "Righto then, you come with me," he said, pointing to me, "I'll take you first."

By the end of that morning, both Brian and I had passed … we were elated. We were also relieved, we'd taken a risk and got away with it; no cross-checking was done, as everybody seemed too involved with the emergency situation. I looked at the little slip of paper in my hand that the officer had given me.

"Ye-eah!" I chuckled with sheer delight. "I've done it … I've done it!"

*   *   *

Just a couple of days later, we were all informed that our regiment was being posted to the Cameroons. I was pleased in a way, because at least I would get to see another part of the world, and – as a bonus – we all got ten days' embarkation leave.

When I got home I felt at a loose end, as most of my friends were serving abroad in the Forces. However, I was determined to enjoy my last Saturday night in England before I too was shipped out of the country. That afternoon, whilst downtown, I bumped into another mate of mine, Martin Grogan, who came out with some intriguing news.

"All reight, Johnny," he greeted me, "how's it going?"

"Oh not so bad Martin, an' you?" I asked, "are you still playing football nowadays?"

"Aye I am, but not in Civvy Street. I'm in th'army now doing mi National Service."

"Bloomin' 'eck, Martin, so am I. What regiment are you with?"

"I'm in th'infantry serving with the King's Own Borderers and I'm stationed at Barnard Castle up in Durham ... which one are you with?"

"I'm in the Medics and I'm stationed in Plymouth down in Devon. I weren't keen on th'idea at first, but it's all reight now; in fact, I'm quite enjoying it."

"Yeah, you will be you lucky bugger," he joked, "it's just like thi to get a cushy number."

"You wouldn't say that Martin, if you knew where I were going next week."

"How's that then, where are you off to?"

"To a place called the Cameroons somewhere in West Africa near to the Belgium Congo."

"You're joking!" he laughed. "That's incredible, I don't believe it."

"Why not, what's so funny about that, Martin? Soldiers are geddin posted abroad all the time."

"Oh I know that, John," he laughed, "but the thing is ... I'm geddin posted there as well!"

"You're joking!" I said responding as he had. "You mean to say you're on embarkation leave too?"

"I am that and I get shipped out next Thursday on the *Devonshire* from Southampton."

"Flamin' Emma, this is geddin more uncanny by the minute," I grinned, "that's the same boat as I'm going on ... you never know, we'll be sharing the same bunk next."

"Bloomin' 'eck that's great John!" he said excitedly. "We're gonna have to do somet about it ... how about a celebration tonight?"

"I'm all for that, Martin. Have you owt planned?"

"Aye, I have as a matter o' fact ... I've bin told it's a great night o'er in Rawtenstall at the Astoria Ballroom. What d'you think?"

"Aye, why not, it sounds all reight to me … what bus d'you wanna catch?"

"Well, I'll catch the seven o'clock bus from th'end o' Trafalgar … how about you?"

"Yeah fair enough, I'll catch it further up Manchester Road outside the Rose and Crown."

"Sounds good enough to me," said Martin, "I'll see thi later then … think on, don't forget."

"There's no danger o' that," I grinned, "I'm lookin' forward to it as much as you are."

The bus was on schedule and as arranged we arrived in Rawtenstall around half-past seven.

"How about having a couple o' pints in the Queens?" Martin suggested. "It's usually packed in there with a good atmosphere."

"Yeah, I'm with you there Martin," I replied, "it's the same pub I've always gone in with mi mates Pete Holly and Dave Whittaker."

We entered the pub full of enthusiasm, but to our disappointment there were only a few people stood around the bar.

"Bloomin' 'eck John, it's flamin' dead in here," moaned Martin. "I wonder what's goin' on … I've never known it this empty afore."

"No, neither have I, it's usually jam-packed by this time. Still, give it another half an hour … things might buck up."

However, before we'd finished our first pint, Martin became a little edgy. He realised something was wrong.

"Bloomin' 'eck John," he whined again, "whose flamin' idea were it to come to this pub?"

"Well, if I remember rightly, Martin it were …."

"Aye I know it were me," he laughed, "don't remind me. Still, I wonder where everybody is … I can't weigh it up."

"No, neither can I. Anyroad, I don't know about you, but I'm bursting ... I'll have to nip to the loo."

"Aye, me too," said Martin, "I'll join thi"

We both made our way to the gents, where we got talking to Joe Frankland's another lad from Burnley.

"All reight Joe," said Martin, "it's flaming dead in here tonight, innit?"

"Aye I know it is," replied Joe, "and I know why too. I've just found out that most people have gone down the Nelson Imp, cos Johnny Dankworth and Cleo Laine are playin there tonight. It'll be no good goin' to th'Astoria. It'll be as dead as a dodo in there."

"Charming," retorted Martin, "flamin' charming! We've come all the way o'er here to have a rave-up and everybody's back o'er in our neck o' th'woods."

"Blast it," I moaned, "that's put the tin hat on it! What are we gonna do now?"

"There's not much we can do," replied Martin, looking at his watch. "By the time we caught the bus back to Burnley and then to Nelson it'd all be o'er bar the shouting. We'll just have to mek the best of a bad job."

"P-p-pth," I pouted, "just our flamin' luck. And on our last Saturday night out in England for ages!"

"Not to worry, lads," put in Joe with a grin on his face, "if you wanna go down th'Imp, I'll tek you there."

"How d'you mean, Joe," asked Martin. "How canya do that?"

"Well, I've got a van outside, I only bought it two days ago. It's only an old banger, but it gets me fro' A to B and that's all I'm bothered about."

"Oh great!" enthused Martin. "That'll do us ... as long as it gets us down th'Imp, that's all we're bothered about as well."

I was as keen as Martin to get to the Nelson Imperial and so, after quickly downing our pints, we clambered onto the back of Joe's rickety old van and headed back up Burnley Road. It was a bumpy ride but we arrived at the Nelson Imperial about ten o'clock to find it absolutely packed to the doors.

"Yeah!" exclaimed Martin excitedly, "this is more like it, the place is buzzing!"

"You're not kidding," I agreed. "I've never seen it as packed as this afore ... it's absolutely heaving, innit?"

It was a great atmosphere all right ... you could feel the dance floor moving up and down with the sheer weight of all the young folk doing their own thing. Little did Martin and I know that we were to meet two girls that night, who were to become our future wives!

Shortly after arriving, I lost Martin in the crowd and didn't see him again that night. In fact, the next time I saw him was when we were sailing to Africa together on the *Devonshire*.

"What happened to you, Martin, when we got to th'Imp? I lost you once we'd got into the ballroom."

"Aye. No bloomin' wonder, John, in that crowd ... it were superb, weren't it? Anyroad, the first person I saw on entering the ballroom was a girl called Mary Smith, who was dancing with her sister. We clicked right away and after dancing with her all night I made a date with her."

"Bloomin' 'eck Martin, somet similar happened to me. After losing you I spotted a girl I've fancied for ages – they call her Edna Simpson. I've seen her loads o' times down th'Empress Ballroom, but I was always too scared to ask her for a dance. When I saw her this time, though, I plucked up the courage. I thought blow it, what have I got to lose, I won't be coming home again for at least a year."

"Aye, and what happened then?"

"Well, I asked her onto the floor and everything just flowed. I found her dead easy to get on with. We had a couple of bops during the rock 'n' roll session and I even attempted a quickstep, and then I asked if I could take her home and we danced the last waltz. We chatted easily and, after making a date to see her on Sunday night, I met her under the clock outside the Palace and we went for a drink in the Hall Inn and the Coach and Horses. We had a really good night and decided to swap addresses so we could write to each other whilst I'm away in Africa." It seemed that Martin and I were gaining more and more in common with each passing day!

*　*　*

In reminiscense, my embarkation leave soon passed and the day arrived when I had to make my way back to the barracks in Plymouth. Setting off for the station, I was full of nostalgia, as everything about my life seemed to be changing so quickly.

My grandparents and Dad had died, my Albion Street days had come to an end and now I was being shipped off to the Cameroons in West Africa. It might as well have been the other side of the moon!

Before making my way to the railway station I decided to call in at number 14 Albion for a last look. My old home was still vacant and the front door still locked. However, not to be put off I walked around the back and entered the house via the fourteen stone cellar steps. As I stood in the living room the house seemed to come alive as nostalgic memories flooded through my head.

My mind flashed back to my childhood days: My Uncle Ted; the Workhouse; Mum's stories; my schooldays; playing on the front street; working down the pit; all my fond teenage memories of Sandygate Youth Club. And finally, my home leave from the army.

"Well John lad," I lamented, sighing deeply, "I've spent a lot of happy times here, a lot of hard ones mind, but happy all the same." I looked at the flag floors and the old cast-iron fireplace, which triggered off even more memories within me – I saw all my brothers' and sisters' happy smiling faces and I could hear their laughter. The old gas lamp was still hanging from the ceiling, covered in dust, never to be lit again.

And then I saw Dad in one of his frivolous moods, dancing a kind of Irish jig in front of the fire, with his trousers folded above the knees. He looked so funny as he danced on the old pegged rug ... his legs were so skinny, just like picking sticks. I saw myself laughing – I used to think there was more meat on a ginny spinner's legs than on Dad's! The laughter turned to chuckles as I remembered the time he'd brought Peggy, our horse, into the living room when he was drunk, and the time, when he was equally drunk, when he got stuck in the coal-chute, trying to get into the house after Mum had locked him out.

"Aye Dad," I murmured to myself, my eyes welling up, "when you were like that, you were great ... absolutely great, I wouldn't o' swapped thi for any other dad in the world! Anyroad, I'm going now, Dad, but I'll never forget you, you'll always be in my thoughts and my prayers wherever I go ... and I know I'll gain strength from that."

Then I walked upstairs and glanced for the last time over the rooftops of all the other streets. The distant hills of Cliviger and the Bacup hills beyond reminded me of my cycling days.

In the chimney alcove nearest to the window I smiled, noticing the pencil marks that my two brothers and I had scribbled there over the years, indicating the progress of our growth. By the side of the marks were excited comments by whoever had grown the most.

The cracks in the ceiling were still apparent and my imagination could still conjure up many different shapes as I recalled the happy hours we'd spent playing 'I spy with my little eye'. The bare wood floors looked so sparse and yet all I could think of were the good times I'd had there. The hours we'd played about with candles, hanging up pillowcases on Christmas Eve in preference to stockings. I even pictured our Jimmy playing there, happy and contented, with his bag of dried peas spread all over the wooden boards, pretending they were regiments of soldiers. Finally I looked at the place where my bed had been and where I'd prayed every night alongside my two brothers before going to sleep.

At that I got down on my knees and said my last prayer in that humble house. I thanked God that we had all come through it safely, and asked Him to keep His holy light shining around my family and me and to guide us on our way throughout the rest of our lives.

I was brought back to reality when I heard the Town Hall Clock and Watt's Clock chiming simultaneously on the hour, as I'd heard them so many times in the past.

I smiled to myself and sighed at the same time. "A-ah well I'd better be off … let's see what life holds in store for me in the Cameroons."

I descended the multicoloured staircase and finally walked through the lobby. I unbolted the front door and closed it for the last time, leaving it unlocked, as it had always been throughout my young life. On reaching the bottom of Albion Street I took my last look at the humble abode and, taking a deep breath, made my way to the Barracks Station.

I felt rather sad as I meandered along Trafalgar, passing all the familiar cobbled streets Rowley Street, Whitaker Street, Derby Street, Sandygate, Mile Street and finally Lord Street where the Pawnshop, sporting the three balls above its shop window, still stood on the corner. Memories of all the poor folk, who had pledged heirlooms and other valuable objects just to make ends meet flooded through my head; I could picture them as plain as day, bartering with the smug pawnbroker.

Before leaving Lord Street, my thoughts were on my young friend Derek Ratcliffe, who had been tragically killed on Trafalgar whilst riding the butcher's bike at the age of sixteen.

"My, how time flies," I thought to myself. "That's over five years ago. May God bless you, Derek … I know I'll never forget you!"

As I passed the Alhambra Picture House, I reflected on the Saturday afternoon matinees and the times I'd spent there with my friends David Whittaker, Ronnie Hopkinson, Kenny Clayton and Bobby Cheetham. And finally, just before reaching the Mitre Junction, I stopped at the Ribble bus stop at the side of Mullen and Durkin's Builder's Yard.

"U-um," I thought, "many's the time that I've caught the Accrington bus here during my working days at Thorney-Bank Colliery." I lingered a while longer, reflecting on more nostalgic memories, and then tried to compose myself. "A-ah well, never mind John," I mused, "it all seems rather sad but still, look on the bright side. You've made a lot of new friends in the army and most of 'em are going off to West Africa with you." At that moment, my thoughts were interrupted by a voice from behind me. I turned, and there stood Jack Lofthouse.

"All reight Johnny Cowell," he said, as bright and cheerful as always, "where are you goin' in that army uniform?"

"Oh hiya Jack, how's it going? It's a long time no see!"

"It is that, too. Long gone are the days when we used to raid th' Paper Mill. By 'eck, but they were good days, weren't they Johnny?"

"They were that, Jack. We fairly got into some scrapes didn't we?"

"We did that, it were really good fun. Anyroad, you still haven't told me where you're off to."

"Well, believe it or not Jack, I'm making my way back to Plymouth on the train and as from next week I'm being shipped off to the Cameroons in West Africa."

"You lucky so-and-so, you're nowt else. I wish I were comin' abroad with you, cos there's nowt round here worth stoppin' for anymore. Anyroad," he added as he walked off, "let me know if there's any good paper mills o'er yonder, ha, ha, ha!" Then on a more serious note, he called out, "All the best Johnny ... go and show 'em what the Trafalgar wallers are made of!"

"What the 'eck!" I thought, "I'm just turned twenty-one and as fit as a fiddle. The world's my oyster. Come on John lad, go for it!"

I smiled and walked on with a spring in my step, eager to enter a new chapter in my life!

EPILOGUE

I spent fifteen months in the Cameroons and made many friends of the local natives. My upbringing held me in good stead amongst these deprived impoverished people.

I enjoyed every aspect of working in the army field hospitals, which got me to thinking how much I would like to pursue nursing in 'Civvy Street' after being discharged.

I did eventually follow my dream but much later than anticipated, the reason being that on leaving the army I went into a courtship, got married and started a family. Money was scarce and so I decided to enter the building trade.

I undertook a government training course and eventually got a job with Lancashire Shopfitters, a reputable firm in Oswaldtwistle. Along with another joiner, I spent the next few years driving the length and breadth of England, Scotland and Wales, refitting out shops. During this time I managed to pay off my mortgage and save a substantial amount of money.

In 1972 I started working for myself as a joiner. Using all the business expertise that Dad had taught me I worked very hard and prospered. At first I was very tentative but then I remembered some of Dad's advice. "Lad ... you've got to speculate to accumulate. Never be afraid o' venturing into something or you'll never get anywhere in this world. If you've got a gut feeling about anything ... go for it!"

This I did ... I wasn't afraid anymore. Being self-employed wasn't easy ... it had its ups and downs, but overall I enjoyed the challenge and liked being my own boss.

By 1977 I had done quite well and felt I could now pursue my nursing career. I eventually qualified in 1980 as a state registered nurse. My first post was on the Accident and Emergency Department, better known as Casualty.

Lots of incidents, both happy and sad, occurred during my army and working career. The years took their toll but on the whole my life has been full, interesting and satisfactory.

THE YOUNG MINER

I left school at fifteen years of age,
To go down the pit was all the rage.
I left for work with head held high,
And wanted to show the whole world why.
I worked very hard in every way,
And can honestly say I deserved my pay.
My first task was as a tackle lad,
Taking from me all the strength I had.
Steel girders and props I had to carry,
For every Tom, Dick and Harry.
The colliers were a happy lot,
So long as I was on the dot.
But woe betide if I was late,
Getting tackle to the bottom gate.
The gate was likened to a tunnel,
Running from the coalface like a funnel.
Throughout the tunnel ran a conveyor belt,
Onto which the coal was spilt.
Alongside this ran a small steel track,
To help carry the tackle right to the pack.
The pack consisted of shale and stone,
To help sustain the weight in that lower zone.

*   *   *

Tackle lads always worked as a pair,
This was better as far as wear and tear.
Working as hard as one can,
The boy very soon became the man.
The weekly wage was just a fiver,

No one could be called a skiver.
A bonus which helped boost this cash,
Each collier gave us some 'pey-brass'.
For carrying all those props and bricks,
Each miner handed over 'two and six'.

*   *   *

Till the age of eighteen I kept up the pace,
Then commenced training on the coalface.
Seven yards of rubble I had to haul,
In order to shift sixteen tons of coal.
Water leaked in from the layers above,
One could say ours was an act of love.
Working in conditions that were wet and dusty,
It's little wonder ... one's knees were rusty.
Toiling in seams only eighteen inches high,
Many a back felt broken ... no one wondered why.
Seven and half hours we had to strive,
In order to keep our hopes alive.
An extra bonus was given to shift the lot,
An incentive to keep us on the dot.
Colliers and tackle lads worked as a team,
Their goal ... to completely strip the seam.
Because of the friendship we were seldom beat,
Working together we completed this special feat.
At the time I often wondered why
Those men always appeared so home and dry.
Looking back over my own life's span,
I know the miner is a special kind of man.
Working deep down in the bowels of the earth,
With a deep commitment for all his worth.

Beneath the ground ... each one like a brother,
The life of each one ... dependent on the other.
Since then I've worked everywhere you can name,
But the comradeship has never been the same.

Also by John Cowell, the bestselling *The Broken Biscuit* – a true story of poverty, tragedy, love and humour.

The Broken Biscuit is a remarkable story of a remarkable woman. A woman of true courage, generosity and spirit; a woman who throughout her life has pitted herself against poverty and hardship to become a role model to young and old alike.

In the vein of *Angela's Ashes* and *A Child Called It*, *The Broken Biscuit* is the heart-rending story of one woman's struggle and refusal to succumb to adversity – the beatings of a violent husband, the crippling poverty of the age – to raise six children and devote a lifetime to charity and good works. A truly heart-warming tale, it captures the imagination of everyone who picks it up.

The Broken Biscuit is a book that will move, amuse, inspire and entrance – a true classic.

'A very clever book – I kept it under my pillow. I enjoyed reading it very much.' Dame Thora Hird

'If you read one book this year, read *The Broken Biscuit*.' *Runcorn Weekly News*

'… *The Broken Biscuit* will stand out from the rest as one of the best examples of history brought to life by personal experience. It is sure to become a classic …' *The Preston Citizen*

To order your copy, please send a cheque for £6.99, made out to John Blake Publishing Ltd, to:

John Blake Publishing Ltd
3 Bramber Court
2 Bramber Road
London W14 9PB

To order by credit card, please call our order hotline on 020 7381 0666.